# THE BOOK
## OF OLYMPIC
# LISTS

# THE BOOK
# OF OLYMPIC
# LISTS

## David Wallechinsky
## and Jaime Loucky

First published in Great Britain
2012 by Aurum Press Ltd
7 Greenland Street
London NW1 0ND
www.aurumpress.co.uk

ISBN 978 1 84513 773 1

1   3   5   7   9   10   8   6   4   2
2012   2014   2016   2015   2013

Text design: www.timpeters.co.uk
Typeset in Interstate and Sabon by Tim Peters
Printed and bound by CPI Group (UK) Ltd,
Croydon, CR0 4YY

# Contents

## OLYMPIANS AT WAR 179

## AFTER THE OLYMPICS 196

The authors would like to thank Dr Bill Mallon
for sharing his Olympic databases, which were used
to create the lists in the Record Book chapters

The International Olympic Committee does not
recognize the 1906 Intercalated Games that were
held in Athens, although most Olympic historians
do because of their importance to the development
of the Olympic Movement. In this book the authors
have included stories from the 1906 Olympics,
but the results from that year have been excluded
from the Record Book chapters.

# Number of Nations and Events in the Summer Olympics 1896-2012

|      |             | NATIONS | EVENTS |
|------|-------------|---------|--------|
| 1896 | Athens      | 14      | 43     |
| 1900 | Paris       | 28      | 75     |
| 1904 | St Louis    | 12      | 84     |
| 1906 | Athens      | 20      | 74     |
| 1908 | London      | 22      | 109    |
| 1912 | Stockholm   | 28      | 102    |
| 1920 | Antwerp     | 29      | 154    |
| 1924 | Paris       | 44      | 126    |
| 1928 | Amsterdam   | 46      | 109    |
| 1932 | Los Angeles | 37      | 116    |
| 1936 | Berlin      | 49      | 129    |
| 1948 | London      | 59      | 136    |
| 1952 | Helsinki    | 69      | 149    |
| 1956 | Melbourne   | 72      | 151    |
| 1960 | Rome        | 83      | 150    |
| 1964 | Tokyo       | 93      | 163    |
| 1968 | Mexico City | 112     | 172    |
| 1972 | Munich      | 121     | 195    |
| 1976 | Montreal    | 92      | 198    |
| 1980 | Moscow      | 80      | 203    |
| 1984 | Los Angeles | 140     | 221    |
| 1988 | Seoul       | 159     | 237    |
| 1992 | Barcelona   | 169     | 257    |
| 1996 | Atlanta     | 197     | 271    |
| 2000 | Sydney      | 200     | 300    |
| 2004 | Athens      | 201     | 301    |
| 2008 | Beijing     | 204     | 302    |
| 2012 | London      | 302     | 302    |

# Olympic
# Athletes

# 6 Athletes Whose Names Destined Them for Their Sports

**1 Walter Bathe, Great Britain**

In 1912 swimmer Walter Bathe earned gold medals in the 200-meter and 400-meter breaststroke.

**2 Lewis Moist, Great Britain**

A swimmer, Moist was eliminated in the heats of the 1908 1,500-meter freestyle.

**3 Eugene Swift, USA**

In 1996 Swift was 6th in the 110-meter hurdles.

**4 Ernest Fast, Sweden**

Fast finished third in the 1900 marathon. He was an electrical engineer working in the Swedish section of the Paris World's Fair, but was also the national champion at 10,000 meters.

**5 Nathan Leeper, USA**

Leeper placed 11th in the high jump in 2000.

**6 Samson N'Dicka Matam, Cameroon/France**

A weightlifter, Matam competed in three Olympics. In 1996 he represented Cameroon and in 2000 and 2004 France. His best performance was sixth place in his final appearance.

# 10 Noteworthy Names

## 1 Man Afraid Soap, Canada

Lacrosse was included in the Olympic program in 1904 and 1908. One of the three teams entered in 1904 was a squad of Mohawk Indians from Ontario, Canada. Among Man Afraid Soap's teammates were Snake Eater, Almighty Voice and Rain in Face.

## 2 Lucky Willie Bhembe, Swaziland

Lucky Willie Bhembe finished 51st in the 2000 marathon. Three other athletes whose legal name was Lucky have competed at the Olympics: Zambian boxer Lucky Mutale (1980), Zambian footballer Lucky Msiska (1988) and Nigerian relay sprinter Nnamdi Lucky Anusim (2000). None was fortunate enough to win a medal.

## 3/4 Calvin Coffey and Mike Staines, USA

Rowers Coffcy and Staines won silver medals in the coxless pairs event in 1976. They probably should have got together with . . .

## 5 Kleanthis Bargkas, Greece

A cyclist, Kleanthis was a member of the 3-man team that placed fourth in the Olympic sprint event in 2000. Kleanthis Ierissiotis represented Greece in the hammer throw in 1976.

*Like the Kleanthises, some athletes' names only sound odd if pronounced in English. Here are three more examples.*

## 6 Odd-Even Bustnes, Norway

Odd-Even was a member of Norway's coxless fours rowing crew in 1996.

## 7 Sylvie Pissis, France

She represented France in archery in 2000.

## 8 Gregor Fucka, Italy

Fucka was a member of the Italian basketball team in 2000.

*And here are two record-setters.*

## 9 Prapawadee Jaroenrattanatarakoon, Thailand

At 31 letters, weightlifter Prapawadee Jaroenrattanatarakoon of Thailand set the record for the longest name of any Olympic champion. It was so long that it did not fit on the digital scoreboard at the Beijing Games . . . so she was listed as "J." She was actually given a different name at birth: Junpim Kuntatean. After failing to make the Thai Olympic team in 2004 and coming second at the 2005 world championships and the 2006 Asian Games, Kuntatean was told by a fortune-teller that if she changed her name she would win an Olympic gold medal. She took the advice, legally taking the name Prapawadee Jaroenrattanatarakoon ("Good Girl, Prosperous"). It worked.

## 10 O Il, North Korea

At the other end of the scale is the athlete with the shortest name in Olympic history. O Il represented North Korea in men's table tennis in 2004.

# 3 Medal Winners Who Were Simultaneously Famous and Unrecognized

### 1 Percy Williams, Canada, 100 Meters, 1928

Percy Williams was one of the most popular winners of the Amsterdam Games. Not considered a serious threat by the experts, the slim, almost frail-looking 20-year-old from Vancouver, British Columbia, caught the fancy of the crowd early on. In the final he took the lead immediately and kept it the entire way. In the days before television, an unexpected winner like Williams could be famous and unrecognized at the same time. Only a few hours after his Olympic victory, Williams and a friend noticed a large crowd gathered in front of his hotel. "We joined the mob," Williams later recalled, "looking over their shoulders. I asked a person in front of me why they were there and he said, 'We're waiting for the Canadian runner Williams to come out of the hotel.' I didn't tell him who I was. I stood around waiting for him, too, and talking to some of the people—it was much more fun."

### 2 George Roth, USA, Club Swinging, 1932

Club swinging was included in the gymnastics program the first two times the Olympics was held in the United States. The 1932 winner, George Roth, was unemployed and nearly starving in the midst of the Great Depression. He would go to the Olympic Village each day, collect some food, and sneak it home to his wife and baby daughter in East Hollywood. After receiving his gold medal before 60,000 cheering spectators Roth walked out of the stadium and hitchhiked home.

### 3 Reg Harris, Great Britain, Match Sprint Cycling, 1948

The reigning world champion, Harris was beaten in the Olympic final by Mario Ghella of Italy. Harris immediately turned professional and won the professional world sprint title four times. He retired from competition in 1957, but returned 14 years later and, incredibly, in 1974 won the British sprint championship at the age of 54. Harris was remarkably well-known considering that he excelled at a sport which was not terribly popular in Great Britain. His name became synonymous with cycling speed, and any youngster who rode his bicycle fast would be good-naturedly nicknamed, "Reg." Harris, in his mid-sixties but as aggressive as ever, was cycling on the streets one day when he jumped a red light and was pulled over by a police officer, who approached him and asked, "Who do you think you are, Reg Harris?"

# 6 Athletes of Ambiguous Gender

### 1 Stella Walsh, Poland, Women's 100 Meters, 1932-1936

Stanisława Wałasiewicz was born in Rypin, Poland, on April 3, 1911. When she was still an infant her family moved to the United States and settled in Cleveland, Ohio, where she grew up and became known as Stella Walsh. In 1930 she was the first woman to run 100 yards in less than 11 seconds, and, competing for Poland, her performance in Los Angeles in 1932 did not disappoint. Running with what the Canadian official report called "long man-like strides," she equaled Tollien Schuurman's two-month-old world record in every one of her three races. On December 4, 1980, Stella Walsh went to a discount store in Cleveland to buy ribbons for a reception for the Polish national basketball team. In the parking lot she was shot dead during an attempted robbery. When an autopsy was performed it turned out that Walsh had a condition known as "mosaicism," having both male and female chromosomes. She had a tiny penis and testes, but no female organs. All the while that she had been setting 11 world records, and winning two Olympic medals (gold in 1932, silver in 1936), she was, by current rules, a man.

### 2 Herman "Dora" Ratjen, Germany, Women's High Jump, 1936

Fourth-place finisher Dora Ratjen was barred from competition in 1938, when it was announced that she was a hermaphrodite, a rare sexual group for which international athletics has made no provisions. In 1957 Ratjen revealed that she was really Herman Ratjen and that he had been ordered to pose as a woman by officials of the Nazi Youth Movement.

### 3 Ewa Kłobukowska, Poland, Women's 100 Meters and 4 x 100-meter Relay, 1964

Double medalist Kłobukowska was later the subject of much controversy. On September 15, 1967, she was barred from international competition after failing a sex chromosome test. Although she passed a visual examination she was subsequently stripped of all her records.

## 4 Edinanci Silva, Brazil, Women's Heavyweight Judo, 1996-2008

Nineteen-year-old Edinanci Silva was forced to undergo extraordinary measures to ensure that she passed gender and doping tests. Although clearly a woman, Silva, upon reaching puberty, discovered that she had testicles. Three months before the 1996 Olympics, according to Brazilian newspaper accounts, she underwent an operation to remove her testicles, as well as to reduce the size of her clitoris. She eventually competed in four Olympics, placing seventh each time.

## 5/6 Tamara and Iryna Press, Soviet Union, Women's Track and Field, 1960-1964

Between them, Tamara Press and her younger sister Iryna set 26 world records and won five Olympic gold medals and one silver in four different events. Unfortunately, when sex tests were instituted at international competitions the careers of both Press sisters came to a sudden halt, and they never competed again.

# 8 Athletes Who Had Trouble Producing Urine for Drug Tests

## 1 Chris Finnegan, Great Britain, Middleweight Boxing, 1968

Finnegan's most difficult challenge was not winning the gold medal, but his post-competition urine test. As Finnegan put it: "Now if there's one thing I've never been able to do, it's have a piss while someone's watching me. I can never stand at those long urinals you get in gents' bogs, with all the other blokes having a quick squint." Sure enough, he was unable to produce. People turned on water faucets, whistled, whispered encouragement. He drank several glasses of water. Still nothing. Then he downed three or four pints of beer, but still without the desired result. After giving a television interview, Finnegan was hauled off to a local restaurant for a victory meal; two Olympic officials tagged along with the necessary collection equipment. Finally, at 1:40 a.m., Finnegan jumped up and shouted, "Who wants some piss?" The officials followed him to the men's room, secured their sample, and returned to the lab. The test, of course, proved negative.

## 2 David Hemery, Great Britain, 400-meter Hurdles, 1968

After winning the 400-meter hurdles in world record time, David Hemery found that his system was "most uncooperative." He drank water, coke and orange juice, but was unable to produce a urine sample until after the medal ceremony.

## 3 Daniel Bautista, Mexico, 20,000-meter Walk, 1976

Daniel Bautista brought Mexico its first-ever track and field gold medal. He was so dehydrated at the end that he had to drink ten cans of soft drinks before he could produce enough urine for the drug test.

## 4 Tony Willis, Great Britain, Welterweight Boxing, 1980

Bronze medalist Tony Willis required three hours, an orangeade, and a glass of water to produce enough urine to be used for a drug test. He passed.

## 5 Alex Baumann, Canada, 400-meter Individual Medley, 1984

Gold medal-winner Baumann was unable to meet reporters after the race because he needed almost two hours to produce a urine sample for drug-testing. In the middle of his third beer, medical officials discovered that, at 20 years old, he was under age and forced him to switch to soft drinks.

## 6 Clint Robinson, Australia, K-1000 Singles Canoeing, 1992

Robinson, a 20-year-old from Maroochydore, Queensland, upset twice world champion Knut Holmann by staying close to the Norwegian throughout the race and then surging ahead at the end. He pushed himself so hard that, for the first time in his life, his whole body went numb. He was also so dehydrated that it was six hours before he could produce a urine sample for doping control.

## 7 Andreas Wecker, Germany, Parallel Bars, 1992

It took gymnastics silver medalist Andreas Wecker only 30 seconds to earn his medal, but five hours to produce a urine sample for drug testing.

## 8 Rod Dixon, New Zealand, 1,500 Meters, 1972

The surprise bronze medalist was Rod Dixon of New Zealand, who began sobbing when he realized that his dream of an Olympic medal had come true. Still weeping, he was ushered backstage for the urine test. After producing a meager sample, Dixon sheepishly asked the German official if it was enough. "For the gold medal, no," was the reply, "but for the bronze medal, it will do."

# 13 Witty Olympians

### 1 Bob Mathias, USA, Decathlon, 1948-1952

Bob Mathias was only 17 years old when he won the decathlon at the London Olympics. He was the youngest winner of a men's track and field event in the history of the Olympics. In the dressing room afterward, the exhausted teenager was asked how he intended to celebrate his victory. He replied, "I'll start shaving, I guess." He successfully defended his championship four years later.

### 2 Emil Zátopek, Czechoslovakia, Distance Running, 1948-1956

One of the legends of long-distance running, Emil Zátopek is the only person in history to win the 5,000 meters, the 10,000 meters and the marathon at the same Olympics. Whenever he ran, his face was always contorted by a grimace, and his shoulders and body looked hunched with pain. Observers, on first seeing Zátopek, were sure that he was on the verge of collapse, but it turned out that that was just his style. Years later Zátopek was asked about this idiosyncrasy. He replied, "I was not talented enough to run and smile at the same time."

### 3 Dana Zátopková, Czechoslovakia, Women's Javelin Throw, 1948-1960

Shortly before the 1952 competition began, Dana Zátopková's husband, Emil Zátopek, was awarded a gold medal for winning the 5,000 meters. After the ceremony, she rushed up to him and said, "You've won! Splendid! Show me that medal." After examining it, she added, "I'll take it with me for luck." She put it in her bag and left. On her first throw she set an Olympic record and earned a gold medal of her own. That evening Emil claimed that he deserved partial credit for his wife's gold medal because he had inspired her. Naturally, Dana was quite offended and replied, "What? All right, go and inspire some other girl and see if she throws a javelin fifty meters."

### 4 Earlene Brown, USA, Women's Shot Put and Discus Throw, 1956-1964

Los Angeles housewife Earlene Brown made a great impression on the

Australians in 1956 and became a local favorite. Arriving in Melbourne early, she took part in the shot put in a regional meet and won. When a fan informed her that she had just broken the Victoria state record, Brown replied, "I'm sorry, honey. If I'd known I was going to do that I wouldn't have thrown it so far."

## 5 John Carlos, USA, 200 Meters, 1968

When bronze-medal-winner John Carlos and fellow American Tommy Smith staged a Black Power protest at the medal ceremony in Mexico City, they were joined by silver medalist Pete Norman of Australia, who asked if he could wear a symbolic badge too. Thirty-two years later, Carlos told Mike Wise of The New York Times, "To wear the badge as a white individual, it made the statement even more powerful. During a crucial time in our lives, he was compassionate, understanding and he showed his manhood. I'll always respect and love him for that. Pete became my brother at that moment. . . . But the most amazing thing was . . . I didn't know there was a white guy who could run that fast."

## 6 Jürgen Croy, East Germany, Football, 1976

The victory of East German Waldemar Cierpinski in the marathon came as a shock even to his fellow countrymen. Back in the Olympic Village, the East German soccer team watched the race on television while waiting for their final match against Poland. Goalkeeper Jürgen Croy later recalled, "We just sat there staring at each other, thinking that if this living example of mediocrity can lift himself up and win the marathon, and we don't beat Poland, we are never going to hear the end of it." They won.

## 7 Miruts Yifter, Ethiopia, 5,000 Meters and 10,000 Meters, 1972, 1980

The winner of both the 5,000 meters and the 10,000 meters at the 1980 Olympics, Miruts Yifter kept his birth date a secret. His age was variously reported as 33, 35, 36, 37, or 42. When asked for a definitive answer, Yifter would only reply, "I don't count the years. Men may steal my chickens, men may steal my sheep. But no man can steal my age."

## 8 Yasuhiro Yamashita, Japan, Open Class Judo, 1984

Yasuhiro Yamashita dominated the world of judo, going undefeated for seven years leading up to his Olympic victory in Los Angeles and winning

194 matches in a row at national and international level. Despite his ferocity on the mat, Yamashita was known for his gentlemanly manner and his kind smile. However he once explained, "When I was training for competition, I had to smile. If I showed my real feelings of determination on my face, no one would practice with me."

## 9 Mike Swain, USA, Lightweight Judo, 1984-1992

At the 1988 Seoul Olympics world champion Mike Swain was defeated in a bronze-medal match by Kerrith Brown of Great Britain, but when Brown was disqualified for failing his doping test, Swain was moved up to a medal position. When asked how he felt about backing into a bronze medal, Swain was philosophical. "I didn't want to win it this way," he said. "But I can always lie to my grandchildren."

## 10 Derek Redmond, Great Britain, 400 Meters, 1992

Redmond described sprinter Linford Christie as "Britain's best-balanced athlete, because he has a chip on both shoulders."

## 11 Huang Zhihong, China, Women's Shot Put, 1988-1992

The winner of the silver medal in 1992, Huang was a welcome contrast to obsessed athletes. "I didn't like the shot at all," she once said. "How could anyone like those heavy metal lumps? If I knew the shot put would make me so fat, I wouldn't have taken it up." After she won the 1991 world championship, she was asked how it felt to be the first Asian to win a world athletics title. She replied, "What I have done is no more newsworthy than if I had swallowed 500 eels."

## 12 Ato Boldon, Trinidad, Sprints, 1992-2004

Boldon took the bronze medal in the 200 meters in 1996, crossing the finish line in 19.80 seconds, yet he was far behind Michael Johnson, who smashed his own world record with a time of 19.32 seconds. Boldon went straight up to Johnson and bowed down in homage. "19.32, Boldon marveled. That's not a time. It sounds like my dad's birthday."

## 13 Michael Johnson, USA, 200 and 400 Meters, 1992-2000

Johnson, who won four Olympic gold medals, once said that he did not have a pre-race ritual but he did have a post-race ritual: "I stand on the podium and have them put a gold medal around my neck."

# 3 Olympians Who Had Songs Written About Them

## 1 Dorando Pietri, Italy, Marathon, 1908

A small man from the small town of Carpi, near Modena, Dorando Pietri was the first runner to enter the stadium in the 1908 Marathon, but struggled to finish the race, collapsing repeatedly on the track. When he started to collapse a fifth time, just short of the finish, Jack Andrew, the head organizer of the race, caught him and carried him across the line. Pietri was ultimately disqualified for receiving assistance, but nevertheless became an international celebrity. Even in the United States, songs were written about him, including one by Irving Berlin. Unfortunately, Berlin completely missed the point of what had happened, entitling his song "Dorando, He's a Gooda for Not" and portraying the courageous Italian as a "bigga de flop."

## 2 Hasely Crawford, Trinidad, 100 Meters, 1976

As Trinidad's first Olympic champion, Crawford received more than his share of honors. He was awarded the Trinity Cross, his picture appeared on two postage stamps, an aircraft was named after him, and six different Calypso songs were written in his honor.

## 3 Michelle Smith, Ireland, Women's 400-meter Freestyle, 1996

At the 1996 Atlanta Games Irish swimmer Michelle Smith won four Olympic medals: three golds and one bronze. When she flew back to Dublin, she was met at the airport by Ireland's president, Mary Robinson, and a local folk group sang a song composed in her honor: "The Great Michelle, our golden girl, the princess of our tide." In Smith's home village of Rathcoole, south-west of Dublin, the celebration, which had already been going on for days, surpassed the one for the Pope's visit in 1979. Smith's performances were ultimately discredited when she was banned for having manipulated a doping test by adding alcohol to her urine sample.

# 9 Summer Olympic Competitors Who Appeared in *Playboy*

### 1 Hortência, Brazil, Basketball, 1992-1996
The most famous women's basketball player of her era, Hortência Marcari was the first future Olympic athlete to appear in *Playboy*, specifically in the January 1988 edition of the Brazilian version.

### 2 Aurelia Dobre, Romania, Gymnastics, 1988
Only 14 years old at the time she won the 1987 world championship, Romania's Aurelia Dobre seemed to be on track to become a bigger celebrity than her predecessor, Nadia Comaneci. Besides being the best female gymnast in the world, she was charming, graceful and unusually beautiful. However, a knee injury forced her to undergo three operations, and the pressure to produce a winner led her coaches to ignore the advice of doctors and make her resume training before she was fully recovered. In Seoul she was already only a shadow of her former self. She placed sixth in the All-Around competition, went home without an individual medal and was ignored by the television cameras of the world. Three years later, however, she did earn a place in sports history when, in September 1991, she became the first Olympic athlete to appear nude in *Playboy* magazine—even if it was only in the Dutch edition.

### 3 Natalya Meshcheryakova, Russia, Freestyle Swimming, 1992-1996
With the encouragement of her husband, gold-medal swimmer Vladimir Pyshnenko, Natalya Meshcheryakova appeared in the Russian edition of *Playboy* just before the Atlanta Games. She had won a bronze medal in the medley relay in 1992. In 1997 both Meshcheryakova and Pyshnenko were suspended when they tested positive for anabolic steroids.

### 4 Svetlana Khorkina, Russia, Gymnastics, 1996-2004
Svetlana Khorkina entered the 2000 Olympics as the queen of international gymnastics. She had won the 1997 world championship, the 1998 European championship, and, four months before the Olympics, she successfully defended her European championship. In addition, at the age of 18, she had enhanced her image by appearing topless in the November 1997 issue of the Russian edition of *Playboy*. At the 2000 Games, Khorkina was the victim of

an unfortunate apparatus mix-up, in which the horse vault had been set to the wrong height. After two falls in the vault and a poor uneven bars score she dropped out of medal contention in the All-Around competition. However, she did successfully defend her Olympic title on the uneven bars.

### 5 Vanda Hadarean, Romania, Gymnastics, 1992

Vanda Hadarean, a member of the 1992 silver-medal-winning Romanian Olympic team, appeared nude in the September 2000 Romanian edition of *Playboy*.

### 6 Susen Tiedtke, Germany, Long Jump, 1992, 2000

Tiedtke placed eighth in the long jump in 1992 and fifth in 2000. She appeared in the August 2001 German edition of *Playboy*, as well in the US and international editions in September 2004.

### 7 Amy Acuff, USA, High Jump, 1996-2008

Four-time Olympian Amy Acuff was one of eight female Olympians to appear nude in *Playboy*'s September 2004 "Women of the Olympics" pictorial. Among the others were American backstroke swimmer Haley Cope, who earned a silver medal by swimming in the qualifying round of the 2004 medley relay, Ineta Radevica, who represented Latvia in the long jump and triple jump, and Ukrainian sprinter Zhanna Pintusevich-Block, who competed from 1995 to 2004.

### 8 Amanda Beard, USA, Swimming, 1996-2008

A four-time Olympian, Amanda Beard won two gold medals, four silvers and one bronze. After her victories, Beard started modeling, appearing in the *Sports Illustrated Swimsuit Edition* and the July 2007 edition of *Playboy*, among others. "I told my dad," she said, "that I'd take like black tape and kind of mark out certain things, so he doesn't feel awkward looking at it. He's like, 'Could ya?'" In 2008 Beard posed nude in an anti-fur campaign for animal rights organization PETA.

### 9 Nicole Reinhardt, Germany, Canoeing, 2008

The September 2008 German edition of *Playboy* featured photos of four Olympic athletes who competed at the Beijing Games, including Reinhardt, who went on to earn a gold medal in the kayak fours event. The others were Petra Niemann (sailing), Romy Tarangul (half-lightweight judo) and Katharina Scholz (field hockey).

# 5 Misrepresentations in *Chariots of Fire*

*The story of the victories of Eric Liddell and Harold Abrahams in Paris in 1924 is well told in the beautiful film* Chariots of Fire. *Unfortunately, despite its claim of being "a true story," the film contains several factual distortions.*

## 1 Eric Liddell

In the film, Eric Liddell is portrayed as a devout Christian who learns, as he is boarding a ship en route to the Paris Olympics, that the heats of the 100-meter dash, his specialty, will be run on a Sunday. Because of his respect for the Sabbath, he refuses to run. Finally another member of the British team, a cinematic version of Lord Burghley, offers Liddell his spot in the 400 meters. This highly dramatized rendition of Liddell's Olympic experience bears only a slight resemblance to reality. Liddell was in fact a devout Christian, and it is true that he withdrew from the 100 because he wouldn't run on a Sunday. He dropped out of the relays for the same reason. However, he did *not* find out the Olympic schedule at the last minute. In real life Liddell learned the schedule more than six months in advance, and, once he had made his decision not to enter the 100, he was able to concentrate his training on the 200 and 400. As for Lord Burghley, he wasn't even entered in the 400 meters.

## 2 Jackson Scholz

There is one scene in *Chariots of Fire* in which Jackson Scholz, just before the start of the 400 meters, approaches Eric Liddell and hands him a piece of paper inscribed with a religious message. Scholz who later made his living as an author of "pulp" fiction, actually did no such thing—he wasn't even religious. This put him in a difficult situation. When *Chariots of Fire* became a hit, the 84-year-old Scholz, by now living in Delray Beach, Florida, was inundated with mail from people requesting spiritual inspiration. "I'm afraid," he told reporters, "that my religious background was rather casual." Indeed, when asked what he best remembered about Harold Abrahams, who had finished in front of him in the 1924 100 meters final, Scholz replied, "I remember his ass."

### 3 Harold Abrahams

Abrahams did not race around the great courtyard of Trinity College at Cambridge. He did not look at the 100-meter contest as a chance to redeem himself after his failure in the 200 meters, since in real life the 100 meters was run before the 200 meters. Although Abrahams did feel himself an outsider because he was Jewish, a much more important motivating factor in his quest for victory was a desire to do better than his two older brothers, both of whom were well-known athletes and one of whom had represented Great Britain in the long jump at the 1906 and 1912 Olympics.

### 4 Evelyn Montague

The sixth-place finisher in the 1924 3,000-meter steeplechase event, Evelyn Montague is introduced in the film as a good friend of Harold Abrahams, whose acquaintance he makes when they both arrive at Cambridge as freshmen. In reality, Abrahams and Montague were rivals, as Montague attended not Cambridge, but Oxford.

### 5 Lord Burghley

Heir to the Marquess of Exeter, David George Brownlow Cecil, Lord Burghley, first appeared in the Olympics in 1924, when he was eliminated in the first round of the 110-meter hurdles. In 1927, during his last year at Cambridge, he caused a sensation by running around the Great Court at Trinity College in the time it took the Trinity clock to toll 12 o'clock. In *Chariots of Fire* the feat is credited to Harold Abrahams. For this reason Lord Burghley, who was then 76 years old, reportedly refused to view the film. Actually Lord Burghley was not the first person to accomplish the Great Court run. It had been done in the 1890s by Sir Walter Borley Fletcher, but in Sir Walter's time the clock took five more seconds to complete its toll. Burghley was an extremely colorful character who is believed to be the first hurdler to place matchboxes on hurdles and practice knocking over the matchboxes with his lead foot without touching the hurdle. It is not true, despite his portrayal in *Chariots of Fire*, that he put glasses of champagne on the hurdles as well. In the words of his daughter, Lady Victoria Leatham, "He was never one to waste champagne."

# 8 Athletes Who Overcame Injuries or Disease

**1 George Orton, Canada, Steeplechase and Hurdles, 1900**

Paralysed as a child after falling out of a tree, George Orton regained his motor skills when he was twelve years old and ran everywhere, earning the nickname "The Boy Who Never Walked." Canada's first Olympic medalist, he won the 2,500-meter steeplechase and finished third in the 400-meter hurdles.

**2 Dimitrios Tofalos, Greece, Super-heavyweight Weightlifting, 1906**

Tofalos, the son of a count, had been run over by a wagon as a young boy. His upper arm was crushed, and doctors wanted to amputate it, but Tofalos's father wouldn't allow it. Dimitrios recovered the use of his arm, even though it was two-and-a-half inches shorter than his uninjured arm. After winning at the Olympics he turned professional and eventually went to America, where he entered vaudeville and became a wrestler. In a match against world champion Frank Gotch, Tofalos got caught in one of Gotch's famous toe-holds, but refused to submit. His stubbornness cost him six months in hospital with a dislocated hip. He became a US citizen in 1921 and remained a popular figure in professional wrestling and physical culture circles for the rest of his life.

**3 Károly Takács, Hungary, Rapid Fire Pistol Shooting, 1948-1956**

Károly Takács was a member of the Hungarian world champion pistol shooting team in 1938 when, during army training, a grenade shattered his right hand—his pistol hand. Takács taught himself to shoot with his left hand and, ten years later, he won an Olympic gold medal in the rapid-fire pistol event. He repeated his victory at the 1952 Olympics.

**4 Wilma Rudolph, USA, Women's Sprints, 1956-1960**

Wilma Rudolph was born prematurely and weighed only 4½ pounds at birth. Polio caused her to lose the use of her left leg, and from the age of six she wore a brace. Her mother learned from doctors that rubbing her daughter's leg might help, so each day Wilma received four leg rubs from her brothers, sisters, and mother. Eventually she graduated from a brace to an orthopedic shoe, and she joined her brothers playing basketball whenever she could. When Wilma was 11 her mother returned home one day to find her daughter playing basketball barefooted, having thrown away her corrective shoe. By the time she was 16 Rudolph had developed into a star runner and had qualified for the US Olympic team, winning a bronze medal in 1956 and three sprint gold medals (the 100 meters, 200 meters and 4 × 100-meter relay) in 1960.

## 5 Silken Laumann, Canada, Women's Single and Double Sculls Rowing, 1984-1996

Having won the 1991 world championship by more than three seconds, 27-year-old Silken Laumann was considered the overwhelming favorite to win the single sculls at the Barcelona Games. But on May 16, 1992, just 73 days before she was scheduled to race for the first time at the Olympics, Laumann was the victim of a horrific accident. In a poorly supervised warm-up area in Essen, Germany, her shell was rammed by the shell of the German coxless pair, Peter Holtzenbein and Cohn von Ettingshausen. A piece of wood ripped through her lower right leg, fracturing the bone, cutting the muscles in her calf and causing extensive nerve and tissue damage. The wound was so gruesome that Holtzenbein and Ettingshausen, after helping to save Laumann, both fainted. Doctors told Laumann she would need at least six months to recover. But she insisted that she wanted to compete again at the Olympics.

In 1984, rowing with her sister, Laumann had earned a bronze medal in double sculls. In 1988 she placed seventh in the same event. For 1992 her goal was reduced to finishing ahead of at least one other rower. Miraculously, after five operations and some two-and-a-half months after the accident, she made it to Barcelona, although she walked with a cane and was advised to avoid standing up for more than fifteen minutes at a time. Surprisingly, she finished second in her qualifying heat and then won her semi-final. In the final, she came from behind to earn the bronze medal.

## 6 Gail Devers, USA, Women's Sprints, 1988-2004

In June 1988 Gail Devers began getting migraine headaches. She also experienced dizziness and temporary loss of sight in one eye. She managed to qualify for the Olympics in her specialty, the 100-meter hurdles, but in Seoul she was eliminated in the semi-finals. At first it had been easy to assume that Devers' symptoms were the result of stress, but her condition continued to deteriorate. Unfortunately, it was two years before doctors finally came up with a correct diagnosis: Graves' disease. In order to control her hyperactive thyroid, Devers began radiation therapy on September 12, 1990. The therapy worked, but then she developed awful reactions to the radiation. She hemorrhaged blood clots, her weight fluctuated dramatically, and she experienced second-degree burns on her feet, which became infected and swollen. Incredibly, after missing two-and-a-half years of training, Devers returned to competition, and at the 1992 Olympics she won 100 meters in a photo-finish. She defended her title in 1996 and added a third gold medal in the 4 × 100-meter relay.

## 7 Cliff Meidl, USA, Kayak Canoeing, 1996–2000

When Cliff Meidl was 20 years old, he was electrocuted while working for a construction company in Southern California. He received 30,000 volts of electricity (electric chair executions use 1,500 volts) and experienced three cardiac arrests. He was unable to walk unaided for three years. Ten years later he competed in the K-4 1,000 meters at the Atlanta Olympics and in 2000 in the K-2 1000.

## 8 Jérôme Thomas, France, Flyweight Boxing, 2000–2008

Two-time Olympic medalist (bronze in 2000 and silver in 2004) Jérôme Thomas was born with Poland syndrome, which left him with one hand that would not close, one pectoral muscle too few and a left arm that was seven centimeters shorter than his right arm. He underwent 15 operations as a child—including seven on his left hand alone. Thomas claimed that his mismatched arms were actually an advantage because after a few jabs with his left hand, an opponent would be unprepared when they were followed with a hard blow from his surprisingly long right arm.

# 11 Disabled Athletes Competing in the Olympics

**1 George Eyser, USA, Gymnastics, 1904**

One of the most remarkable athletes of the St Louis Games was the American gymnast George Eyser, who won three gold medals, two silvers and one bronze. What made his feats particularly impressive was that his left leg was made of wood. His leg had been amputated after he was run over by a train.

**2 Olivér Halassy, Hungary, Water Polo, 1928-1936**

Olivér Halassy played on three Hungarian Olympic water polo teams, winning three medals (two golds and a silver) despite the fact that one of his legs had been amputated below the knee after a streetcar accident when he was 11.

**3 Lis Hartel, Denmark, Equestrian Dressage, 1952**

Lis Hartel was one of the first women allowed to compete against men in the equestrian dressage. Although paralysed below the knees after an attack of polio in 1944, when she was 23, Hartel learned how to do without the affected muscles, improving so much that she was chosen to represent Denmark in the 1952 Olympics. She responded by earning the silver medal, even though she had to be helped on and off her horse.

**4 Ildikó Rejtö, Hungary, Women's Foil Fencing, 1960-1976**

Ildikó Rejtö was born deaf on May 11, 1937. When she began fencing at age 14 her coaches communicated their instructions on pieces of paper. She competed in five Olympics, earning two gold medals, one silver and two bronzes. She also holds the unusual distinction of being the only Summer Olympian to win medals using three different names, having married twice during her Olympic career.

**5 Jeff Float, USA, Freestyle Swimming, 1984**

Swimming the third leg for the US in the 4 × 200-meter freestyle relay, was Jeff Float, who had lost 80% of his hearing in his right ear and 60% in his left ear after contracting viral meningitis at the age of 13 months.

So great was the roar of the hometown crowd as Float lengthened the US lead during the Olympic final that, for the first time in his life, he heard the crowd cheering him on.

## 6 Neroli Fairhall, New Zealand, Women's Individual Archery, 1984

Finishing in 35th place was New Zealand's Neroli Fairhall, the first athlete to take part in the Olympics after previously competing in the Paralympic Games. Paralysed from the waist down after a motorbike accident, she competed while seated in a wheelchair.

## 7 Paola Fantato, Italy, Women's Archery, 1996

Wheelchair-bound since the age of eight as a result of polio, Paula Fantato was the first athlete to compete in the Olympics and the Paralympics in the same year.

## 8 Terrence Parkin, South Africa, 100-meter Butterfly, 2000

Silver-medal-winner Terence Parkin was 100 percent deaf since birth, so a strobe light was used to communicate to him the start of the race.

## 9 Marla Runyan, USA, Women's Running, 2004-2008

Legally blind as a result of Stargardt's disease, Marla Runyan had already won five gold medals in the Paralympics when she qualified for the US team at 1,500 meters at the Athens Olympics. She placed eighth in the final. Four years later she competed at 5,000 meters.

## 10 Natalie du Toit, South Africa, Women's Open Water Swimming, 2008

Sixteenth place finisher Natalie du Toit had an inspiring path to the Olympics. As a teenager she had narrowly missed a spot on South Africa's Sydney 2000 Olympic team. A year later she was hit by a car while riding her scooter and lost her left leg below the knee. She continued swimming, winning five gold medals and one silver at the 2004 Paralympics and qualifying for the Beijing Olympics after finishing fourth at the 2008 world championships.

## 11 Natalia Partyka, Poland, Women's Table Tennis, 2008

Born without a right hand and forearm, Natalia Partyka won the Paralympic championship in 2004 before competing in the Beijing Olympics in 2008.

# 6 Unlikely Olympic Champions

## 1 John Pius Boland, Ireland, Tennis, 1896

John Pius Boland was a student at Christ's College, Oxford, when he invited a Greek friend, Thrasyvoulos Manos, to speak at the Oxford Union on the subject of the forthcoming Olympic Games. During the Easter holidays Boland traveled to Athens as a spectator. One night at dinner he met a Greek from Alexandria named Dionysios Kasdaglis, who convinced him to enter the tennis tournament, and he was enrolled the following morning, the day before play began. Boland competed wearing leather-soled shoes with heels. He won three matches and then found himself in the final against none other than his new friend Kasdaglis. Because it was Kasdaglis who had arranged for him to enter in the first place, Boland considered forfeiting, but decided this would be improper because "the game was of an international character." Boland won 6–2, 6–2 and then teamed with Fritz Traun of Germany to win the doubles tournament as well.

## 2 Edgar Aabye, Denmark, Tug of War, 1900

The competition consisted of a single contest between France and Sweden. Edgar Aabye of Denmark was a journalist covering the Games for *Politiken*. The Swedes asked him to join their side and he ended up on the winning team.

## 3 Zimbabwean Women's Field Hockey Team, 1980

When five of the six nations scheduled to compete in the inaugural women's field hockey tournament withdrew as part of the Jimmy Carter boycott, it set the stage for a true Cinderella story. As white-ruled Rhodesia, Zimbabwe had been banned from the Olympics, but when the black majority took power, the ban was lifted. Desperate to fill the field, the Soviet Union and the International Olympic Committee contacted Zimbabwe five weeks before the start of the Games and offered to subsidize the sending of a team, the members of which were not selected until the weekend before the Olympics opened. Ironically, the team that represented Zimbabwe was all white. They were held to ties by Czechoslovakia and India, but they were the only team to avoid defeat. A 4–1 victory over Austria assured them of the gold medals.

## 4 Andrzej Wronski, Poland, Heavyweight Greco-Roman Wrestling, 1988

Andrzej Wronski was one of the most unexpected winners of the Seoul Olympics. Before 1988 he had never placed in the top eight of a major international competition. His most noteworthy accomplishment was finishing *third* in the 1987 Polish championships. Meanwhile, the Olympic field was filled with winners, most notably the defending Olympic champion, Vasile Andrei; the defending world champion, Guram Gedekhauri; the world championship runner-up, Dennis Koslowski; the 1986 world champion, Tamás Gáspár; the 1986 European champion, Jožef Tertei; and the 1987 European champion, Ilia Georgiev. None of these worthies made it to the final. Wronski himself lost once when he was pinned by Gedekhauri (in fact, he was the only wrestler at the 1988 Olympics to win a gold medal despite having lost a match). What Wronski did do was to register three upset victories: 1–0 over Tertei, 1–0 over Koslowski, and a passivity win over Andrei. In the final he scored all his points when he lifted Germany's Gerhard Himmel from a prone position and threw him to the mat.

## 5 Rod White, USA, Archery, 2000

The US Olympic Trials were held in September 1999, with the top three finishers qualifying for the Olympic team. Rod White, who had earned a gold medal in the team event in 1996, finished a disappointing fifth. White tossed his bow into his basement and tried to get on with his life. Then Shane Parker, who had placed third, was suspended for cheating (he shot two extra arrows at the Trials), and White was moved up to team alternate. In March 2000 Justin Huish, who had finished second at the Trials, withdrew after being arrested for selling marijuana. Suddenly White, who had not picked up his Olympic bow for six months, found himself on the US team after all. He began shooting 200–300 arrows a day to get back "in quiver." The team went on to win the bronze medals.

## 6 Greek Synchronized Springboard Diving Pair, 2004

As the host nation, Greece was automatically allowed to enter a pair in the synchronized springboard diving event without participating in a qualifying tournament. The Greeks were represented by Nikolaos Siranidis, who had placed 36th in the 2000 springboard event and fellow Athenian Thomas Bimis, who had placed 32nd. Leading by twelve points with one dive remaining, China's Peng Bo and Wang Kenan seemed a certainty for Olympic victory, particularly as they had never lost a major international competition together. However, Wang lost control on his final dive, earning zero points from the judges and dropping the pair to last place. Next, the reigning world champions, Dmitri Sautin and Aleksandr Dobroskok of Russia, botched their final dive when Sautin hit his head on the board, dropping them to seventh place. With a chance for gold, the US team of Justin and Troy Dumais were stymied because of a poor takeoff by Troy, leaving them in fifth place. Siranidis and Bimis, encouraged by the wild support of the crowd, performed a spectacular last dive—an inward 3½ somersault tuck—and unexpectedly won the event by 2.40 points. The upset nature of their victory was underscored a week later, when Siranidis took part in the individual springboard event. With 32 divers in the competition, he ended up in 28th place.

# 8 Athletes Unfamiliar with Olympic Rules or Equipment

## 1 Bakhaavaa Buidaa, Mongolia, Lightweight Judo, 1972

Buidaa lost a silver medal when he became the first person in judo history to fail a drug test. He tested positive for excess caffeine. Buidaa was so unschooled in judo tradition that he wrapped his belt around his waist only once instead of twice.

## 2 Secundino Borabota, Equatorial Guinea, 400 Meters, 1984

Innocent Egbunike of Nigeria, one of the secondary favorites, thought he had prepared for any eventuality. But shortly after the start of the third heat of the first round, Egbunike, running in the inside lane, found himself cut off by Secundino Borabota of the small, impoverished West African nation of Equatorial Guinea. After yelling at Borabota for 100 meters, Egbunike finally squeezed by on the inside and went on to win the heat. After the race, Borabota, evidently unaware that 400-meter runners are supposed to stay in the same lane from start to finish, explained rather cryptically that an injury led him to switch lanes temporarily. "Lane one is a good lane," he added.

## 3 Derrick Tenai, Solomon Islands, Archery, 1988

Security guard Derrick Tenai had never seen a modern bow until he arrived in Seoul for the Olympics. In the open round, he hit the target 89 times and missed it 55 times. None of the other 83 contestants missed the target more than 5 times, and 65 of them had no misses at all.

## 4 Gilda Montenegro, Costa Rica, Kayak Slalom Canoeing, 1992

Gilda Montenegro accumulated 470 penalty points on her first run, and then spent most of the second run upside-down before giving up with 11 gates to go. At one point, she hit her head on the bottom of the course with such force that her helmet cracked. Some observers wondered how Montenegro could have qualified for the Olympics. In fact, she didn't. She was working as a raft guide for Rafael Gallo, who happened to be the manager of the Costa Rican canoe team. One month before the Barcelona Games, Gallo learned that Costa Rica had been awarded an extra entry. Gallo offered the place to Montenegro even though she had never trained for slalom. Montenegro was so shaken by her Olympic experience that she didn't get into a slalom boat again for a year and a half. Then she decided to try to return to the Olympics in 1996 and complete a run without missing a gate. She succeeded on her second run and placed 28th of 30.

## 5 Josia Thugwane, South Africa, Marathon, 1996

Josia Thugwane was abandoned by his parents and began working at the age of nine, tending cattle. When he was seventeen he switched from playing soccer to running, having learned that it was possible to earn money racing. His first success was in a local half-marathon that brought him 50 rand ($14). He attracted the attention of a nearby coal mine who wanted him for contests against other mines. He was given a job as a kitchen worker and built a shack for his wife and children in Mzinoni Township in the highlands east of Johannesburg. At 1.58 meters (5 feet 2 inches) and 47 kilograms (99 pounds), Thugwane was the smallest of the 123 runners who started the 1996 Atlanta marathon. He won by three seconds, the closest marathon in Olympic history. In an age of television coverage and shoe contracts, Josia Thugwane was still so unaware of the significance of the Olympics that he was preparing to leave the stadium when officials informed him that there would be a medal ceremony on the field, and when his name was announced as the gold-medal-winner, he remained standing on the ground until another official motioned him to climb the platform. He celebrated his victory by buying a CD player and thirty CDs.

## 6 Eric Moussambani, Equatorial Guinea, 100-meter Freestyle Swimming, 2000

Perhaps the most unexpected celebrity of the Sydney Olympics was Equatorial Guinea's Eric Moussambani. With the encouragement of the International Olympic Committee, the International Swimming Federation allowed each nation to enter two swimmers even if they did not meet the official qualifying times. In Equatorial Guinea, three trial races were held in a 20-meter hotel pool. Two of them were won by 22-year-old Eric Moussambani, who did not start swimming until January 2000. Because he could not afford the fee to use the hotel pool, he was only able to practice once a week for one hour at 6 a.m. on Sundays.

Moussambani arrived in Sydney expecting to compete in the 50-meter freestyle, but his coach ordered him to enter the 100 meters, a distance he had never attempted.

So, on the morning of September 19, Moussambani found himself on the starting line of heat one of the 100 meters, alongside two other extreme outsiders, Karim Bare of Niger and Farkhod Oripov of Tajikistan. Bare jumped into the pool too soon and was disqualified. Thinking the race had started, Oripov did the same, and he too was disqualified. Moussambani, who had the presence of mind to stay on the podium until the gun went off, was left to swim the race alone. Swimming with his head above the water, he managed to complete the first 50 meters in 40.97 seconds, but he had expended almost all of his strength and the second 50 turned into an adventure. His speed, not great to begin with, diminished dramatically. He flailed and thrashed and, ten meters from the finish line, he stopped moving forward. Swim officials began to wonder if they should intervene, but then Moussambani heard the crowd shouting encouragement and he called up an extra burst of energy and made it to the wall. His time, 1:52.72, was more than 50 seconds slower than the next slowest swimmer.

## 7 Barila Bolopa, Equatorial Guinea, Women's 50-meter Freestyle Swimming, 2000

Like her better-known Equatorial Guinean teammate Eric Moussambani, Barila Bolopa had no formal training and had never swum in a full-size pool. She completed her 50-meter lap in 63.97 seconds: ten seconds more than it took Inge de Bruijn to win the 100-meter race, not to mention more than 28 seconds slower than the second slowest swimmer in the 50 free, Aissatou Barry of Guinea.

## 8 Fatema Hameed al-Gerashi, Bahrain, Women's 50-meter Freestyle Swimming, 2000

Hameed was the youngest athlete at the 2000 Olympics: 12 years old. Before arriving in Sydney, she had never swum in front of men. Understandably nervous before thousands of people on the morning of her race, she wobbled on the starting block rather than remaining still and was disqualified.

# 3 Laconic Olympic Champions

### 1 George Goulding, Canada, 10,000-meter Walk, 1912

George Goulding, an English-born Canadian, had competed in the 1908 Olympics as both a walker and a runner, placing fourth in the 3,500-meter walk and 22nd in the marathon. In 1912 he kept up such a rapid pace in the 10,000-meter walk that three of the ten finalists dropped out and another three were disqualified for lifting. After his victory, he sent a telegram to his wife which read simply, "Won—George."

### 2 Pierre Coquelin de Lisle, France, Prone Small Bore Rifle Shooting, 1924

Following his gold medal victory, 23-year-old Pierre Coquelin de Lisle sent the following succinct cable to his mother: "Am Olympic champion. World record beaten. Will arrive Tuesday morning."

### 3 Percy Williams, Canada, 200 Meters, 1928

Running his eighth race in four days, and two days after he won the 100 meters, Percy Williams won the 200-meter final by almost a yard. That night Williams wrote in his diary: "Telegrams galore. The girls' team sent flowers to me. Hot dog!"

# 5 Competitors Who Shaved Their Heads During the Olympics

**1 Japanese Wrestling Team, 1960**

The entire Japanese wrestling team had their heads shaved after an all-round poor showing at the 1960 Rome Olympics.

**2 Elvira Ozolina, Soviet Union, Women's Javelin, 1964**

Representing the Soviet Union, defending Olympic champion Elvira Ozolina of Latvia fouled on her last four attempts and had to settle for fifth place. She was so distressed by her performance that she went straight to the hairdresser at the Olympic Village and asked to have her head shaved. When the Japanese hairdresser refused, Ozolina took the clippers herself and removed a chunk of her long tresses. The hairdresser finished the job and Ozolina left the parlor bald, refusing a scarf to hide her shame.

**3 David Rigert, Soviet Union, Middle Heavyweight Weightlifting, 1972**

The clear favorite, world-record-holder David Rigert of the Soviet Union, set an Olympic record in the press of 187.5 kg. However, he failed at all three of his attempts to snatch 160 kg, despite the fact that he held the world record of 167.5 kg. Rigert was so upset that he literally pulled his hair out and banged his head against a wall. He was finally restrained by his colleagues, but the next day he threw another fit and had to be sent home.

**4 USA Volleyball Team, 1992**

In the opening match between the United States and Japan, umpire Laert de Souza of Brazil, issued a yellow card to United States middle blocker Bob Samuelson for arguing a call. Because Samuelson had already received a yellow card earlier in the game, he should have been ejected from the match, and Japan should have been awarded a point—a point that would have given Japan the victory. But referee Ramis Samedov of Azerbaijan didn't want to end a match on a penalty point and instead waved for play to continue. The Americans fought off match point and went on to win in five games. Japan protested, and the next day the International Volleyball Federation control committee voted unanimously to award the victory to Japan. Samuelson suffered from alopecia universalis, a condition that left him bald. As a show of solidarity, the other eleven members of the United States team showed up for their second match with their heads completely shaved. The Americans won their next five matches, but were beaten by Brazil in the semi-finals.

## 5 Robert Esmie, Canada, 4 x 100-meter Relay, 1996

Canada's Robert Esmie was replaced by Carlton Chambers in the early rounds of the 1996 Atlanta Olympics. When Chambers was injured in the semi-final the team brought Esmie back to run the first leg of the final. Esmie celebrated this honor by shaving his head to read "RELAY BLAST OFF."

# 5 Athletes Who Bit
# Their Opponents

## 1 Roger Brousse, France, Middleweight Boxing, 1924

Olympic boxing has a long and glorious history of protests, demonstrations and general outrages. But of all the incidents and controversies, the real gold-medal-winner was the Brousse-Mallin Affair, which occurred in Paris in 1924. Harry Mallin, the defending champion, was a 32-year-old London policeman. In the quarter-finals he faced 23-year-old Roger Brousse of France. As soon as the fight ended, Mallin approached the Belgian referee and displayed several well-defined teeth marks on his chest. The referee ignored him and proceeded to award the bout to Brousse, 2–1. Examination of Mallin's chest revealed that he had most definitely been bitten, and quite robustly at that. In fact, in his previous bout Brousse had also been accused of biting his opponent, Manolo Gallardo of Argentina. Brousse's supporters claimed that he had an odd habit of snapping his jaw whenever he threw a punch. What had happened, they said, was that Mallin had ducked one of Brousse's punches and, coming back up, bumped his chest against Brousse's snapping mouth. The Jury of Appeal ruled that Brousse's bite had been unintentional, but disqualified him anyway. Mallin went on to win the gold medal. The British press had a field day with the affair. "It was found necessary," said the *Daily Sketch*, "to substitute for a mere boxer a man-eating expert named Brousse, whose passion for raw meat led him to attempt to bite off portions of his opponents' anatomies." Another reporter wrote, "Having got his teeth into a piece of Argentine meat during one of the earlier contests, M. Brousse decided to vary the menu by sampling some of the unroasted human beef of Old England."

## 2 Ezio Gamba, Italy, Lightweight Judo, 1980

European champion Neil Adams needed less than four minutes to defeat his first three opponents, but in the final he lost a unanimous decision to his 21-year-old nemesis, Ezio Gamba. The most noteworthy confrontation between Gamba and Adams occurred at the 1977 European Championships when Gamba, in a desperate attempt to avoid submission, bit Adams on the backside. A shocked Adams won anyway but, Adams later recalled, "I still wonder how far Gamba would have gone if I had continued holding him down. I'm just glad I wasn't lying on top of him the other way around."

### 3 Matt Lindland, USA, Middleweight Greco-Roman Wrestling, 2000

Matt Lindland lost the final in the US trials 2–1 to Keith Sieracki, but protested that Sieracki had used his legs to trip him. Sieracki countered that Lindland had bitten his ear. In the midst of arbitration, Lindland won a rematch 8–0. The case was appealed all the way to the US Supreme Court, and eventually it was Lindland who was allowed to compete in the Olympics. He went on to win the silver medal.

### 4 Emilio Correa, Cuba, Middleweight Boxing, 2008

Cuba's Emilio Correa had two points deducted for biting his opponent James DeGale's shoulder in the first round of the final. DeGale was also penalized two points for holding in the third round, but was still ahead by two points going into the final round. The bout deteriorated quickly as both boxers began to tire, falling over each other no less than five times as DeGale held on to his lead to win the gold medal.

### 5 Dzhakhon Kurbanov, Tajikistan, Light Heavyweight Boxing, 2008

Eventual bronze medalist Yerkebulan Shynaliyev had an unpleasant experience in his quarter-final bout: he was leading 12–6 in the third round when his opponent, Dzhakhon Kurbanov, bit him on the shoulder and was disqualified.

# 2 Olympians Aboard the *Titanic*

## 1 Cosmo Duff Gordon, Great Britain, Épée Fencing, 1906

Cosmo Duff Gordon was 43 years old when he helped the British team to second place at the 1906 Athens Games. On the night of April 15, 1912, Duff Gordon and his wife Lucille, a noted fashion designer, were passengers aboard the *Titanic* when the doomed ship struck an iceberg. Amid the panic the Duff Gordons found an emergency lifeboat that was being prepared away from the throng. Along with Lady Duff Gordon's secretary, Miss Francatelli, they were hoisted aboard and the lifeboat was lowered into the water. Although the boat was big enough to accommodate forty people, there were only twelve inside: seven crew members, two American gentlemen, and the Duff Gordon party of three. Despite the fact that there was room for twenty-eight more people, they made no attempt to save any of the passengers who were drowning and freezing to death in the icy water. Indeed, they seemed to make a point of rowing away from the screams and wails of the victims. After they were saved by the *Carpathia*, Duff Gordon gathered the seven crew members from the lifeboat and gave them each a check for £5, presumably to help them replace their lost kits (tools and uniforms). A group photo was taken, and the crew members autographed Lady Duff Gordon's lifebelt. Upon their arrival in New York City the Duff Gordons established themselves in a suite at the Ritz Hotel and immediately threw a dinner party, complete with champagne and caviar. But a few days later, word spread about the payment Duff Gordon had made to the crew members, and he was accused of having bribed the crew to row away from the sinking ship. The Duff Gordons found themselves booed when they tried to walk in the streets, and many staff members of the Ritz refused to serve them. Back in London, a Board of Trade inquiry absolved Cosmo of bribery. However, although he lived for another nineteen years, he was never able to fully escape his public image as a coward.

## 2 Dick Williams, USA, Tennis, 1924

Dick Williams was 21 years old in 1912 when, with his father Charles, he boarded the *Titanic* in Cherbourg and headed for New York. After the ship hit an iceberg, Williams watched as his father was killed by the collapse of a huge funnel. He dived into the freezing water and, wearing a fur coat, swam fifty feet to a collapsible lifeboat. Along with about 25 to 30 others, he clung to the boat for six hours. When the *Carpathia* finally arrived to save them, only eleven were still alive; the rest had frozen to death. The *Carpathia*'s doctor wanted to amputate both Williams' legs to avoid gangrene, but Williams refused. Instead, he exercised daily and recovered. He returned to the US the following year as a member of the 1913 Davis Cup team. During World War I, Williams joined the US Army and served with distinction, earning the Croix de Guerre and the Legion of Honor. With all this behind him, the stress of playing in the Olympics must not have fazed Williams. He sprained his ankle in the semi-finals and suggested to his partner, Hazel Wightman, that they withdraw from the final. She refused. "She told me to stay at the net," Williams later recalled, "and she'd cover everything else. I didn't move much, but Hazel ran everywhere and won the match and the [gold] medals for us."

# 16 Royal Olympians...
# and one honorable mention

*Numerous barons, counts, dukes and other members of nobility have competed in the Olympics. Here are a few of the higher-ranked members of royal families.*

## 1 Prince Friedrich Karl of Prussia, Germany, Equestrian Jumping, 1912

Prince Friedrich Karl earned a bronze medal as a member of Germany's jumping team. He was a fighter pilot during World War I, was taken captive by Australian troops and died in captivity.

## 2 Grand Duke Dmitri Pavlovich Romanov, Russia, Equestrian Jumping, 1912

The grandson of Tsar Alexander II, he tied for ninth place in the individual jumping competition in Stockholm. Four years later, he was involved in the assassination of the mystic Rasputin. When the Russian Revolution overthrew his family in 1917, Dmitri Pavlovich was fortunate to be out of the country and avoided execution.

## 3 Prince Esper Beloselsky-Belozersky, Russia, 10-meter Sailing, 1912

Prince Esper earned a bronze medal at the Stockholm Games five years before the Russian Revolution forced him to flee to a lesser life in Paris.

## 4 Crown Prince Olav, Norway, 6-meter Sailing, 1928

Crown Prince Olav of Norway was part of the crew that won the 6-meter yachting event. He later became a symbol of Norwegian resistance to the Nazis during World War II and, after succeeding to his father's throne in 1957, was a popular king for 34 years until his death in 1991.

## 5 Crown Prince Gustav Olaf, Sweden, Equestrian Jumping, 1936

A member of Sweden's jumping team at the Berlin Olympics, Gustaf Olaf died in an aircraft accident in 1947, three years before his father became king of Sweden. His own son ascended to the throne in 1973.

**6** **Prince Adegboyega Folaranmi Adedoyin, Nigeria,**
**Long Jump, 1948**
Fifth-place finisher Prince Adegboyega Folaranmi Adedoyin was a
member of the royal family of the kingdom of Ijebu-Remo in Nigeria.
A medical student at Queen's University in Belfast, he represented Great
Britain, since Nigeria was then a British colony (it gained independence
in 1960).

**7/8** **Prince Bhanubandh Birabongse and Princess Arunhee,**
**Thailand, Sailing, 1956-1964, 1972**
The grandson of King Mongkut of Siam, Prince Bhanubandh first took
up Formula One racing. In 1955 he switched to sailing, representing his
country in four Olympics. His wife, Princess Arunhee, joined him as
crew in the Dragon class event in 1964.

**9** **Crown Prince Konstantinos, Greece, Dragon Class Sailing, 1960**
A member of the gold medal-winning Greek boat, twenty-year-old
Crown Prince Konstantinos received the traditional victory dunking by
being pushed into the water by his mother Queen Frederika. Four years
later he succeeded to the throne as King Constantine II and served until
the Greek monarchy was abolished in 1973.

**10** **Crown Prince Harald, Norway, Sailing, 1964-1972**
Crown Prince Harald finished in eighth place in the 5.5-meter class in
1964 and eleventh in 1968, and tenth in the Soling class in 1972.

**11** **Crown Prince Juan Carlos, Spain, Dragon Class Sailing, 1972**
Prince Juan Carlos and his crew finished in 15th place. Three years later
he ascended the throne as King Juan Carlos I.

**12** **Princess Anne, Great Britain, Equestrian, 1976**
Princess Anne placed 24th of 49 in the three-day event.

**13** **Princess Cristina of Spain, Tornado Class Sailing, 1988**
Princess Cristina placed 20th of 23.

**14** **Prince Felipe, Spain, Soling Class Sailing, 1992**
Princess Cristina's brother, Prince Felipe, heir to the Spanish throne, was

a member of the sixth-place Spanish crew. His full title was Crown Prince Felipe Juan Pablo Alfonso de Todos los Santos Borbón Schleswig-Borbón Sonderburg Glucksburg.

## 15 Prince Abdul Hakeem, Brunei, Skeet Shooting, 1996–2000

In 1988 and 1992 the Sultanate of Brunei participated in the Olympics, but sent only officials—no athletes. Sensitive to criticism that they were using the Olympics for their own pleasure, the National Olympic Committee of Brunei solved the problem by entering an athlete in the 1996 skeet event: the sultan's nephew, Prince Abdul Hakeem. Abdul Hakeem caused something of a sensation in 1993 when he reputedly sent his private jet from Glasgow to London to purchase a jar of his favorite brand of mustard. He arrived in Atlanta with two $35,000 gold-inlaid Krieghoff shotguns. He ended up in a tie for 49th place. In 2000 he moved up to 45th place.

## 16 Princess Nathalie of Sayn-Wittgenstein-Berleburg, Denmark, Equestrian Dressage, 2008

The niece of Queen Margrethe II of Denmark, Princess Nathalie earned a bronze medal in team dressage at the Beijing Olympics.

## Honorable Mention: Prince Octopus Dzanie, Ghana, Featherweight Boxing, 2008

Although he failed to advance beyond the first round and was not actually royal, Ghana's entry in the featherweight competition attracted attention for his unusual name: Prince Octopus Dzanie. Ghana has sent other "princes" to the Olympics. In 1972 Prince Amartey won a bronze medal in middleweight boxing, and in 1996 Prince Koranteng played for the Ghanaian football team.

# Family
# Life

# 8 Olympic Families

## 1 Kellers, Germany, Field Hockey, 1936-2008

Andreas Keller of the 1992 gold medal-winning German field hockey team was the third generation of his family to medal in the event. His grandfather Erwin earned a silver medal in 1936, and his father Carsten represented Germany in three Olympics and was a member of the 1972 gold-medal-winning squad. Andreas himself won silver in 1984 and 1988 before picking up his own gold. As if that weren't enough, in 2004 Andreas's step-sister Natascha won gold with Germany's women's team, and in 2008 their brother Florian became the fifth member of the family to earn a gold medal in the sport.

## 2 Roycrofts, Australia, Equestrian, 1960-1996

In 1968 Australia's bronze medal-winning team included the father-son combination of Bill and Wayne Roycroft. The pair repeated their performance in 1976, when father Bill was 61 years old. Two more of Bill Roycroft's sons competed in the Olympics: Clarke in 1972 and Barry in 1976 and 1988. Wayne's wife, Vicki, took part in 1984, 1988 and 1996.

## 3 Montanos, Italy, Sabre Fencing, 1936-2004

In 2004 25-year-old Aldo Montano, from Livorno, won the gold medal in the individual sabre competition. He was the third generation in his family to win an Olympic medal in the sabre: his grandfather, also named Aldo, earned silver medals in the team event in 1936 and 1948, and his father, Mario, won a team gold and two silvers between 1972 and 1980.

## 4 Vandernottes, France, Coxed Fours Rowing, 1936

The coxswain for the French bronze medalists was 12-year-old Noël Vandernotte, whose father, Fernand, and uncle, Marcel, were also members of the crew. Noël also coxed for the pair-oared shell.

## 5 Lundes, Norway, Sailing and Skiing, 1924-1994

Eugen Lunde, who won a gold medal in 6-meter sailing in 1924, spawned one of the most successful families in Olympic history. His son, Peder, won a silver medal in 1952 in the 5-meter class; his grandson Peder, Jr., won gold in the 1960 Flying Dutchman and silver in the 1968 Star class; and his great-granddaughter, Jeanette, represented Norway in downhill skiing at the 1994 Winter Olympics.

### 6 Bogen/Gerevich, Hungary, Fencing, 1912-1980

The 1932 individual foil bronze medalist Erna Bogen was the daughter of Albert Bogen, who won a silver medal in team sabre in 1912. She later married seven-time sabre gold medalist Aladár Gerevich. Their son, Pál, earned two bronze medals in team sabre in 1972 and 1980.

### 7 Simions, Romania, Boxing, 1984-2000

Sydney 2000 light heavyweight silver-medal-winner Marian Simion came from a boxing family. His father Gheorghe competed in the 1984 Olympics, and his younger brother Dorel earned bronze medal in 2000. Marian himself had won a bronze as a welterweight at the 1996 Olympics and a gold medal at the 1999 world championships.

### 8 Phinneys, USA, Cycling, 1984-2008

The seventh-place finisher in the 4,000-meter individual pursuit at Beijing in 2008, Taylor Phinney, came from a prominent cycling family. His father, 1984 Olympian Davis Phinney, was the first American to win a stage of the Tour de France, and his mother, Connie Carpenter-Phinney, won the gold medal in the inaugural women's road race at the 1984 Games. She also competed in speed skating at the 1972 Sapporo Olympics.

# 10 Notable Parent-Child Combinations

## 1 Oscar and Alfred Swahn, Sweden

In 1908 Oscar Swahn was already 60 years old when he won his first Olympic gold medals, earning a total of two golds and one bronze in running-target shooting. In 1912 he won one gold and one bronze, and in Antwerp in 1920, at the age of 72, he won his first silver medal as part of the Swedish double-shot running deer team. Oscar's son Alfred had an even more successful Olympic career. Between 1908 and 1924 he won nine medals: three golds, three silvers and three bronzes.

## 2 Bill and Frank Havens, USA

Bill Havens was a member of the Yale University eights rowing team that won the right to represent the United States at the 1924 Olympics. However, he chose not to make the trip to Paris because his wife was expecting their first child. That child, a boy named Frank, was born five days after the close of the Paris Olympics. Twenty-eight years later Frank competed in the Canadian singles 10,000 meters canoeing event at the 1952 Helsinki Olympics. Frank moved into the lead in the home stretch of the last lap and won by about 18 yards. After the race, Frank sent a telegram from Helsinki to his father that ended, "I'm coming home with the gold medal you should've won."

## 3/4 Paul and Hilary Smart, USA, and Carlos de Cárdenas Jr. and Sr., Cuba

Two father-and-son teams won the gold and silver medals in Star class sailing at the 1948 London Olympics. Paul Smart was a 56-year-old lawyer from New York. His 23-year-old son, Hilary, was a student at Harvard. The silver-medal-winning Carlos de Cárdenas and Carlos de Cárdenas Junior were also father and son.

## 5 Márton Homonnai and Katalin Szoke, Hungary

The winner of the 1952 women's 100-meter freestyle, 16-year-old Katalin Szoke had been well-known in Hungary for quite some time. Her mother had introduced her to swimming when she was only six months old, and she became known as "Kati, the World's First Waterproof Baby." She was able to stay afloat unaided before she was two years old. Szoke's father, Márton Homonnai, was a member of Hungary's gold medal-winning water polo team in 1932 and 1936, and her husband, Kalman Markovits, was a member of Hungary's gold-medal-winning water polo team in 1952 and 1956.

## 6 Mike and Andre Agassi, USA

Emanoul "Mike" Agassi represented Iran as a boxer at the 1948 and 1952 Olympics, losing his first fight both times. A member of Iran's Armenian minority, Agassi emigrated to the United States, settling first in Chicago and then in Las Vegas. He was obsessed with turning one of his four children into a tennis star. After traumatizing the three oldest, he hit the jackpot with the youngest, Andre. By the time he was three years old, Andre, with a racket taped to his hand, was volleying with his father. He turned professional at the age of sixteen and made it to the semi-finals of the 1988 French and US Opens when he was eighteen. By 1996 Andre had signed a $100 million contract with Nike. He flew around in his own jet, hobnobbed with celebrities and was going steady with actress Brooke Shields (they would later marry and divorce). By the time the 1996 Atlanta Olympics rolled around, Agassi was in another of his slumps. However, despite his glitzy lifestyle, he was firmly committed to representing the United States. He managed to win two tie-breaks to beat Jonas Björkman of Sweden; he lost the opening set to Andrea Gaudenzi of Italy and he struggled against Wayne Ferreira before prevailing 7– 5, 4–6, 7–5. As it turned out, the final was his easiest match, lasting only 77 minutes. Agassi was on the top of his game, and Sergi Bruguera of Spain, a clay court specialist, was unable to cope.

## 7 Imre and Miklos Németh, Hungary

Miklos Németh was less than two years old when his father Imre won the gold medal for the hammer throw at the 1948 Olympics in London. His father pressed him to take up the hammer, but Miklos preferred the javelin, and by 1967 he was ranked second in the world. But he never performed well in major championships. At the 1968 Olympics an elbow injury kept him from qualifying for the final. In 1972 he was one of the favorites, but finished a disappointing seventh. Finally in 1976 Miklos not only won the javelin event, but broke the world record. In so doing he became the first son of a track and field gold medalist to win a gold of his own.

## 8 Paul and Trine Elvstrøm, Denmark

Paul Elvstrøm was the first person in Olympic history to win the same individual event four times, having triumphed in Finn class sailing in 1948, 1952, 1956 and 1960. He also competed in 1968 and 1972. He returned to the Olympics in 1984, this time in the two-person Tornado class with a new partner—his daughter Trine. They finished in fourth place and took part once more in 1988.

## 9 Lennox and Inger Miller, Jamaica/USA

Running the third leg of the women's 4 × 100-meter Relay in 1996, Inger Miller put the US in front and, anchor Gwen Torrence extended the margin. Miller's gold medal completed the set for her family: her father, Lennox Miller, won a silver in the 1968 100 meters and a bronze in 1972.

## 10 Butch and Misty May, USA

Misty May competed at the 2000 Olympics as part of the US women's indoor volleyball team. Four years later she and partner Kerri Walsh swept through the women's beach volleyball event, winning all seven of their matches without losing a single set. They successfully defended their title in 2008. Misty May's father, Butch May, was a member of the 1968 US Olympic volleyball team, and her cousin on her mother's side, Taylor Dent, placed fourth in the men's tennis singles event in Athens in 2004.

# 7 Teams with
# 3 or More Brothers

## 1 British Footballers, 1906
The 1906 football team from Smyrna was an international one, including players from Great Britain, France, Armenia and Greece. The five British players were all members of the Whittal family. Albert, Edward and Godfrey were the sons of Edward Whittal; Donald and Harold were the sons of Edward's brother, Easton. The team placed second after the team from Athens refused to play off for second place.

## 2 British Cyclists, 1928
The British men's pursuit team set an Olympic record of 5:11.2 in the quarter-finals but finished third in the final. Three of the four British riders were the Wyld brothers from Derby: Frank, Leonard and Percy.

## 3 Swedish Footballers, 1948
By 1948 the best players of Western Europe and South America were turning professional, and Olympic soccer began to be dominated by the state-sponsored "amateur" teams of Eastern Europe. Sweden was the last non-Communist team to win an unboycotted Olympic football tournament until 1992. Their team included three brothers, Gunnar, Bertil and Knut Nordahl, as well as three firemen, including Gunnar Nordahl.

## 4 Peruvian Basketball Players, 1964
The Peruvian team sported four brothers, Ricardo, Enrique, Raul and Luis Duarte.

## 5 Swedish Cyclists, 1968
The four Swedish silver medalists in the 1968 men's team time trial were all brothers: Erik, Gösta, Sture and Tomas Pettersson. They won the world championship in 1967, 1968 and 1969. Three of them subsequently changed their last names from Pettersson to that of their home village, Fåglum.

## 6 Australian Field Hockey Players, 1968

The second-place Australian team included three brothers: Eric, Gordon and Julian Pearce. A fourth brother, Mel, represented Australia in 1956.

## 7 Swedish Sailors, 1968-1972

The three Sundelin brothers, Jörgen, Peter and Ulf Sundelin, from the small resort town of Ektorp, won the 5.5-meter sailing event at the 1968 Mexico City Olympics. Four years later they competed in the 1972 Dragon class event, placing sixth.

# 17 Sets of Twins in the Olympics

**1/2 Bernd and Jorg Landvoigt (East Germany) and Yuri and Nikolai Pimenov (Soviet Union), Coxless Pairs Rowing, 1980**

Observers of the medal ceremony for the 1980 men's coxless pairs might have been excused for rubbing their eyes. Both the gold- and the silver-medal teams were identical twins. Bernd and Jorg Landvoigt of East Germany took first place, while Yuri and Nikolai Pimenov of Russia finished second. The Landvoigt twins were 25-year-old steelworkers from Potsdam and had also won the gold medals at the 1976 Olympics.

**3 Sonia Robertson and Sandy Chick, Zimbabwe, Women's Field Hockey, 1980**

Sonia Robertson and Sandy Chick of the Zimbabwe team became the second set of identical twins ever to win Olympic gold medals—just four days after Bernd and Jörg Landvoigt earned theirs.

**4 Madeline and Margaret de Jesus, Puerto Rico, Women's 4 x 400-meter Relay, 1984**

The Puerto Rican coach refused to let his team take part in the final when he discovered that the woman who ran the second leg for the Puerto Ricans in their qualifying heat was not team member Madeline de Jesus, but her twin sister Margaret. After being injured in the long jump, Madeline had asked her sister, who was in Los Angeles as a spectator, to take her place in the relay.

**5 Alvin and Calvin Harrison, USA, 4 x 400-meter Relay, 2000**

Among the Athens 2000 gold-medal-winning US 4 × 400-meter relay team were 26-year-old twins Alvin and Calvin Harrison. The pair were champions of perseverance. They both dropped out of high school in Salinas, California, and tried to run track at a local college. In 1995 they were forced to quit and make a living. They both landed jobs—Alvin handling hazardous materials and Calvin at a sporting goods store—but for a while they had to live in their 1987 Ford Mustang: Calvin in the front seat, Alvin in the back. In Sydney, Alvin earned the silver medal in the 400 meters, and the twins finally came together to share gold in the relay. Calvin's 43.55 third leg was the fastest leg of the race.

## 6 Tyler and Cameron Winklevoss, (USA), Coxless Fours Rowing, 2008

Sixth-place finishers Tyler and Cameron Winklevoss are better known for their long-running legal battle with Mark Zuckerberg, creator of the popular social media site Facebook, whom they accused of stealing their idea for the website while classmates at Harvard. Their story was popularized in the 2010 movie *The Social Network*. In 2011, after seven years of lawsuits, the Winklevoss twins agreed to a $65-million settlement.

## 7 Pavol and Peter Hochschorner, Slovakia, Canadian Slalom Pairs Canoeing, 2000-2008

Twins Pavol and Peter Hochschorner won the 2000 Canadian Slalom gold medal, and then easily defended their title at both the 2004 and 2008 Olympics. They even celebrated in unison, pumping their right fists into the air.

## 8 Ann and Janet Osgerby, Great Britain, Women's 100-meter Butterfly, 1980

Ann and Janet Osgerby were 17-year-old twins from Chorley, Lancashire. Ann was 20 minutes older and 0.69 seconds faster. In the final they placed fourth and eighth.

## 9 Georgina and Caroline Evers-Swindell, New Zealand, Women's Double Sculls Rowing, 2004-2008

Twenty-five-year-old identical twins Georgina and Caroline Evers-Swindell arrived at the Athens Games with a three-year winning streak. They won the 2004 championship by just under a second, and then came back four years later to successfully defend their Olympic title at the 2008 Beijing Olympics.

## 10 Tõnu and Toomas Tõniste, Soviet Union, 470 Sailing, 1988

The previously unknown Tõniste twins from Estonia were in first place with one race remaining. All they had to do to win gold medals was finish ahead of French pair Thierry Peponnet and Luc Pillot in the final race, which was sailed in near-gale conditions. The Tõnistes were in the lead with less than a lap to go when they suffered a severe capsize and were forced to retire; they ended up with silver medals.

## 11 Arne and Åke Borg, Sweden, Freestyle Swimming, 1924

Arne and Åke Borg, who finished second and fourth in the 400-meter freestyle, were twin brothers. They both gained bronze medals as members of Sweden's 4 × 200-meter relay team. Arne, who eventually competed in three Olympics and won one gold medal, two silvers and two bronzes, was an extremely popular athlete in Sweden and abroad. Once he was called up for military service, but ignored the notice in order to take a tour of Spain. Imprisoned upon his return to Sweden, he received so many gifts of food and wine during his incarceration that he gained 17 pounds before he was finally released.

## 12/13 Karen and Sarah Josephson (USA) and Penny and Victoria Vilagos (Canada), Synchronized Swimming, 1992

Both the top two pairs comprised identical twin sisters. The Josephsons, undefeated since gaining silver medals at the 1988 Olympics, and having won 15 straight meets, took the gold medals. The Vilagoses had come back after five years away from competition to prepare for the 1992 Olympics. It was the first time two sets of twins took gold and silver since the Landvoigt and Pimenov twins won the men's coxless pairs rowing at the 1980 Games.

## 14 Paul and Morgan Hamm, USA, Gymnastics, 2000-2004

Paul Hamm and his fraternal twin brother Morgan competed in their first Olympics in Sydney. At the time, Morgan reached the finals of the floor competition, while Paul finished 14th in the all-around. Four years later, Paul won the individual all-around gold medal and both earned silver medals in the team event.

## 15 John and Tom Anderson, Australia, Sailing, 1972

At the same time that John Anderson was winning a gold medal in the Star class, his identical twin brother, Tom, was winning a gold medal in the Dragon class on a different course.

## 16 Anatoly and Serhei Bilohlazov, Soviet Union, Freestyle Wrestling, 1980

After winning his first two matches on decisions, Ukrainian Anatoly Bilohlazov needed only 4 minutes and 54 seconds to dispose of his last four opponents. Twenty-four hours and 48 minutes after Anatoly won the Flyweight gold medal, his twin brother, Serhei, won the Bantamweight tournament.

## 17 Kazimierz and Jozef Lipien, Poland, Greco-Roman Wrestling, 1976-1980

Kazimierz and Jozef Lipien both won Olympic medals in Greco-Roman wrestling, Kazimierz earning gold in 1976 and Jozef silver in 1980. At the 1975 World championships the Poles were accused of substituting Jozef for Kazimierz in one match. Their accusers should have known better, since Jozef always parted his hair on the left side, while Kazimierz parted his on the right.

# 6 Olympic Romances

## 1 Cold War Warmth: Harold Connolly and Olga Fikotová

American Harold Connolly won the 1956 hammer-throw gold medal, but gained far more international attention for his Olympic Village romance with Czechoslovakian discus champion Olga Fikotová. After a great deal of pressure, the Iron Curtain was drawn open long enough for Olga and Harold to wed. Forty thousand well-wishers attended their civil ceremony in Prague, which was followed by two more services, one Catholic and one Protestant. The couple then settled in the United States. Harold eventually took part in four Olympics and Olga in five. After they divorced in 1973 Harold married three-time Olympian Pat Daniels.

## 2 A Couple of Rivals: Camilla Andersen and Mia Hundvin

The first day of the Sydney 2000 women's team handball competition saw an unusual occurrence: for the first time in Olympic history, a married couple played against each other. Three months before the Sydney Games, Camilla Andersen of Denmark and Mia Hundvin of Norway became "registered partners" in Copenhagen. As expected, Norway won the match, but Denmark came back to win the gold medals. The couple separated in 2003.

## 3 Taking the Plunge: Elizabeth Becker and Clarence Pinkston

Elizabeth Becker Pinkston of the United States balanced her 1924 springboard gold with first place in the platform diving four years later. Between Olympics she had married fellow American Clarence Pinkston, whom she had met when both were members of the 1924 US diving team in Paris. Husband and wife eventually won seven Olympic medals between them.

## 4 Royal Introduction: Iñaki Urdangarín and Princess Cristina

During the 1996 Atlanta Olympics Spanish handball star Iñaki Urdangarín met Princess Cristina, daughter of King Juan Carlos of Spain, who had competed in sailing at the 1988 Olympics. The couple married in October 1997. In 2012 Urdangarín was investigated in connection with a corruption allegation in which he was accused of making millions of Euros by using his royal position to win contracts from regional governments for his non-profit foundations and then subcontracting the work to companies he oversaw.

## 5 Another Royal Couple: Prince Albert and Charlene Wittstock

Charlene Wittstock, who swam the lead leg for South Africa in the Sydney 2000 women's 4 × 100 meter medley relay, went on to marry Prince Albert of Monaco, the five-time bobsled Olympian and son of Grace Kelly and Prince Rainier.

## 6 Better than a Medal: Matthew Emmons and Katerina Kurková

Matthew Emmons missed a chance to win two gold medals in a single Olympics. With a healthy three-point lead going into the final shot of the three position small-bore rifle event, Emmons, who had won the prone event two days earlier, accidentally aimed and fired at the wrong target, earning zero points and dropping to eighth place. His blunder did come with a silver lining. After the competition, Czech shooter Katerina Kurková came over to offer her condolences. The pair started dating and married in 2007.

# 6 Olympic-Related Weddings

### 1 First Wedding at Olympics: Diana Yorgova and Nikolai Prodanov

The 1964 Tokyo Games saw the first Olympic wedding, between two Bulgarian athletes, long-jumper Diana Yorgova and gymnast Nikolai Prodanov. The ceremony took place in the Olympic Village in front of a huge Olympic flag and a photo of the Olympic flame. The couple honeymooned in Kyoto, but returned to Tokyo in time for the Closing Ceremony.

### 2 Public Adoration in Mexico: Vera Cáslavská and Josef Odložil

The undisputed heroine of the Mexico City Olympics was defending All-Around gymnastics champion Vera Cáslavská. After one of Cáslavská's performances on the balance beam received a 9.6, the audience spent ten minutes booing, howling, and chanting "Ver-a, Ver-a," until finally her mark was upped to 9.8. She eventually earned four gold medals and two silvers to add to the three golds and two silvers she had won four years earlier in Tokyo. Twenty-four hours later Cáslavská topped off her week by marrying Czechoslovak 1,500-meter champion Josef Odložil. After a civil ceremony at the Czechoslovak ambassador's house, the happy couple pushed their way through a mob of 10,000 people to get to the altar of the Roman Catholic church in Xocalo Square. The couple divorced in 1992. The following year their teenage son Martin killed Odložil during a fight in a pub.

### 3 16-medal Marriage: Roland Matthes and Kornelia Ender

Roland Matthes of Erfurt, Thuringia, was 16 years old when he set his first backstroke world record on September 11, 1967. Over the next six years he broke records in the 100-meter and 200-meter backstroke 16 times. He also won four Olympic gold medals, two silver, and two bronze. In 1978 Matthes married four-time Olympic champion Kornelia Ender. Their first child, Franziska, was born later that year, the product of parents who, between them, had earned eight gold medals, six silvers, and two bronzes. The couple divorced in 1982.

#### 4 Sydney-Themed Wedding: Candra Wijaya and Maria Caroline Indriani

A few months after winning the 2000 gold medal with Tony Gunawan in men's badminton doubles, Candra Wijaya married his sweetheart, Maria Caroline Indriani, in a Sydney Olympics-themed wedding. Both Gunawan and Wijaya's former badminton partner Budiarto served as groomsmen, while the bride's gowns were designed with Olympic themes: the shoulders of her morning gown were covered with a replica of the Sydney Opera House and her evening gown included on the shoulders an imitation of Sydney's Harbour Bridge made of pleated fabric.

#### 5 Sports Stadium Ceremony: Gezahgne Abera and Elfenesh Alemu

After winning the 2000 marathon gold medal Gezahgne Abera became so popular that, when he married fellow Olympian marathoner Elfenesh Alemu in 2003, the ceremony was held in the Ethiopian national football stadium and was attended by 25,000 people. The train of Alemu's wedding dress measured 300 meters and was carried by 600 students.

#### 6 Walking to the Altar: Jared Tallent and Claire Woods

Two weeks after winning the silver medal in the 2008 high jump, Tallent married his fiancée, Claire Woods, who competed in the women's 20-kilometer walk. The couple held their wedding in an appropriately named suburb of Adelaide: Walkerville.

# 9 Women Who Won Gold after Having a Baby

## 1 Fanny Blankers-Koen, Netherlands, Track and Field, 1948

A farmer's daughter, Fanny Koen was 18 years old when she was chosen to join the Dutch team for the 1936 Olympics in Berlin. She tied for sixth place in the high jump and was part of the 4 × 100-meter relay team that finished fifth. When the Olympics resumed after a 12-year break, Fanny was the holder of six world records—in the 100 yards, the 80-meter hurdles, the high jump, the long jump and two relays. In the interim she had also married her coach, Jan Blankers, and given birth to two children. Aged 30, she was thought by some to be too old to win the Olympic sprints, despite her string of records. She silenced her critics almost immediately by recording the best time of the opening round (12.0 seconds) in the 100-meter dash. Later in the week she also won gold medals in the 80-meter hurdles, the 200 meters, and the 4 × 100-meter relay. When she returned to Amsterdam she was driven through the crowded streets in an open carriage drawn by four gray horses. Her neighbors gave her a bicycle, "so she won't have to run so much."

## 2 Pat McCormick, USA, Diving, 1956

Eight months before the Melbourne Olympics, Pat McCormick gave birth to a baby boy. She had continued training throughout her pregnancy and swam a half-mile a day up until two days before the birth. In 1956 she repeated her double-gold-medal performance of 1952.

## 3 Valerie Brisco-Hooks, USA, Sprints, 1984

In 1982 Valerie Brisco-Hooks was a retired runner, forty pounds overweight after giving birth to a baby boy. Encouraged by her family and her coach, she returned to the track the following year and found that childbirth and motherhood had actually increased her strength. In 1984 she seemed to come out of nowhere to make the US team. Three days after winning the 400 meters, she overcame a mediocre start to become the first person to achieve a 200-/400-meters double win in the Olympics, before going on to a third gold medal in the 4 × 400-meter relay.

## 4 Tania Dangalakova (Bogomilova), Bulgaria, Breaststroke, 1988

In 1987 Tania Dangalakova, the reigning European champion in the 200-meter breaststroke, made a move not uncommon among 23-year-old female swimmers: she put aside her competitive career to have a baby. But the following year she did something rare among swimmers: she made a successful comeback. In the preliminary round she set an Olympic record of 1:08.35. In the 100-meter breaststroke final world-record-holder Silke Hörner swam the first 50 meters in 31.58, faster than world record pace. Dangalakova was right behind her. Before her pregnancy, Dangalakova had had a reputation for swimming a fast first half and then dying badly for the remainder of the race; this time, though, it was Hörner who struggled to the finish line, while Dangalakova took the lead at 80 meters and went on to become Bulgaria's first Olympic swimming champion. She was so overcome by emotion after her victory that she collapsed in tears and was unable to speak to the press.

## 5 Svetlana Masterkova, Russia, Middle-Distance Running, 1996

In 1991 Svetlana Masterkova recorded the fastest time of the year at 800 meters, but at the world championships she only placed eighth. In 1993 she was second at the indoor world championships, but injury kept her out of the outdoor meet. A notorious over-racer, she then took two years off to have a baby—after which she won two gold medals at the 1996 Olympics, in the 800 meters and the 1,500 meters.

## 6 Ekaterina Karsten (Khodatovich), Belarus, Single Sculls Rowing, 2000

After winning the single sculls at the 1996 Olympics, Ekaterina Khodatovich added the 1997 world championship and then took a year off to marry German Wilfred Karsten and give birth to a baby girl. She returned to competition in 1999 and won the world championship by a whopping three seconds. At the 2000 Olympics she fell victim to the flu and struggled through the early rounds. In the final, she and Rumyana Neykova appeared to finish in a dead heat. The judges' decision-making process took three times as long as the race itself. Eventually they decided that Karsten had won by 12 thousandths of a second. The Bulgarians protested, but their complaint was rejected. Karsten added a silver medal in 2004 and a bronze in 2008.

### 7 Maurren Maggi, Brazil, Women's Long Jump, 2008

Maurren Maggi's father was a big fan of The Beatles and named his daughter after drummer Ringo Starr's first wife, Maureen. A spelling error on her birth certificate, however, turned the name to Maurren. Maggi made her first Olympic appearance in Sydney in 2000 but was injured in the qualifying round. In 2003 she tested positive for the anabolic steroid clostebol and received a two-year suspension (she blamed the positive test on a skin cream she used after cutting herself during a hair removal process). During her ban from competition she met and married Formula 1 racer Antonio Pizzonia and gave birth to a daughter. She returned to competition in 2006, winning the South American championships and finishing sixth at the 2007 world championships. In 2008 she won the women's long jump, becoming the first Brazilian woman to win an Olympic athletics medal.

### 8 Kirsten van der Kolk, Netherlands, Lightweight Double Sculls Rowing, 2008

After winning the bronze medals together at the 2004 Athens Olympics, Kristen van der Kolk and Marit van Eupen went their separate ways. Van Eupen focused on the lightweight single sculls, winning three consecutive world titles in 2005, 2006 and 2007, while Van der Kolk left competition to have a daughter. The pair reunited in 2008 to win the double sculls gold medal.

### 9 Dara Torres, USA, Swimming, 2008

Dara Torres first competed in the Olympics as a 17-year-old in 1984, winning a gold medal as a member of the US 4 × 100-meter freestyle relay squad. She won two more medals in 1988 and another in 1992, after which she retired. She returned to the Olympics in 2000, earning five medals including two golds. Then she retired again. She gave birth to a daughter in 2006 and then came out of retirement once more, now at the age of 41, to take home three silver medals from the 2008 Olympics.

# 4 Olympian Parents of Famous Actors or Actresses

## 1 Charles Simmons, Great Britain, Team Gymnastics, 1912

Simmons was one of 24 gymnasts who secured third place for the British team at the Stockholm Olympics. His daughter, Jean Simmons, starred in numerous films, including *Great Expectations* (1946), *The Big Country* (1958), *Elmer Gantry* (1960) and *Spartacus* (1960)

## 2 Jack Kelly Sr., USA, Single and Double Sculls Rowing, 1920-1924

Jack Kelly, who once won 126 straight races, was barred from competing in London's famous Diamond Sculls race at Henley in 1920 because the Vesper Boat Club of Philadelphia, of which he was a member, had been accused of professionalism. Kelly got his revenge a few weeks later in the Olympics, when he defeated the Diamond Sculls winner, Jack Beresford, in the final. The two men were so exhausted after the race that they were unable to shake hands. Nevertheless, Kelly managed to recover sufficiently to win a second gold medal in the double sculls 30 minutes later. He repeated his double sculls victory four years later at the 1924 Paris Games. Kelly had two illustrious offspring. His son John Jr., who competed in four Olympics himself, brought his father great joy when he won the Diamond Sculls at Henley in 1947 and 1949. His daughter was Grace Kelly, the famous film actress who later became Princess of Monaco. Before retiring to a life of royalty she won an Academy Award for her performance in *The Country Girl* (1954), although she is better known for two other films released that year, both directed by Alfred Hitchcock, *Dial M for Murder* and *Rear Window*.

## 3 Frank Kurtz, USA, Platform Diving, 1932

Frank Kurtz began supporting himself when he was 12 years old. At 14 he was selling newspapers in Kansas City, Missouri, and diving at local meets when Johnny Weissmuller saw him and advised him to find a good coach in California. Kurtz hitchhiked to Los Angeles and was taken in by coach Clyde Swendsen. Seven years later, Kurtz won a bronze medal at the 1932 Olympics. During World War II he became one of the US's most famous fighter pilots, flying a plane called the Swoose. When his wife gave birth to a daughter in 1944, they named her Swoosie after the plane. Swoosie Kurtz grew up to be a well-known actress who has won two Tony awards for her roles in the plays *Fifth of July* (1982) and *The House of Blue Leaves* (1986). She has also been nominated for Emmy awards ten times.

## 4 Ran Laurie, Great Britain, Coxless Pairs Rowing, 1948

Jack Wilson and Ran Laurie were best friends who joined the Colonial Service and were sent to the Sudan. Returning to London on leave in 1938, they entered the Henley Regatta and took first place. Then they went back to the Sudan and didn't touch an oar for ten years. In May 1948 they returned to Britain on another leave and decided to take up rowing again. After six weeks' training they entered the Henley Regatta and won again. This gained them an invitation to represent Great Britain at the Olympics, and they were granted six months' leave to prepare. Rowing on their favorite course at Henley, "the Desert Rats," as they were known, won the coxless pairs gold medals. Laurie was the father of Hugh Laurie, the actor and comedian best known for playing the title role in the hospital drama series *House M.D.*

# Sport-Specific
# Lists

# 11 Unusual Olympic Sports and Events

*In the early days of the modern Olympics, the sporting program was not standardized, and the host nations were free to add sports and events of their own choosing.*

**1 100-meter Freestyle Swimming for Members of the Greek Navy, 1896**

This exceedingly specialized event attracted three entrants.

**2 Croquet, 1900**

The 1900 croquet tournament was noteworthy for the participation of three women: Jeanne Filleaul-Brohy, Marie Ohier and Madame Després, the wife of the tournament's organizer. The Official Report of the Paris Games used their inclusion as part of its defense of croquet as a sport. "This game," it explained, "French in name and origin . . . has hardly any pretensions to athleticism . . . One would be wrong, however, to disdain croquet. It develops a combinative mind—one has only to see it transform young girls into reasoners and from reasoners into reasonable people." The events were not well-attended. There was apparently one paying spectator: an English gentleman who travelled to Paris from Nice to watch the early rounds.

**3 200-meter Swimming Obstacle Race, 1900**

This quaint event required the participants to struggle past three sets of obstacles. First they had to climb over a pole, then they had to scramble over a row of boats, and finally they had to swim *under* another row of boats. Gold-medal-winner Freddy Lane of Australia grew up around boats in Sydney's harbor and put this experience to good use in the obstacle race. Rather than clamber over the middle of the boats, he crossed them at the stern, where the going was smoother. Lane was better known for his victory in the unimpeded 200-meter freestyle.

**4/5 Equestrian Long Jump and High Jump, 1900**

The former event was won by Constant van Langhendonck of Belgium, who guided his horse, Extra Dry to a distance of 6.10 meters (20 feet ¼ inch). The latter resulted in a tie between Dominique Maximien Gardères of France and Giovanni Giorgio Trissino of Italy, who, on their horses Canela and Oreste, cleared 1.85 meters (6 feet ¾ inch).

## 6 Tug of War, 1900-1920

Tug-of-war was first held in Paris in 1900 and was eventually included in five Olympics, as well as the Intercalated Games of 1906. Olympic tug-of-war rules changed from Games to Games, with team sizes varying from five to eight a side. In fact it was the lack of clarity regarding the rules that led to repeated controversies and the eventual elimination of the seemingly innocent sport from the Olympic program.

## 7 Plunge for Distance, 1904

Probably the least spectator-friendly event in Olympic history, the plunge for distance demanded that contestants begin with a standing dive into the swimming pool and then remain motionless for 60 seconds or until their heads broke the surface of the water, whichever came first. Then the length of their dives was measured. William Dickey of the United States won with a plunge of 19.05 meters (62 feet 6 inches).

## 8 56-Pound Weight Throw, 1904, 1920

The first winner of this event was Montréal policeman Étienne Desmarteau. Refused a leave of absence from his job to compete in the St Louis Games, Desmarteau went anyway and was fired. When it was learned that he had won a gold medal, his dismissal notice was conveniently lost. The second and last winner, 16 years later, was another policeman, Patrick McDonald of New York. Aged 42 years and 26 days, he remains the oldest person to win an Olympic track and field gold medal.

## 9/10/11 Standing Jumps, 1900-1912

Included in four Olympics, as well as the 1906 Intercalated Games, the standing high jump, long jump and triple jump were dominated by the amazing Ray Ewry of the United States, who earned 8 gold medals and 2 more in 1906. Ewry contracted polio as a boy and it was thought that he would be confined to a wheelchair for the rest of his life. However he began exercising on his own and not only regained the use of his legs but eventually grew up to be a superb athlete. He made a great impression at the 1900 Paris Olympics and was dubbed "The Human Frog." Ewry also held the amateur record for the backward standing long jump— 9 feet 3 inches (2.8 meters).

# 4 1,500-meter Winners Overcome by Emotion

## 1 Josy Barthel, Luxembourg, 1952

The 1952 1,500 meters was up for grabs. Coming up to the back straight Germany's Werner Lueg had opened up a three-yard lead and held it around the final turn. However, almost unnoticed, two outsiders, Josy Barthel and American Bob McMillen, had sprinted up from the very back of the field to within striking distance. Fifty yards from the finish, Lueg began to tie up. With the crowd screaming wildly, first Barthel and then McMillen passed him. Barthel could feel McMillen literally breathing down his back as the American inched closer with every stride until he was only a foot and a half behind:

Let Josy Barthel tell the rest of the story: "Five meters to run, the victory is mine, and, just as I had always dreamed in secret, I raised my arms, I smiled and I crossed the finish line. Afterward, I didn't appreciate right away that I had won. For me, as for the public, it was a surprise. I sat down, without being excited, on a bench in the middle of the infield. Then, no longer able to contain my joy, I cried. My friend Audun Boysen asked me, 'Eh bien, Josy, why are you crying? Are you ill?' It was only then that I truly understood. 'No,' I replied. 'I am crying because I won.'"

## 2 Ron Delany, Ireland, 1956

Before the race, the great Australian sportsman John Landy gave a pep talk to Ron Delany, the youngest of the four-minute milers, and told him, "I think you can win this one, Ron." The twelve finalists were so well matched that at the start of the final lap less than eight yards separated the leader from the last man. The official in charge of signaling the beginning of the final lap was so excited that he forgot to ring the bell. Delany was boxed in at tenth place. His coach at Villanova University, Jumbo Elliott, had always told him that if he was ever in a box just to relax. So Delany relaxed, even though there were only 300 yards left in the race. Just then the runner in front of Delany, Gunnar Nielsen of Denmark, realizing that he himself couldn't win the race, turned around and motioned Delany to pass him on the inside. Gradually Delany moved up; then, 120 meters from the finish, he burst out with all he had, flying past the tiring leaders to win by three yards. After crossing the finish line, Delany fell to his knees. John Landy, thinking Delany was ill or injured, rushed up to help him, only to discover the new Olympic champion was actually deep in prayer.

### 3 Pekka Vasala, Finland, 1972

Pekka Vasala was known in Finland as "Mr. Unpredictable." He had competed in the Mexico City Games but, struck down by "Montezuma's Revenge," had finished last in his heat. Nevertheless, he had been very moved by the Opening Ceremony and vowed to himself that "someday, somewhere, I would accomplish something great." In Munich, Kenya's Kip Keino made his move after 600 meters and Vasala followed close behind, dogging the defending Olympic champion all the way until the home stretch, when he moved ahead to win by about three meters. Vasala recalled, "When I walked into the dressing room after the race . . . . I realized in a second I had won. Somehow I had not fully understood it on the track. All became misty and I was crying uncontrollably. I had completely lost control of myself. I was still confused on the victory stand. It was not until I put the gold medal into my pocket and grabbed it in my fingers that I finally woke up."

### 4 Hicham El Guerrouj, Morocco, 2004

Known as the "King of Middle Distance Running," Hicham El Guerrouj won the 1,500-meter world championship four consecutive times between 1997 and 2003 and set world records in the 1,500 meters and the mile. Before the 2004 season, he had lost only three of 87 race finals in eight years, but two of those losses had been in the Olympics: 12th in 1996 and second in 2000. In the 2004 final El Guerrouj made his move with a lap-and-a-half to go. Bernard Lagat of Kenya stayed with him, even as El Guerrouj began to increase his speed. In the last half lap Lagat challenged and managed to move half a stride ahead with only 50 meters to go. El Guerrouj drew level again, and then surged ahead at the finish, collapsing onto the track and bursting into tears. After the victory, El Guerrouj leapt into the stands to kiss his 19-year-old wife and three-month-old daughter Hiba, whose name means "gift from God." As he later said, "It's amazing to think that in Sydney I was crying tears of sadness, and here I am crying tears of joy. I'm like a five year-old with a toy, living something wonderful with the people I love and people who love me."

# 9 Track Relay Incidents

**1 Thomas Hicks, 1904**

The first Olympic relay race was actually a medley relay. The first two runners each ran 200 meters, the third 400 meters, and the last runner 800 meters. The runners did not pass a baton, but touched hands instead. One member of the winning US team was John Taylor, the first African-American athlete to win a gold medal.

**2 4 x 400 Meters, 1920**

Although only six teams entered the competition, the officials in charge insisted that a semi-final round be run, with the top three in each semi qualifying for the final. Needless to say, all six teams qualified.

**3 Women's 4 x 100 Meters, 1928**

The first women's relay was won by Canada. Training restrictions for the Canadian runners were so strict that they were not allowed to drink soda pop.

**4 Women's 4 x 100 Meters, 1936**

In the opening round the German women set a world record that would last for 16 years. But in the final Ilse Dorffeldt dropped the baton Watching in the stadium, Adolf Hitler was so moved by the sight of Dörffeldt sobbing on the track, that he called the team members to his box and comforted them.

**5 4 x 100 Meters, 1936**

Marty Glickman and Sam Stoller, the only Jewish members of the US track team, were scheduled to run only in the relay. On the morning of the heats US coaches dropped them from the squad. They were the only members of the US squad who left Germany without competing.

**6 4 x 100 Meters, 1948**

The US won by six meters, but British officials disqualified them for passing the baton outside the appointed zone. Gold medals were awarded to the British team. The US protested and a Jury of Appeal, after viewing film of the race, upheld the protest and returned the victory to the Americans.

## 7 Women's 4 x 100 Meters, 1996

The Australian team set a world record in the opening heat, but dropped the baton during the final changeover. Marjorie Jackson caught the baton on the bounce and raced on, but finished fifth.

## 8 4 x 100 Meters, 1996

Previously the only US losses in the men's 4 × 100 had been the result of disqualification or boycott. In Atlanta in 1996 Canada became the first team to beat the Americans in an Olympic final. None of the four Canadian finalists was born in Canada: Donovan Bailey and Robert Esmie were born in Jamaica, Glenroy Gilbert in Trinidad and Bruny Surin in Haiti.

## 9 4 x 400 Meters, 1996

The Jamaican team was in second place midway, but their third runner, Greg Haughton, was tripped by incoming runner Robert Martin and fell. Remarkably, Haughton did a shoulder roll and bounced back onto his feet, allowing Jamaica to hold onto third place.

# 3 Americans Who Won the Marathon Although Not the First to Enter the Stadium

*Only three Americans have ever won the Olympic marathon, and none of them was the first to enter the stadium.*

### 1 Thomas Hicks, 1904

Fred Lorz crossed the finish line after 3 hours and 13 minutes and was immediately hailed as the winner. He had already been photographed with Alice Roosevelt, the daughter of the President of the United States, and was about to be awarded the gold medal when it was discovered that he had actually stopped running after 9 miles, hitched a ride in a car for 11 miles, and then started running again. Lorz readily admitted his practical joke, but AAU officials were not amused, and he was slapped with a lifetime ban. The real winner of the 1904 Olympic marathon was Thomas Hicks, an English-born brass-worker from Cambridge, Massachusetts. Ten miles from the finish Hicks begged to be allowed to lie down, but his handlers wouldn't allow it, even though he had a lead of a mile and a half. Instead they gave him an oral dose of strychnine sulfate mixed with raw egg white. Hicks was forced to slow to a walk when faced with a final, steep hill two miles from the stadium, but a couple more doses of strychnine and brandy revived him enough to win the race by six minutes.

### 2 Johnny Hayes, 1908

After 26 miles of running, the first man to enter the stadium was Dorando Pietri of Italy. But Dorando, as he came to be known, collapsed on the track five times and was finally carried across the finish line by well-meaning officials. He was disqualified for receiving outside aid, but he did become an international celebrity. The real winner of the race was Johnny Hayes, a 22-year-old who was paid to train by Bloomingdale's department store in New York City, Hayes had prepared for the big race by resting in bed for two days.

### 3 Frank Shorter, 1972

Munich-born Yale graduate Frank Shorter, annoyed by the slow pace, took the lead before the 15-kilometer mark and pulled away steadily as the race progressed. He was never challenged. Quite naturally, he entered the stadium expecting to be greeted by cheers and applause. Instead, all he heard was whistling and booing, and he wondered what he had done wrong. Unknown to Shorter, a hoaxer had appeared on the track a couple of minutes before him and run a full lap before being hustled away by security guards; the sounds of derision were aimed at the hoaxer, not Shorter. After the race, Shorter went back to his room and celebrated his victory by drinking three gins in the bath.

# 4 US Track Medalists who became Stars in Professional Sports

### 1 Buddy Davis, 1952

Buddy Davis won the 1952 high jump by clearing 2.04 meters (6 feet 8½ inches). After the Olympics the 6-foot 8-inch Davis, already an All-American basketball player from Texas A. & M., was drafted by the Philadelphia Warriors of the National Basketball Association (NBA). However, he refused to turn professional until he had set a world record in the high jump. On June 27, 1953, Davis jumped 2.13 meters (6 feet 11⅝ inches) to break the 12-year-old world record. A few days later he signed a contract with Philadelphia and won NBA championships with both the Warriors and the St Louis Hawks.

### 2 Bob Hayes, 1964

Bob Hayes equaled the world record in winning the 100 meters and six days later ran a stunning anchor leg to lead the United States to victory in the 4 × 100-meter relay. After the Olympics, he became the first Olympic champion to make a successful transition to professional football. He played nine years for the Dallas Cowboys and was twice chosen All-Pro as a wide receiver. He is the only athlete to earn both an individual Olympic gold medal and a Super Bowl victory ring. Hayes was so fast that opposing teams had to abandon their traditional man to man pass defenses and create a double zone defense.

### 3 Michael Carter, 1984

Six days after winning the shot-put silver medal, Michael Carter was playing in his first professional football pre-season game, and six months later, he was taking part in the San Francisco 49ers' Super Bowl victory. He went on to earn two more Super Bowl rings and was selected for three Pro Bowls as a nose tackle.

### 4 Michael Bates, 1992

The bronze medalist at 200 meters, Michael Bates was actually a football player who ran track to stay in shape. He went on to a successful 10-year professional football career, primarily with the Carolina Panthers. He earned places in the Pro Bowl five times as both a kickoff returner and as a defensive kick coverage specialist.

# 10 Outrageous Boxing Protests

## 1 Welterweight, 1924

The first two rounds of the final match belonged to Belgium's Jean Delarge, as Argentina's Héctor Méndez tried unsuccessfully to land his notorious knockout right. He finally caught the Belgian in the third round and pummeled him around the ring. But it was too late. Delarge wouldn't go down, and he had already built up a big enough lead to secure the victory. When the verdict was announced, pandemonium broke loose as thousands of Argentinians began chanting, "Méndez! Méndez! Méndez!" A furious Belgian rushed in among them and unfurled a Belgian flag, which led to further chaos. The demonstration went on for more than fifteen minutes before order was restored. This incident was actually a mere anticlimax after what had occurred following a preliminary match three days earlier. On that day an English referee, T.H. Walker, disqualified an Italian boxer named Giuseppe Oldani for persistent holding of his opponent. Oldani fell to the floor, sobbing, while his supporters pelted Walker with sticks, coins, and walking-stick knobs. This went on for almost an hour, until Walker was finally escorted from the arena by a contingent of British, American, and South African boxers, headed by the 265-pound wrestler Con O'Kelly.

## 2 Middleweight, 1924

In the semi-finals, Roger Brousse of France was disqualified for biting his opponent, Harry Mallin of Great Britain (see 5 Athletes Who Bit Their Opponents). When this decision was announced at the Vélodrome d'Hiver the evening following the bout, Brousse leapt to his feet and burst into tears. Immediately the hall became a scene of turmoil. Brousse was hoisted upon the shoulders of his loyal fans and paraded about the arena. Hundreds of demonstrators hooted and hollered and attempted to enter the ring. They were repulsed by the police. After about a half hour the commotion died down, but Brousse's supporters continued to launch attacks against the judges and referees for the rest of the evening.

### 3 Bantamweight, 1928

Controversy developed when Harry Isaacs of South Africa was announced the winner of his semi-final bout with John Daley of the United States. In what the US Official Report would refer to as "a demonstration never equaled in Olympic history," American supporters stormed the judges' table demanding that the decision be reversed. After several minutes, it was announced that one of the judges had transposed his figures for the two fighters. Daley was declared the victor. He moved on to the final while Isaacs went home certain that he had been robbed. It was, in the words of the London *Daily Express*, "an example of vacillation unprecedented in the history of a meeting of such worldwide scope." In the final, Daley, perhaps rattled by his earlier experience, fought below his usual standard and Vittorio Tamagnini of Italy was given a narrow victory. Again the Americans howled their disapproval. Complained one British reporter, "For more than two hours, there was little else save din and clatter, screeching and raving, and several skirmishes with the police . . . " This time it was to no avail: the decision stood.

### 4 Middleweight, 1928

In the final, Jan Hermánck of Czechoslovakia appeared to be the winner, but Italy's Piero Toscani was awarded the gold medal. Hermánek was lifted onto the shoulders of his countrymen and dumped at the feet of the judges, where he argued his case while the demonstration spread, erupting into violence in the back of the hall. While the light heavyweight finalists prepared for their bout, Hermánek's seconds tried to push him back into the ring. Finally the police intervened, and action *inside* the ring resumed.

### 5 Featherweight, 1948

Following the announcement that American Eddie Johnson had been declared the winner over 33-year-old Basilio Álves of Uruguay in their second-round match, the crowd booed for more than fifteen minutes. Meanwhile, Álves's supporters raised him onto their shoulders and stormed the table of the Jury of Appeal. In the semi-finals, it was the turn of the Argentinians to protest. Upset over the defeat of Francisco Núñez by Dennis Shepherd of South Africa, they grabbed Núñez, who had refused to leave the ring, lifted him to their shoulders and attempted a Uruguayan charge toward the Jurors' table. Repulsed by a phalanx of twelve attendants, the Argentinians listened to speeches by two of their officials and were finally convinced to end their protest by an Argentinian member of the Jury of Appeal, Señor Oriani.

## 6 Flyweight, 1964

After one minute and six seconds of the first round of his quarter-final bout against Stanislav Sorokin of the Soviet Union, South Korean boxer Choh Dong-kih was disqualified for holding his head too low. Unable to accept this verdict, Choh sat down in the middle of the ring and refused to leave. His sit-down strike continued for 51 minutes, until officials persuaded him to abandon his protest. Ironically, Sorokin was forced to withdraw before his next fight because of a cut that wasn't healing.

## 7 Featherweight, 1964

After all the hoopla and uproar that had gone on as a result of unpopular decisions in Olympic boxing, it was left to Spanish featherweight Valentín Lorén to register the ultimate protest. Disqualified for repeated holding and open-glove hitting in the second round of his first fight, Lorén turned on the Hungarian referee, György Sermer, and punched him in the face. This unfortunate indiscretion caused the Zaragoza southpaw to receive a lifetime ban from international boxing.

## 8 Light Welterweight, 1984

In a preliminary bout Jorge Maisonet of Puerto Rico was declared a split-decision winner over Nigeria's Charles Nwokolo. While the crowd chanted references to animal excrement, Colonel J. Whyte Ukor, the president of the Nigerian Boxing Association, rushed towards the jury waving his walking stick. After striking at least one boxing official, he was restrained by his coaches and removed from the arena.

## 9 Bantamweight, 1988

In 1988 a new twist was added to the history of ringside ugliness when a referee was attacked, not by spectators, but by South Korean boxing officials and security guards. The incident was rooted in the 1984 Los Angeles Olympics, when the South Korean team became upset by what they perceived as biased judging against their boxers. They were particularly incensed by the dubious victory of light welterweight Jerry Page of the US over Kim Dong-kil.

Four years later the wound was reopened when Korean light flyweight favorite Oh Kwang-soo was narrowly upset by Michael Carbajal of the US. The day after the Carbajal–Oh fight, South Korean bantamweight Byun Jong-il faced one of the division favorites, Alexander Hristov of Bulgaria. The fight was not a pretty one. There was much pushing, shoving, grabbing and general brawling. Referee Keith Walker of New Zealand tried to control the bout, cautioning both boxers, but he focused his reprimands on Byun. After warning Byun three times to stop using his head as a battering ram, Walker ordered the judges to deduct a point from the Korean's score. Another head butt in the final round led to the deduction of a second point. As it turned out, those two points decided the outcome of the fight. Without the penalties Byun would have won the decision; instead, he lost 4–1.

As soon as the verdict was announced, South Korean boxing trainer Lee Heung-soo charged into the ring and struck Walker on the back. Other Koreans, apparently under the mistaken assumption that Walker had also refereed the Carbajal–Oh fight, followed suit. Within seconds the ring was filled with angry Koreans pummeling Walker. Walker's fellow referees came to his aid and held off his attackers until security personnel could escort him out of the arena. Unfortunately, some of the security guards also took part in the riot, one of them aiming a kick at Walker's head as he fled. After the ring was cleared of unauthorized personnel and miscellaneous debris, Byun sat down in the middle of the ring and staged a silent protest. After 35 minutes he was given a chair. He finally left after 67 minutes, breaking the Olympic sit-in record set in 1964 by his countryman, flyweight Choh Dong-kih. Before leaving the arena, Byun returned to the ring and bowed to the remaining spectators. As for Walker, he went straight from the arena to his hotel, checked out and took the next flight to New Zealand. Eventually, five Korean boxing officials were suspended, the president of the Korean Olympic Committee resigned, and the South Korean government apologized to the government of New Zealand.

## 10 Featherweight, 1992

Paul Griffin, Ireland's first European champion in 42 years, was eliminated in his first bout. After Zambia's Steven Chungu knocked him down twice in the second round, the ring doctor stopped the fight. Griffin was so outraged that he kicked his gumshield into the fourth row, engaged in abusive language, and had to be restrained from attacking the doctor. This outburst earned him a six-month suspension.

# 9 Boxing Oddities

## 1 Eating Binge

In the opening round of the lightweight division of the 1936 boxing tournament Thomas Hamilton-Brown of South Africa lost a split decision to Carlos Lillo of Chile. However, it was later discovered that one of the judges had mistakenly reversed his scores for the two boxers, and that Hamilton-Brown was in fact the winner and thus eligible to move on to the next round. Unfortunately, Hamilton-Brown, who had had trouble making the weight limit, had softened the disappointment of his loss by going on an eating binge. By the time the South African manager found him it was after midnight, and the boxer had already put on nearly five pounds (2.27 kilograms). Desperately his trainer tried to boil him down, but it was no use. The next day Hamilton-Brown, still over the weight limit, was disqualified, and Lillo was allowed to advance in his place.

## 2 Getting a Buzz

Because there were so many entrants in the 1988 boxing tournament, two rings were used simultaneously until the quarter-finals. To avoid confusion, the end of a round was announced by a bell in ring A and a buzzer in ring B. The system did not work perfectly, leading to a bizarre incident in the round of 16 during the bout between Todd Foster of the United States and Chun Jin-chul of South Korea. The match was held in ring B. With 17 seconds left in round one, the bell sounded in ring A. In ring B Foster, Chun, and the Hungarian referee, Sandor Pajar, hesitated for a moment. Chun dropped his hands and took a step toward his corner. The referee called "Stop." Foster, realizing that Chun and the referee had made a mistake, blasted Chun with a left hook that caught the Korean in his eye. Chun looked to his corner, and then collapsed to the canvas, pretending to be knocked down in an attempt to have Foster disqualified for a late blow. Pajar began to count Chun out, but stopped at four and walked over to the judges for a consultation. Jury president Emil Jetchev called the bout a no-contest and ordered a rematch. Two and a half hours later, the fight began again. This time Foster knocked out Chun in the second round.

### 3 The Worst Decision
In 1992 American Eric Griffin entered the Olympics as the two-time defending champion in the light flyweight division and the overwhelming favorite. But in Barcelona he ran into an opponent he couldn't beat: the new computerized scoring system. Before 1992 each judge scored a bout separately, and the fighter who earned the higher score from a majority of judges was declared the winner. In 1992 the International Amateur Boxing Association introduced computerized scoring. Each judge was given a console. Whenever a boxer connected with a punch, the judge pushed a button corresponding to that boxer. If three of the five judges pushed their buttons within one second, the boxer automatically received a point. Whichever boxer registered the most points at the end of three rounds was declared the winner. In his second fight, Eric Griffin faced Rafael Lozano of Spain. All five judges gave Griffin the advantage: 19–9, 18–9, 26–17, 8–5 and 10–9, but he lost the bout anyway, 5–6, because the judges didn't push the buttons of their consoles at the same time.

### 4 Too Poor to Protest
At the 1968 Mexico City Games, Aboriginal light flyweight boxer Joe Donovan of Australia lost a disputed decision in the quarter-finals to Hubert Skrzypczak of Poland. Donovan wanted to file a protest but was told he would have to pay the $50 appeal fee himself. He was unable to afford it, so the decision went unchallenged.

### 5 Man of Many Identities
Ivailo Hristov, a 28-year-old sailor, used a quick left jab and clever counterpunching to earn a gold medal in the light flyweight division in 1988. However, he was aided by a secret weapon: his frequent changes of name. Few ringside observers in Seoul were aware that Hristov was the same fighter who won an Olympic bronze medal in 1980 using the name Ismail Hjuseinov, a world championship in 1982 as Ismail Mustafov, and a silver medal at the 1985 European championship as Ivajlo Marinov. The name changes were not meant to cause confusion or to put his opponents off their guard—Hristov, a member of Bulgaria's Turkish minority, was forced to change his name because of the Bulgarian government's attempt to crush all remnants of Turkish ethnic identity.

### 6 Referee Apologizes
American bantamweight Joe Lazarus of Cornell University had the

unusual misfortune of knocking out his opponent, Oscar Andrén of Sweden, at the 1924 Olympics and yet being declared the loser. As Andrén was being revived, the referee, Maurice Siegel of France, announced that Lazarus was disqualified for striking the knockout punch while breaking from a clinch. Siegel later apologized to US officials for his mistaken call and Andrén and the Swedish team manager urged Lazarus to file a protest. Moved by the Swedes' good sportsmanship, Lazarus declined, as did the US officials.

## 7 Unprepared

The official records show that 26 light heavyweights competed in the 1992 Olympic tournament. In fact, 27 showed up in the arena. Ali Kazemi of Iran made it to the ring in time for his opening bout with Ashghar Muhammad of Pakistan. Unfortunately, he wasn't wearing any gloves. His handlers frantically searched for a pair, but he was disqualified after five minutes for not being ready on time.

## 8 Best Friends

At 16, Jackie Fields, whose real name was Yonkel—or Jacob—Finkelstein was the youngest boxer at the 1924 Paris Olympics. Back home in Los Angeles he and the boxer he faced in the final, Joe Salas, were best friends. Salas later recalled, "We had to dress in the same room. When they knocked on the door to call us to the fight, we looked up at each other and started to cry and hugged. Ten minutes later we were beating the hell out of each other." After his victory over Salas, Fields was so upset at having defeated his buddy that he went back to the dressing room and cried again. Fields and Salas died eight days apart in June 1987.

## 9 The Other Ali

One unusual highlight of 1988 super-heavyweight tournament was the appearance of 5-foot 11-inch, 260-pound Ali Albaluchi of Kuwait. Clearly outclassed by the more athletically shaped Aleksandr Miroshnichenko of the Soviet Union, the good-natured Albaluchi took advantage of his moment in the spotlight to imitate Muhammad Ali. While Kuwaiti supporters chanted, "Ali, Ali," Albaluchi performed the rope-a-dope and the Ali Shuffle. He dropped his gloves, stuck out his chin and dared Miroshnichenko to hit him. Miroshnichenko won the fight easily, but it was Albaluchi who received the only standing ovation of the entire 429-match Seoul tournament.

# 5 Violent Water Polo Incidents

### 1 Unpleasantness in Antwerp, 1920
The United Kingdom team's 3–2 victory in the final over the home team was not popular. Afterwards Belgian spectators attacked the British and Irish players, who had to be taken away under the protection of armed guards.

### 2 Unhappy Brazilians, 1932
The team from Brazil, having lost 7–3 to Germany, gave a cheer for their conquerors, climbed out of the pool, and physically attacked the Hungarian referee, Béla Komjadi. They didn't let up until the police arrived. Needless to say, the entire Brazilian team was suspended, and their remaining games were forfeited.

### 3 Blood in the Water, 1956
On November 4, 1956, 200,000 Soviet troops invaded Hungary to put down a major revolt against Communist rule. The bitter feelings between the Hungarians and Soviets carried over into the Olympics in Melbourne, which were held less than three weeks later. Hostilities culminated in the water polo match between the two countries on December 6. Although the players on the two teams had previously been on friendly terms, the game quickly turned into a brawl and was halted by the referee before completion, with Hungary leading 4–0. Hungary was credited with a victory; however the police had to be called in to prevent a riot, as the 5,500 spectators wanted to punish the Soviets further.

### 4 Foul Play, 1972
The Munich tournament included a bloody match between Yugoslavia and Cuba, and a contest between Hungary and Italy in which eight players were suspended within one 38-second span.

### 5 Overtime Scuffling, 1992
Host-country team Spain faced Italy in the final. The match was tied 7–7 at the end of regulation play. After 42 seconds of overtime, Italy's Mario

Fiorillo fouled Jordi Sans, and Spain's star, four-time Olympian Manuel Estiarte, converted the penalty throw. The predominantly Spanish crowd went wild, but their joy was short-lived. Nine seconds later, Sans was excluded and Italy capitalized on their one-man advantage when Massimiliano Ferretti evened the score via a backhand shot with 20 seconds on the clock. During the break before the next overtime period, nerves were raw, and scuffling broke out between the two teams. Back in 1920 a tense tied match between Italy and Spain had ended abruptly during the second overtime period when the Italian team left the pool in a protest against the referee. Seventy-two years later, the Italian team had no intention of repeating the incident; back into the pool the two teams went. Italy finally won in the sixth overtime period.

# 6 Football Riots and Protests

## 1 Antwerp, 1920

The final matched the hosts, Belgium, against Czechoslovakia, who had outscored their opponents 15–1 on their way to the final. From the Belgian point of view, the football final was the highlight of the Antwerp Olympics. The stadium, built to accommodate 40,000 spectators, was filled to capacity two hours before kick-off. Not to be denied, a group of youthful fans dug a tunnel under an outside fence, and soon every free space was overrun with supporters of the home team. A cordon of Belgian army troops was marched in to surround the field, ostensibly to prevent the crowd from spilling onto the pitch. The team from the recently created Czechoslovak Republic interpreted the soldiers' presence differently and found their conduct on the touch line "provocative and menacing." The Czechoslovaks also objected to the choice of John Lewis of England as the referee. In a pre-Olympic match in Prague Lewis had been physically attacked by Czech supporters, and it was thought, no doubt with some justification, that Lewis might not be able to judge the game objectively. Belgium scored twice, including once on a penalty, when, with six minutes left in the first half, Lewis sent off Czech star Karel Steiner for rough play—whereupon the entire Czechoslovak team walked off the field in protest and were disqualified.

## 2/3 Berlin, 1936

The 1936 tournament was marred by a number of unruly incidents. First came the match between Italy and the United States, in which two Americans were injured. When the German referee, Weingartner, ordered Achille Piccini of Italy to leave the game, he refused to go. Several Italian players surrounded Weingartner, pinned his arms to his sides, and covered his mouth with their hands. The game continued with Piccini still in the lineup, and Italy won 1–0.

This unfortunate affair was nothing compared to what took place five days later, during the quarter-final contest between Peru and Austria. Austria led 2–0 at the interval, but Peru tied the match with two goals in the last 15 minutes. A 15-minute overtime period was then played with no further score, so a second overtime was ordered. By now the small but vocal group of Peruvian spectators had become frantic with emotion. What followed depends on which continent is telling the story. Evidently, some Peruvian fans rushed onto the field while the game was still in progress and actually attacked one of the Austrian players. The Peruvian team took advantage of the chaos to score two quick goals and win the match, 4–2.

Austria protested immediately, and a Jury of Appeal, composed of five European men, ordered the match to be replayed two days later. The jury also decreed that the game be played behind locked doors, with no spectators allowed. The Peruvians refused to show up, and the entire Peruvian Olympic contingent withdrew from the games, as did the Colombians, who supported their South American neighbors. Back in Lima, Peruvian demonstrators threw stones at the German consulate, while Peru's president, Oscar Benavides, denounced "the crafty Berlin decision." When German diplomats appealed to Benavides and pointed out that the decision had been made not by Germans but by officials of FIFA, the International Football Federation, the president changed his tune and blamed the demonstrations on Communists.

## 4 Tokyo, 1964 (Qualifying)

Beginning in 1952, so many nations began applying to compete in the Olympics that pre-Olympic soccer tournaments had to be held to decide the 16 Olympic teams. On May 24, 1964, one such qualifying match, between Peru and Argentina, took place in Lima. Argentina led 1–0, but with two minutes to play Peru scored to tie the game. However, the Uruguayan referee, Angel Eduardo Payos, nullified the goal because of rough play by the Peruvians. While the crowd of 45,000 booed its disapproval, two spectators leaped onto the field and attacked the referee. They were quickly arrested, which angered the crowd even more. Then Payos ordered the game suspended, claiming, with obvious justification, that police protection on the field was inadequate. The incensed crowd surged onto the field while the police hustled Payos and the players to safety.

Some spectators began breaking windows, and before long mounted police appeared and began herding the rioters toward the exits, many of which were, unfortunately, locked. Tear-gas grenades were fired by the police, while the Peruvian soccer fans responded by throwing stones and bottles and setting part of the stadium on fire. The fighting spilled into the streets of Lima, and before the night was out 328 people had been killed and more than 500 injured. Most of those killed had been trampled to death, but at least four were shot by police bullets. The Peruvian government declared a national "state of siege" and suspended the constitution. Meanwhile, demonstrators marched to the National Palace demanding an end to police brutality and the declaration of a tie in the match with Argentina. Neither demand was met. (Argentina, by the way, went to Tokyo but lost both their matches.)

## 5/6 Mexico City, 1968

Morocco qualified for the final tournament, but refused to participate against Israel. They were replaced by Ghana. The Ghana–Israel match, won by Israel 5–3, disintegrated into brawling, which continued back at the Olympic Village. A match between Czechoslovakia and Guatemala was also disrupted by fighting.

The final pitted defending champion Hungary against Bulgaria, who qualified only after their tied quarter-final game with Israel was decided by the toss of a coin. With Hungary leading 2–1, referee Diego De Leo, an Italian born naturalized Mexican, ejected Dimitrov for rough play. Seconds later another Bulgarian, Kiril Ivkov, was thrown out. An angry teammate, Atanas Hristov, kicked the ball toward the referee, and he too was ejected. The Mexican crowd was none too pleased with the actions of Mr De Leo; having already disrupted the third-place match by throwing cushions onto the field, they used the same tactic to show their disapproval and cause delay in the final. Hungary eventually won 4–1.

# 6 Gymnastics Controversies

## 1 Disgruntled Judge: 1980 Women's All-Around

Russian Yelena Davydova's bold routine on the bars put her in first place and gave her a lead that only defending Olympic champion Nadia Comaneci of Romania could hope to overtake, and then only if she also scored 9.95 on her final beam routine. The last time Comaneci had scored that high on the beam in an All-Around final had been at the 1976 Olympics. With the arena in complete silence, Nadia went through an impressive routine with only two small errors, including a step back on landing. The 1980 US Olympic book described the routine as "good but not great." Controversy, however, began when the scores were being tallied. The Romanian head judge, Maria Simionescu, a friend of Comaneci's since 1969, refused to accept the final result and tried to get three other judges to increase their scores. The judges argued for 28 minutes before overruling Simionescu's complaint. Even then she refused to punch the score into the computer. A representative of the Moscow Organizing Committee had to do it while Simionescu looked on in rage. Finally Nadia's score flashed on the computer: 9.85. Davydova had won the gold medal.

## 2 Revenge: 1988 Women's Team

Controversy emerged in the battle for bronze among East Germany, the US and Bulgaria. The problem arose during the compulsory round, while the American women were performing on the uneven bars. It was the responsibility of the US alternate, Rhonda Faehn, to remove the springboard that competing gymnasts used to mount the bars. After Kelly Garrison-Steves had mounted, Faehn took hold of the springboard. But instead of climbing down from the podium, the competition platform, to the bench, she withdrew to the edge of the podium and watched Garrison-Steves go through her routine. Ellen Berger, the East German president of the technical committee of the International Gymnastics Federation (FIG), immediately pointed out that Faehn's presence on the podium was an infraction of the rules and imposed a penalty of five tenths of a point. To apply this rarely enforced rule was petty, but technically correct. Unfortunately, as it turned out, the deduction cost the US the bronze medals—they lost to the East Germans by three tenths of a point. US coach Béla Karolyi was furious. He referred to Berger as a "cow" and called the ruling against the US "a Communist plot."

Actually, the ruling probably involved another factor of a more personal nature. At the 1984 Los Angeles Olympics, Berger and Karolyi had clashed over Karolyi's habit of jumping the press barricade to embrace his pupil, Mary Lou Retton, which was supposed to result in a deduction of three-tenths of a point from Retton's score. However Karolyi had correctly surmised that Berger would not impose the penalty in front of "10,000 screaming Americans." Four years later, Berger got her revenge on Karolyi and six young women were the victims.

### 3 Horsing Around: 2000 Women's All-Around

Svetlana Khorkina entered the 2000 Olympics as the queen of international gymnastics. She began the final with the floor exercise and immediately took the lead. She moved on to the vault and suddenly disaster struck. Khorkina had placed third on the vault in the qualifying round, but she appeared to mistime her leap and ended up on her knees. Stunned, she missed the landing of her second vault too. Khorkina's third apparatus was her specialty, the uneven bars. Distraught, she fell off the bars.

Unbeknownst to Khorkina, there was confusion and controversy brewing back at the vault. Khorkina was only one of many gymnasts who had unexpectedly fallen during the vault (Annika Reeder of Great Britain actually had to be taken away in a wheelchair). During the warm-ups for the third rotation 16-year-old Allana Slater of Australia noticed that there was something wrong with the height of the horse. She told her coach, who told the officials, who measured the horse and discovered that, sure enough, it was 5 centimeters (1.97 inches) too low. It seemed that when the apparatus was shifted from the men's event to the women's, the workmen had mis-set the height, and none of the Australian officials in charge of the competition had noticed. The eighteen gymnasts who had already vaulted were given the opportunity to revault—but for Khorkina it was too late, because she had already recorded a second low score on the uneven bars.

### 4 Scoring Shenanigans: 2004 Vault

The last of the finalists, Marian Dragulescu performed his signature move, which bears his name, a handspring double front with a half turn, which he completed nearly flawlessly to earn a 9.9, the highest score awarded in a world championship or Olympic competition since 1995. Having seemingly clinched the gold medal, Dragulescu attempted an easier second vault, a Katsumatsu-1½ twist. However, he overshot his landing, bounced over the penalty stripe and put both hands to the mat. Considering the automatic deductions that he should have incurred, he was awarded the surprisingly high score of 9.325, winning the bronze medal despite having failed to land one of his two vaults.

On behalf of Kyle Shewfelt, who was in fourth place, Gymnastics Canada immediately lodged a protest, arguing that it was mathematically impossible for Dragulescu to have scored more than 9.1 on his second vault. Under the rules, of the five performance scores given, the high and low scores were thrown out, and the rest had to be within 0.2 points of each other if the score was 9.0 or over. In Dragulescu's case, the scores were outside the 0.2 range, and because two of his scores were 9.5, one of them was included in his final average, boosting it to 9.325. The Canadian protest was largely ignored by the International Gymnastics Federation Technical Director, Adrian Stoica, who, like Dragulescu, was from Romania. Six months after the controversy, four of the judges involved in the vault controversy were given one-year suspensions.

## 5 Protested Protest: 2004 All-Around

America's Paul Hamm arrived in Athens as the favorite, with his main competition expected to come from 2000 silver medalist Yang Wei of China. After taking an early lead in the final, Hamm dropped to 12th place due to a disastrous vault in which he staggered sideways off of two mats and nearly tumbled into the judges' table. Soon after, Yang Wei missed a grip on the high bar, eliminating himself from medal contention. Unexpectedly, this left two South Koreans, Kim Dae-eun and Yang Tae-young, in the top two positions with one rotation remaining. The scoring of Yang Tae-young's fifth round parallel bars routine was to cause a major scandal. Needing to score above 9.512 to take the lead from Kim, Yang Tae-young nailed the most difficult element of his routine, a Stalder-Tkatchev, but finished one of his full pirouettes with a mixed grip instead of an elgrip, dropping his score to 9.475 and putting him in second place. Performing last, Paul Hamm delivered a near-perfect performance, nailing his dismount. "When I finished my routine," he explained later,

"I thought that I had taken the bronze medal." But when Hamm's score, 9.837, was posted, it turned out that it was good enough not for bronze, but for gold. Meanwhile, however, trouble was brewing. As soon as Yang Tae-young finished his parallel bars routine and his score was posted, his coach, Lee Joo-hyung, recognized that something was wrong. Yang's start value for the routine, which had been listed as 10.0 during the qualifying round and the team final, was dropped to 9.9. Kim Dong-min, a Korean judge on the parallel bars, approached the head judge for the apparatus, George Beckford of the United States, and complained about the changed start value. Beckford merely replied that the 9.9 was correct and left it at that. Kim Dong-min then informed a member of the South Korean delegation, Yoo Jae-soo, what had happened, and Yoo presented the problem to the two A-panel judges, Bultrago Reyes of Colombia and Benjamin Bango of Spain. Reyes and Bango reviewed their notes and discovered their error. They had mistakenly identified one of Yang's elements as a Morisue (double back to upper arms) instead of a Belle (giant to double back to upper arms), a difference of .10 points. Had the start value been accurate, he would have won the gold medal.

The South Korean Olympic Committee filed a protest with FIG, who refused to hear a protest against the judges' decision, citing the fact that the protest had been filed after the event had finished. According to FIG rules, protests must be filed immediately, during the competition, to be considered. Two days after the competition the FIG Executive Committee reviewed the case and released a statement admitting that Yang's start value should have been 10.0. They suspended the three judges responsible for the error, but still refused to change the results. Under increasing media pressure and desperate for a resolution, FIG president Bruno Grandi wrote a letter to Paul Hamm, via the United States Olympics Committee (USOC), urging him to voluntarily give his gold medal to Yang. The USOC refused to forward the letter to Hamm, describing it as "a blatant and inappropriate attempt on the part of the FIG to once again shift responsibility for its own mistakes." The Koreans eventually lodged a protest with the Court of Arbitration for Sport (CAS), which upheld the FIG ruling on the basis that they did not have jurisdiction because the FIG decision had been consistent with its published rules that a protest had to filed during a competition. In the end, the Korean Olympic Committee gave Yang a symbolic gold medal and the $20,000 prize awarded to gold medalists.

# 6 Date Lies: 2008 Women's Team

One of the most publicized controversies of the Beijing Olympics involved the Chinese women's gymnastics team. Under the rules in force in 2008 (and still in force in 2012), gymnasts must turn sixteen in an Olympic year to be eligible to compete. Two weeks before the Opening Ceremony *The New York Times* reported that several newspaper and online accounts indicated that He Kexin and Jiang Yuyuan were under age. Gymnast registration lists and at least one newspaper account from *China Daily*, the country's official English-language paper, indicated He's age as fourteen, while an online list of junior gymnastics competitors listed Jiang's birth date as 1 October 1993, which would have made her only fifteen. The official Chinese government sports website had listed He's birthday as 1 January 1994, but before the Olympics it was changed to 1 January 1992. A third gymnast, Yang Yilin, became implicated after state-run China Central Television (CCTV) posted a profile of her indicating that she too was fourteen. The websites were quickly taken down, but not before online security consultant Mike Walker posted backup versions on a public blog. Officials with China's gymnastics federation responded by providing copies of each gymnast's ID card and passport, indicating their ages as sixteen or over. FIG quickly issued a statement saying that the IOC had examined all gymnasts' passports and determined that none were underage. The abundant evidence indicating that these documents might have been forged was ignored. Shrugging off the controversy, the Chinese team finished first. The IOC declined to launch their own investigation into the age of the Chinese gymnasts; instead, a week after the competition, they asked FIG to do so. In October FIG declared that the documentation provided by Chinese authorities was sufficient. Chinese officials blamed the age discrepancies on administrative errors.

# 5 Cycling Medalists Who Also Won the Tour de France

**1 Jacques Anquetil, France**
Olympic Team Road Race: Bronze, 1952
Tour de France: 1957, 1961–1964

**2 Joop Zoetemelk, Netherlands**
Olympic Team Time Trial: Gold, 1968
Tour de France: 1980

**3 Miguel Induráin, Spain**
Olympic Individual Time Trial: Gold, 1996
Tour de France: 1991–1995

**4 Jan Ullrich, Germany**
Olympic Individual Time Trial: Gold, 2000
Tour de France: 1997

**5 Lance Armstrong, USA**
Olympic Individual Time Trial: Bronze, 2000
Tour de France: 1999–2005

# 5 Super-heavyweight Weightlifting Oddities

## 1 First Olympic Controversy, 1896

The first instance of an Olympic judging controversy occurred in the two-handed lift. Viggo Jensen of Denmark and Launceston Elliot of Great Britain tied at 111.5 kg, but Jensen was awarded first place as a result of his better style, Elliot having moved one foot while lifting. Jensen was quite a versatile athlete. In addition to winning the weightlifting competition, he also finished second in the free pistol, third in the military rifle, and fourth in the rope climb. Elliot did win a separate weightlifting event, the one-hand lift, and became Great Britain's first Olympic champion.

## 2 Strong Body, Weak Voice, 1948-1952

John Davis of the United States won the gold medal in 1948 and 1952, recording the heaviest lift in each of the three disciplines, the press the snatch and the jerk. He was undefeated in all competitions between 1938 and 1953. An enthusiastic singer, he once made a record that sold 71 copies.

## 3 The Advantage of Being Slim, 1956

At the Melbourne Games, Paul Anderson of the United States and Humberto Selvetti of Argentina tied with a total of 500 kg. Paul Anderson was a huge man who weighed in at 303¼ pounds (137.9 kg) after losing 60 pounds to get in shape for the Olympics. Ironically, though, he won his gold medal because his bodyweight was actually *less* than that of Selvetti, who was a mammoth 316½ pounds (143.5 kg). On June 17, 1957, at an exhibition in Toccoa, Georgia, Anderson lifted on his back a table carrying 6,270 pounds (2,844 kg).

## 4 The Price of a World Record, 1972-1976

In both 1972 and 1976 Vassily Alekseyev of Russia won the gold medal without being seriously challenged. He was unbeaten between 1970 and 1978. During his lifting career he set 79 world records, each time beating the previous record by the smallest amount possible. This was not surprising considering that the Soviet government paid him a prize of between $700 and $1,500 every time he broke a world record.

## 5 Giving up Heavy Activity, 2000-2004

Hossein Rezazadeh of Iran earned gold medals in both 2000 and 2004, breaking the world record in Sydney and equaling his own world record in Athens. He was so popular in Iran that his 2003 wedding was broadcast live on television. A month before the 2008 Olympics, Rezazadeh announced his retirement from weightlifting, citing his doctor's advice that he should avoid "heavy and stressful activity."

# 3 Dressage Scandals

### 1 Clicking Saddle, 1932

Bertil Sandström of Sweden came in second but was relegated to last place for encouraging his horse, Kreta, by making clicking noises. He claimed that the noises were actually made by a creaking saddle, but the Jury of Appeal was not convinced.

### 2 Non-Commissioned Officer, 1948

In the middle of the competition, Commandant Hector of France, the Secretary General of the International Equestrian Federation, suddenly pointed to Gehnäll Persson of Sweden, who had been entered as an officer, and said, "This man is not an officer. He is riding in the cap of a sergeant." Initially the Swedish team was allowed to keep their gold medals, but eight months later they were formally disqualified and forced to turn over the medals to the French team.

### 3 Nationalist Judges, 1956

In 1956 the judging caused something of a scandal. The German judge, General Berger, ranked the three German riders first, second, and third, and the Swedish judge, General Colliander, ranked the three Swedish riders first, second, and third.

# Before the Competition

# 7 Unusual Fundraising Approaches

## 1 Félix Carvajal, Cuba, Marathon, 1904

Félix Carvajal was a 5-foot-tall (1.52-meter) Cuban mail carrier, who raised the money for his trip to St Louis by walking around the streets of Havana wearing a shirt that asked for donations. He took a boat to the United States and got as far as New Orleans, where he lost the rest of his savings in a crap game. After hitchhiking to St Louis, he arrived on the starting line wearing heavy street shoes, long trousers, a long-sleeved shirt, and a beret. The start of the race was delayed while Martin Sheridan, the American discus thrower, cut off Carvajal's pants at the knees. Carvajal finished in fourth place.

## 2 Billy Sherring, Canada, Marathon, 1906

Determined to compete in the Olympics, Billy Sherring of Hamilton, Ontario, gathered his savings from his job as a railway brakeman, but they weren't enough to pay his way to Greece. A local athletic club raised an extra $75, but it still wasn't enough. In desperation, Sherring turned over the $75 to a friendly bartender named Butch Collier, who bet the money on a horse named Cicely, which won at odds of 6–1. At last Billy Sherring could travel to Athens. He arrived two months early and took a job as a railway station porter, training every other day. He won the gold medal by almost 7 minutes.

## 3 Aubert Côté, Canada, Bantamweight Freestyle Wrestling, 1908

Aubert Côté mortgaged his farm in Québec to pay his way to London. When he returned with a bronze medal, the Canadian Olympic Committee agreed to reimburse him.

## 4 Fanny Durack and Mina Wylie, Australia, Women's 100-meter Freestyle, 1912

The men in charge of naming the Australian team thought it an absurd waste of time and money to send women to the Stockholm Olympics. Eventually the New South Wales Ladies' Amateur Swimming Association voted to let Durack and her friend and rival Mina Wylie go, but only if they paid their own way. A fund was raised to send Durack, and Wylie's family and friends covered her expenses. Durack and Wylie won gold and silver.

## 5 Indian Field Hockey Team, 1932

Following their Olympic triumph of 1928, interest in hockey spread rapidly throughout India. When it came time to raise money to send a team to the Los Angeles Olympics, a journalist representing the Indian Hockey Federation approached Mahatma Gandhi and asked him to issue an appeal to the masses. Gandhi's only reply was, "What's hockey?" Nevertheless, an Indian team did make it to Los Angeles, paying its way by playing exhibition matches in Europe on the way home.

## 6 New Zealand's Coxed Eight Rowing Crew, 1972

The New Zealand team raised the $45,000 needed to support their training and trip to Munich by holding a series of bingo games, as well as a raffle for a "dream kitchen."

## 7 Logan Campbell, New Zealand, Featherweight Taekwondo, 2008

A year after being eliminated in the first round of the men's featherweight division, 23-year-old Logan Campbell caused controversy with the method he chose to raise funds for his 2012 Olympic bid: opening a brothel (legal in New Zealand since 2003).

# 8 Odd Training Regimens

**1 George Larner, Great Britain, Walking, 1908**

Larner broke the 11-year-old world amateur record in the 10-mile walk, and won two gold medals in four days. He practiced unusual training techniques. "When circumstances permit," he advised, "all clothing should be removed for a run round a secluded garden, especially if it is raining at the time."

**2 George Patton, USA, Modern Pentathlon, 1912**

The fifth-place finisher of the 1912 Modern Pentathlon was a 26-year-old army lieutenant, George S. Patton, Jr. who later went on to considerable fame as a general during World War II. During his training for the Olympics, Patton followed a diet of raw steak and salad. On the final day of the competition, he prepared for the cross-country run by receiving an injection of opium.

**3 4 x 400 Meter Relay Team, Great Britain, 1936**

Despite winning the 1936 4 × 400-meter relay gold medal, the British team had an extremely casual view of training. As Godfrey Rampling once recalled, "I remember saying one day: 'Look here, chaps, we really ought to practice some baton-changing.' But we soon got bored and packed it in."

**4 Don Thompson, Great Britain, 50-kilometer Walk, 1960**

Worried about the hot racing conditions facing him in Rome, British race walker Don Thompson decided to acclimatize himself well in advance. Several times each week, the 5-foot 5½-inch fire insurance clerk hauled paraffin heaters, hot water, and boiling kettles into his bathroom, sealed the doors and windows, and did his exercises in steaming 100-degree Fahrenheit (38-degree centigrade) heat. As he would later recall, "Half an hour was more than enough; I was feeling dizzy by then. It wasn't until several years later that I realised I wasn't feeling dizzy because of the heat; it was carbon monoxide from the stove."

## 5 Soviet Women Gymnasts, 1968

In 1994 Olga Karasyova appeared on German television and tearfully revealed that before the 1968 Olympics, she and other Soviet gymnasts were ordered to become pregnant in order to increase their level of male hormones. Then, after ten weeks, they submitted to abortions.

## 6 Lee Kyung-keun, South Korea, Half Lightweight Judo, 1988

Like all the Korean judo team, Lee's training included periodic midnight visits to a cemetery, where he was forced to sit alone for an hour before returning to his dormitory to watch videotapes of his potential opponents.

## 7 Qu Yunxia, China, Women's 1,500 Meters, 1992

Nineteen-year-old bronze medalist Qu Yunxia had been trained by controversial coach Ma Junren. Qu, like the rest of "Ma's Detachment," ran 150 miles a week, ate soft-shell turtle soup, drank an elixir containing caterpillars, made frequent trips to the high altitude of the Qinghai-Tibet Plateau, and was forbidden to pursue romantic affairs until the age of 22.

## 8 Andre Ward, USA, Light Heavyweight Boxing, 2004

The winner of the light heavyweight division at the Athens Games, Andre Ward's training for the Olympics included pushing his trainer's 1999 Cadillac across a parking lot and asking his family to move temporarily from their home in Hayward, California, to Washington State to allow him to focus.

# 3 Heroic Sacrifices

## 1 Ice Cream

Germany's Ilke Wyludda obliterated her opposition in the discus competition at the 1996 Atlanta Olympics. Her first five throws were all better than anything anyone else could produce, and her winning margin was the largest since 1952. After the competition reporters were quick to ask her what changes she had made in her preparations. "I will tell you my secret," she replied. "For six weeks I have not eaten ice cream."

## 2 Karaoke

After winning bronze in an especially close three-position small-bore rifle competition at the 1992 Barcelona Olympics, Japan's Ryohei Koba revealed to the press that during his final weeks of training he had given up not only alcohol but karaoke singing as well.

## 3 Dating

After winning the women's volleyball gold medal at the 1964 Tokyo Olympics, the Japan team captain, 31-year-old Masae Kasai, was invited to the official residence of Japan's prime minister, Eisaku Sato. She confessed to Sato that she wanted to marry, but that her rigorous training schedule had prevented her from meeting any men. Sato promised to help her and subsequently introduced her to Kazuo Nakamura, whom she later married.

# 14 Unusual Injuries

## 1 Dangerous Cologne
Cuban sprinter Silvio Leonard pulled a muscle as he crossed the finish line while winning the 100 meters at the 1975 Pan-Am Games. Hobbling forward, he fell into the ten-foot moat that surrounded the track. Ten days before the 1976 Olympics he stepped on a cologne bottle during a bit of horseplay and cut his foot. Despite being one of the favorites he was eliminated in the quarter-finals.

## 2 The Wave
Herbert Kerrigan, the US favorite in 1906 high jump was injured when a huge wave hit the ship taking him to Athens. He still placed third.

## 3 Excessive Celebration
In 1996 pole vaulter Tim Lobinger of Germany cleared 5.80 meters on his first attempt and was so excited that he injured himself celebrating and failed to clear another height.

## 4 Running over His Own Foot
Three years after he won the gold medal at the 1984 Olympics, boxer Paul Gonzalez broke his ankle and injured his knee when he accidentally engaged the gear shift in his Corvette convertible and ran over his own leg.

## 5 Blood on the Water
In the 1988 springboard diving event, Xiong Ni of China came out of the water after one dive with blood on his face. At first it was thought that he had injured himself, but it turned out that the 14-year-old had broken a pimple.

## 6 Thrown in the Pool
In 2007 defending Olympic Women's 400-meter freestyle champion Laure Manaudou broke a bone in her foot when two of her French team-mates threw her in a pool as a prank.

## 7 Lighting the Cauldron

Twelve years before his appearance in the 1968 Olympics, famed Australian distance runner Ron Clarke, then 19 years old, was chosen to light the cauldron at the Melbourne Olympics. Sparks from the flame singed the hair on his arm and destroyed his T-shirt, but he escaped without serious injury.

## 8 Faulty Elevator

Four years after he earned a gold medal as a member of the US 4 × 400-meter relay team, Walter McCoy received a neck injury in an elevator accident at a Holiday Inn in Tampa, Florida. He sued the hotel owners and the elevator manufacturer, claiming that the injury deprived him of a good shot at a second gold medal at the Seoul Olympics. In July 1994 a jury sided with McCoy and awarded him $900,000.

## 9 Difficult Child

When he was four years old, future pole vaulting great Serhei Bubka almost drowned in a barrel of water used for salting cabbage. He also fell out of a tree and was saved from serious injury only when his suspenders (braces) caught on a branch.

## 10 Bitten in the Night

In the run-up to the 2004 Olympics, British runner Kelly Holmes had a minor scare after suffering a pain in her left leg. Worried it might be a muscle injury, she was relieved when she found a four-inch centipede in her bed that had bitten her during the night. She went on to win both the 800 meters and the 1,500 meters.

## 11 The Perils of Marriage

Early in 2000 British distance runner Paula Radcliffe missed 13 weeks of training because of a bizarre injury: she spent too much time on her knees while writing thank-you notes for wedding gifts and had to undergo minor surgery.

## 12 Fortunate Injury No. 1

The 1984 cycling road race bronze medalist, Dag Otto Lauritzen of Norway, had taken up cycling in 1981 to rehabilitate his knee after suffering an injury while parachute jumping.

## 13 Fortunate Injury No. 2

Shooter Károly Varga of Hungary broke his shooting hand playing soccer two days before his competition at the 1980 Olympics and had to wear a bandage while he shot. After winning the gold medal in the small-bore rifle prone event, he explained that the injury had actually helped him, because it forced him to squeeze the trigger more delicately.

## 14 Unusual Injury Champion

The term "accident-prone" was meant for people like Anne Ottenbrite of Whitby, Ontario. Fortunately for her, all her accidents had been relatively minor. Having previously survived bloody encounters with a plate-glass window and a potato ricer, on May 21, 1984, she dislocated her right kneecap while showing off a new pair of shoes. Unable to take part in the Canadian trials, she was placed on the team anyway. During her brief stay in Los Angeles before the Olympics began, Ottenbrite suffered a whiplash injury to her neck when the van in which she was traveling crashed into the back of another car. Relaxing back at the Olympic Village, she strained a thigh muscle while playing a video game. Despite all these setbacks, she won the gold medal in the 200-meter breaststroke.

# 10 Weigh-In Dramas

## 1 Bantamweight Boxing, 1948

Argentina's Arnoldo Parés, although innocent of any wrongdoing, was the center of much confusion and controversy. At the weigh-in he was found to be overweight. In a panic, his supporters cut off his hair, rubbed him down with a towel, scrubbed the soles of his feet, and blew the dust off the scales. He even wept for a few minutes which further reduced his weight. It was no use: he still couldn't make the limit. The Argentinians filed a protest, and weights and measures experts were sent for. Sure enough, it turned out the scales were inaccurate, and Parés was allowed to compete. In his first match the nearly bald bantamweight won a disputed decision over Vic Toweel of South Africa but he was upset in his next bout by Ireland's Jimmy Carruthers.

## 2 Flyweight Boxing, 1956

About two hours before the weigh-in for the final, it was discovered that Terry Spinks of Great Britain was one and a half pounds overweight. His coach, Jack Roy, shut all the doors and windows in the lounge of the British team house and lit a fire to raise the temperature. Spinks exercised with a skipping rope for more than a half hour without stopping and successfully sweated off enough weight to qualify. In the final he defeated veteran Mircea Dobrescu of Romania.

## 3 Bantamweight Weightlifting, 1956

As weigh-in time approached, 4-foot 10-inch Chuck Vinci of the United States was one and a half pounds overweight. After an hour of running and sweating he was still seven ounces over the limit with 15 minutes to go. Fortunately, a severe last-minute haircut did the trick, and Vinci went on to win the gold medal.

## 4 Kayak Singles 1000 Meters Canoeing, 1976

Before the opening heats Oreste Perri, the world champion from Italy, and Vasile Dîba of Romania were disqualified for using underweight boats. However, the decision was reversed when the judges announced that the super sensitive electronic scales had responded to a change in atmospheric pressure. Both made it to the final, with Dîba placing third and Perri fourth.

## 5 Finn Sailing, 1984

Eventual gold-medal-winner Russell Coutts was almost disqualified at the final weigh-in when his clothing was found to be one pound overweight. However, a third weigh-in, for which Coutts carefully arranged each garment, found him just below the 20 kg maximum.

## 6 Super-heavyweight Freestyle Wrestling, 1984

In a sport where competitors frequently have to go to great lengths to stay below the weight limit for their division, it is sometimes forgotten that super-heavyweights have to make a *minimum* weight. Harouna Niang of Mauritania had the unfortunate experience of traveling ten thousand miles to the Olympics and then being disqualified and prevented from competing because he weighed in at only 216 pounds (97.98 kg).

## 7 Bantamweight Boxing, 1988

Eduard Paululum was to be the first-ever Olympic competitor from the small Pacific island nation of Vanuatu. Unfortunately, he ate a large breakfast before the weigh-in and was disqualified for being one pound overweight.

## 8 Heavyweight Judo, 1996

Judo fans anticipated a hot battle between defending Olympic champion David Khakhaleishvili of Georgia and defending world champion David Douillet of France. But Khakhaleishvili never left the starting gate. On the morning of the competition he travelled from the Olympic Village to the judo venue for the pre-tournament weigh-in only to discover that the weigh-in was actually at the Village. He rushed back, but the weigh-in was over, and he was disqualified. The incident was particularly frustrating considering that heavyweights did not actually have to make weight.

## 9 Women's Half-lightweight Judo, 2000

Before the competition even began, this event was hit by a bizarre controversy. At the practice weigh-in, two hours before the official weigh-in, Debbie Allan, the 1999 European champion from Great Britain, met the qualifying standard. But at the official weigh-in she was 400 grams (14.1 ounces) overweight. Examination of the three practice scales revealed that all three had been tampered with—tissue had been placed underneath the platforms to make the results appear lighter than they really were. Given less than an hour to shed the weight, Allan cut off her shoulder-length hair and stripped naked before climbing back onto the scale. Unfortunately, she was still 50 grams (1.8 ounces) too heavy and was disqualified. The ensuing argument between judo officials and other members of the British team almost led to the blanket disqualification of the entire British squad.

## 10 Half Lightweight Judo, 2004

The clear favorite for gold was two-time reigning world champion Arash Miresmaeili, a 22-year-old who was Iran's first judo world champion. Miresmaeili caused a stir when he arrived at his pre-match weigh-in more than two kilograms (four pounds) over the weight limit and was disqualified. He was later quoted by the Iranian News Agency as saying that he had deliberately failed to make weight to avoid his first-round opponent, Ehud Vaks, because he was from Israel. When he returned to Iran, Miresmaeli was given $125,000 and a ticket to Mecca.

# 6 Unlucky Non-Olympians

### 1 Bruce Kennedy, Zimbabwe/USA, Javelin, 1972-1980

A citizen of Zimbabwe, then known as Rhodesia, Bruce Kennedy went to Munich in 1972 as part of his nation's Olympic team. However, pressure from black African nations opposed to Rhodesia's white minority government prevented the Rhodesians from competing. In 1976 Kennedy was again selected to compete in the Olympics, but again Rhodesia was excluded. Kennedy then moved to the United States, married an American and in 1977 became a US citizen. In 1980 he qualified for the US team, but, for the third time, he was prevented from competing in the Olympics because of politics, as his new country boycotted the Moscow Games. Ironically, Zimbabwe, now ruled by its black majority, was readmitted into the Olympic movement and allowed to take part in the 1980 Olympics. In 1984 Bruce Kennedy, who by this time had earned a master's degree from Stanford University, finally made it inside an Olympic Stadium —as an usher.

### 2 Boyd Gittins, USA, 400-meter Hurdles, 1968

US hurdler Boyd Gittins was eliminated at the 1968 US Olympic semi-trials when a pigeon dropping hit him in the eye and dislodged his contact lens just before the first hurdle. Fortunately, he won a runoff to qualify for the final Olympic trials, and then made the team. Unfortunately, a leg injury forced him to withdraw from his first-round heat.

### 3 Wym Essajas, Suriname, 800 Meters, 1960

Wym Essajas was chosen to be the first person to represent the South American nation of Suriname at the Olympics. Unfortunately he was mistakenly told that the 800-meter heats would be held in the afternoon, so he spent the morning resting. When he arrived at the stadium, the heats were over, and he was forced to return to Suriname without having competed. It was eight years before Suriname sent another athlete to the Olympics.

### 4/5 Bai Yang and Fan Ying, China, Women's Table Tennis, 2004

At the beginning of 2004 men's table tennis stars Ma Lin and Wang Hao were involved in a "dating scandal," dating, according to the Chinese table tennis system, being a threat to training. Ma's 19-year-old girlfriend, Bai Yang, and Fan Ying, Wang's 17-year-old girlfriend, were removed from the national team for dating, but Ma and Wang, because of their high rankings, were allowed to stay on the team. Ma won a gold medal in the doubles event and Wang a silver in singles. The two returned to the Olympics in 2008, finishing one-two in singles and as two members of the winning Chinese trio in the team event. Neither Bai nor Fan ever made it to the Olympics.

## 6 Heino Lipp, Estonia, Decathlon, 1948-1952

Four days after American Bob Mathias won the 1948 Olympic decathlon with 7,139 points, Heino Lipp scored 7,584 points at a meet in Tartu, Estonia. Between 1920 and 1936 Estonia had competed as an independent nation, but it lost its independence during World War II and was annexed by the Soviet Union. The USSR chose not to compete in the 1948 Olympics, and Lipp was left without a country. The USSR did take part in the 1952 Olympics, but Lipp was considered a security risk and was forced to stay home again. After the fall of communism in the Soviet Union, Estonia regained its independence, and it entered a separate team at the 1992 Olympics. When the Estonian team marched into the stadium at the Opening Ceremony for the first time in 56 years, the Estonian flag was proudly carried by 70-year-old Heino Lipp.

# 3 Unusual South Korean Archery Training Methods

## 1 In the Dead of Night

Cho Youn-jeon, the 1992 gold-medal-winner, set a world record of 1375 in the qualifying round. When asked how she calmed her nerves before competitions, Cho replied, "I take long walks at night through the cemetery."

## 2 Biting a Live Snake

In the 1996 women's final Kim Kyung-wook led from start to finish. Along with other members of the South Korean archery team, she had to endure a demanding training regimen. For Kim the low point came in 1994, when she had to pick up a live snake and lightly bite its body. She was so frightened that her trainer had to hold the snake while Kim bit it.

## 3 Screaming Crowds

To prepare their athletes for the noise and distraction of the 2008 Olympic competition South Korean officials built a full replica of the Beijing archery venue at their practice grounds, complete with stands full of screaming spectators and loudspeakers blasting music. The South Korean archers went on to win both the men's and women's team events.

# Competing in
# the Olympics

# 9 Descriptions of the Olympic Experience by Runners

## 1 Arthur Duffey, USA, 100 Meters, 1900

Duffey was leading halfway through the final when he suddenly strained a tendon and fell to the ground. He explained, "I do not know why my leg gave way. I felt a peculiar twitching after going twenty yards. I then seemed to lose control of it, and suddenly it gave out, throwing me on my face. But that is one of the fortunes of sport, and I cannot complain."

## 2 Charley Paddock, USA, 100 Meters, 1920

As they approached the finish line, Paddock was just behind teammate Morris Kirksey. "I saw the thin white string stretched to the breaking point in front of me. I drove my spikes into the soft cinders and felt my foot give way as I sprang forward in a final jump for the tape . . . . My eyes closed as my chest hit the string and when I opened them, my feet were on the ground again and I was yards ahead of the field." Paddock had won the race by 12 inches. He later wrote, "My dream had come true and I thrilled to the greatest moment I felt that I should ever know. . . . The real pleasure had been in the anticipation and in that single moment of glorious realization."

## 3 Tommy Hampson, Great Britain, 800 Meters, 1932

A 24-year-old schoolteacher, Hampson just edged out Canadian Alex Wilson in world record time. Two days after his victory, he recorded his impressions in his diary. "We're in the straight. Oh God, let me get there—mustn't disappoint Winnie [his fiancée]. Ah, goodbye Phil [Edwards, another Canadian]; now for Wilson. Wonder how far from the tape. I can't see. Caught him! Now for it. Harder, harder, harder—shall I do it? Yes, I will. Help me now, darling. I can't drop him; damn the man! At last, just in front—my shadow just ahead. Oh where is that tape? My legs won't take me there. What a row the crowd are making too! Ah, thank God, I felt it break, it must have been. Yes, here's Wilson, patting me: 'Well run, Tommy.'"

#### 4 Helen Stephens, USA, Women's 100 Meters, 1936

Stephens was a 6-foot farm girl from Calloway County, Missouri, who loved to run. After she won the final, she was taken to meet Adolf Hitler in his private glass-enclosed box. "Hitler comes in and gives me the Nazi salute," she later recalled. "I gave him a good old Missouri handshake. Immediately Hitler goes for the jugular vein. He gets ahold of my fanny, and he begins to squeeze and pinch and hug me up, and he said, 'You're a true Aryan type. You should be running for Germany.' So after he gave me the once-over and a full massage, he asked me if I'd like to spend the weekend in Berchtesgaden." She declined.

#### 5 Tom Courtney, USA, 800 Meters, 1956

Trailing Derek Johnson of Great Britain in the home stretch, Courtney was exhausted. "I looked at the tape just 40 yards away and realized this was the only chance I would ever have to win the Olympics." Step by step he gained on Johnson and lunged across the finish line. In a delirium, he turned to Johnson and asked who had won. "Why you did, Tom," came the reply. "It was a new kind of agony for me," Courtney recalled. "I had never run myself into such a state. My head was exploding, my stomach ripping and even the tips of my fingers ached. The only thing I could think was, 'If I live, I will never run again!'" The victory ceremony had to be delayed for an hour until he recovered. Twenty years later, Tom Courtney wrote about his years of competitive running: "It is a world that is gone now, but I still enjoy going out to a local track and taking a run and, with a half lap to go, I kind of savor the idea that I am re-running the last half lap of the best part of my life."

#### 6 Livio Berruti, Italy, 200 Meters, 1960

Berruti was the first non-North-American to win the 200 meters. Thirty-six years later, he looked back on his fellow athletes of 1960: "We were truly all friends, with an equality of souls and races and a desire to exchange ideas and compare our experiences. There was no nationality; we were citizens of the world. We were happy because we took part in sport for pleasure, with enthusiasm, with the primary idea of having a good time. The coach was still our friend, and his scientific and physiological knowledge left a lot to be desired. Now athletes are research laboratories."

### 7 Herb Elliott, Australia, 1,500 Meters, 1960

After winning by a huge margin in world record time, Elliott retired from competitive running at the age of 22. Years later, paying tribute to what he learned from coach Percy Cerutty, Elliott wrote, "I came to realize that spirit, as much as or more than physical conditioning, had to be stored up before a race. I would avoid running on tracks because tracks were spiritually depleting. I never studied my opponents—they were an irrelevancy to me. Poetry, music, forests, ocean, solitude—they were what developed enormous spiritual strength." Of his early retirement he said, "Once I had satisfied myself . . . that my spirit could dominate my body, there was no reason to continue."

### 8 Yuko Arimori, Japan, Women's Marathon, 1996

After the Olympics, bronze medalist Arimori told the Asahi News Service what the Olympics meant to her: "I think the Olympics is a special stage where people of high ability can compete, delight and grieve. It is a field of battle, but I feel something peaceful there."

### 9 Noureddine Morceli, Algeria, 1,500 Meters, 1996

After a disappointing seventh place finish at the 1992 Olympics, Morceli "could not sleep or eat for a week." Four years later in Atlanta, he won the gold medal. He immediately knelt on the track with his hands and forehead down and thanked God. He later told the press, "God teaches you to be dignified in defeat and modest in victory. The records and medals are wonderful, but they are mere trinkets in reality. They cannot feed all the people in the world who are hungry, clothe all those who are cold, comfort all those who are troubled or bring peace to all those who are at war. That is a race we must all run together."

# 7 Descriptions of the Olympic Experience by Non-Runners

## 1 Alfred Hajos, Hungary, Swimming, 1896

The 1896 swimming events were contested in open water in and around the Bay of Zea near Piraeus, which featured 10-foot waves and a water temperature of 13°C (55°F). The winner of the 1,200-meter race, Alfred Hajos of Hungary, later recalled, "My will to live completely overcame my desire to win."

## 2 William Garrett Gilmore, USA, Single Sculls Rowing, 1924

Silver medalist Gilmore had fond memories of the final race. "During the last 200 meters," he later wrote, "when the sun seemed to get hotter with every stroke, and I was making a supreme effort to grasp victory, a kindly breeze swept across the Seine, carrying a strong but pleasant scent from a perfumery which was not within sight. It was truly so strong that it first gagged me, but in a moment I was rowing on as if in a flowing river of the perfume itself."

## 3 Oscar Casanovas, Argentina, Featherweight Boxing, 1936

Casanovas described his emotions after receiving his gold medal and hearing the Argentine national anthem: "My greatest ambition had been achieved. I had succeeded for my country, my parents and my friends. I was overjoyed. Unable to contain myself, I shed a few tears thinking of my dear parents, thanking them in my heart for having brought me into this world. I am sure that if at that moment Death had come to claim me, I would have welcomed him with a smile."

## 4 Isao Okano, Japan, Middleweight Judo, 1964

In his book *Vital Judo*, Okano described his state of mind during major competitions: "By . . . the second or third bout of the tournament, the athlete becomes conscious of an imaginary membrane separating him from all outside things, including the spectators. . . . Surrounded by that imaginary membrane, I found my mind alert and cool. I was like an animal standing alone. Voices and shouts from the crowd had no effect on me. Winning and losing were the only important things. When I reached the semi-final or final stage a tension of an entirely different kind welled up inside me. I was entirely enclosed in a veil of transparency; I felt that I could see through everything. The opponent was nothing but a physical object. The sense of doing battle with myself became clearer in my mind. I sensed a unity with all of the spectators. When I won . . . the world seemed to belong to me, and the single moment of intensely concentrated meaning is unforgettable."

## 5 Kenny Davis, USA, Basketball, 1972

Davis was a member of the US team that lost in the Munich final to the Soviet Union in extremely controversial circumstances. The Americans felt they had been robbed of victory by officials of the International Amateur Basketball Federation (FIBA), and they refused to accept their silver medals. The loss haunted many of the United States players for years to come, but others were able to put it in perspective. In 1992 Davis told *Sports Illustrated*, "I went back to my room and cried alone that night. But every time I get to feeling sorry for myself, I think of the Israeli kids who were killed at those Games. . . .Think of being in a helicopter with your hands tied behind your back and a hand grenade rolling toward you and compare that to not getting a gold medal! If that final game is the worst injustice that ever happens to the guys on that team, we'll all come out of this life pretty good."

## 6 Koji Gushiken, Japan, All-Around Gymnastics, 1984

Gushiken came from behind to edge Peter Vidmar in the closest Olympic All-Around competition in sixty years. "I'm neither a Christian nor a Buddhist," Gushiken later said, reflecting on the medal ceremony, "and suddenly I felt the existence of God. It was clear-cut and exceedingly beautiful."

## 7 Anton Josipovic, Yugoslavia, Light Heavyweight Boxing, 1984

The competition was marred by a controversial semi-final decision in which US boxer Evander Holyfield was disqualified for a late blow, and winner Kevin Barry of New Zealand was prevented from fighting in the final after being declared a knockout victim. As a result, semi-finalist Anton Josipovic, a handsome 22-year-old literature student from Bosnia, was awarded the gold medal by default. After the playing of the Yugoslav national anthem, Josipovic reached down and pulled up a surprised

Holyfield to join him on the gold-medal platform. Afterwards, he told reporters, "It is a great honor to win the gold medal in this city of light and sun. I would have liked to fight Holyfield, to show what I am capable of doing and to win the medal that way. I am a bit disappointed that the audience doesn't realize that this is not the way I wanted it. I took the opportunity to have Holyfield join me on the top step because I believe the Olympics are the spirit of friendliness and goodwill."

# 7 Most Creative Excuses for Failing a Doping Test

## 1 Oral Sex

In June 1996 Daniel Plaza, the Spanish winner of the 1992 20,000-meter walk, tested positive for the steroid nandrolone. Because nandrolone is produced naturally by pregnant women, Plaza claimed that his positive result occurred because he had engaged in oral sex with his wife the night before his race. He was suspended anyway. However, ten years later, in 2006, Plaza was finally exonerated, when the Spanish Supreme Court ruled in his favor and overturned the two-year ban that had been imposed by the Spanish Committee for Sporting Discipline.

## 2 Anti-Scarring Gel

Five years before winning the gold medal in the 2008 long jump, Maurren Maggi tested positive for the anabolic steroid clostebol and received a two-year suspension, she blamed the positive test on hair removal cream. Although she was later cleared by the Brazilian Athletics Federation, the IAAF appealed the ruling to the Court of Arbitration for Sport, and Maggi chose to serve the two-year ban rather than attend the hearing.

## 3 Steroid Orange Juice

In September 2005, a year after winning the silver medal in the K-1 500 meters event, Nathan Baggaley tested positive for the steroids stanozolol and methindione. He blamed the positive test on having accidentally drunk from a container of juice that his brother, who was recovering from a shoulder injury, had mixed with steroids. The International Canoe Federation was unconvinced and banned Baggaley from competition for two years. Just before the ban was lifted, Baggaley faced a second drug charge after police found 762 ecstasy tablets in a car he was driving. He was sentenced to nine years in prison.

## 4 Pork Chops

Two years after her Olympic victory in the women's Heavyweight judo event, Tong Wen was banned for two years by the International Judo Federation after testing positive for clenbuterol. Tong blamed the positive test on eating too many pork chops, pointing to the fact that clenbuterol is used on animals like pigs to keep their meat lean, as well as by athletes to build up muscle.

## 5 Tampered Toothpaste

In October and November 1999 Dieter Baumann, a harsh critic of doping in sports, tested positive for the anabolic steroid nandrolone, which, in addition to being found in his urine, was discovered in his toothpaste. Baumann served out a two-year suspension, while never ceasing to insist that he had been framed.

## 6 Sexual Enhancement Pills

In April 2010 the US Anti-Doping Agency revealed that 2008 400-meters gold medalist LaShawn Merritt had tested positive for a banned substance, DHEA, three times between October 2009 and January 2010. The cause? An over-the-counter "sexual enhancement" product called ExtenZe. Merritt accepted a provisional suspension and then was handed a two-year suspension.

## 7 Massage Cream

In April 2006 Athens 100-meter gold medalist Justin Gatlin tested positive for testosterone after participating in the Kansas Relays. His coach, Trevor Graham, claimed that Gatlin had been doped without his knowledge by Chris Whetstine, Gatlin's massage therapist, whom he accused of sabotaging Gatlin by rubbing steroid-laced ointment onto Gatlin's legs just before the race. *The Washington Post* later claimed to have uncovered evidence that Gatlin's positive test would have been consistent with the use of steroid cream, but noted that it would be impossible to tell conclusively. However, the *Post* also concluded that it would have been foolish for Gatlin to have allowed himself to be rubbed with the cream, as the active ingredient is not known to enhance athletic performance, but is easily detectable in doping tests.

# 9 Athletes Aided by Legal Performance-Enhancing Substances

**1-4** **Sherry and a Raw Egg**

Just before the start of the 1920 men's 100-meter final, the four American runners, Loren Murchison, Morris Kirksey, Jackson Scholz and Charley Paddock, were approached by coach Lawson Robertson, who said, "What you fellows need to warm up is a glass of sherry and a raw egg." Murchison, Scholz, and Paddock were horrified by the suggestion, but when Stanford's Morris Kirksey agreed to try the drink, the others feared it would give him a psychological advantage to be the only one to follow the coach's advice, so they guzzled down the strange concoction as well. Paddock and Kirksey went on to win the gold and silver medals.

**5** **Coffee**

Shortly before the finish of the 1956 javelin competition Norway's Egil Danielsen was offered a cup of strong coffee by fellow competitor Michel Macquet of France. "I never drink coffee," Danielsen later recalled. "After this cup, I almost had a shock. My heart began to beat fast and I was sweating. I took the steel javelin, made a good run and a powerful stroke." Danielsen's enormous throw broke the world record and almost landed on the runway of the pole vault. It would prove to be the longest throw of Danielsen's career.

**6** **Strychnine and Brandy**

The winner of the 1904 Olympic marathon was Thomas Hicks, an English-born brass worker from Cambridge, Massachusetts. Ten miles from the finish Hicks begged to be allowed to lie down, but his handlers wouldn't allow it, even though he had a lead of one and a half miles. Instead they gave him an oral dose of strychnine sulfate mixed with raw egg white. A few miles later he was given more strychnine, as well as some brandy. Hicks was forced to slow to a walk when faced with a final, steep hill two miles from the stadium, but a couple more doses of strychnine and brandy revived him enough to win the race by six minutes.

## 7 Paper

Competing in the 1936 200-meter breaststroke Hideko Maehata brought a small piece of paper with a prayer on it to the starting platform. She read it one last time before the final and then ate it. Maehata was the first Asian woman to win an Olympic gold medal. The Japanese radio commentary on the race gained a special place in history because the NHK announcer became so excited that he kept shouting, "Go Maehata! Go Maehata!" and forgot to describe the progress of the race.

## 8 Mystery Liquid No. 1

During the 1908 high jump competition French athlete Géo André noticed that the US coaches periodically gave to their jumpers sips from blue bottles that they kept hidden underneath their warm-up clothes. André became convinced that this mysterious liquid allowed the Americans to jump with greater elasticity and he was determined to uncover their secret. After the competition was over he slipped over to the American side, stole one of the bottles and hid it in his pocket. Back in his room, André studied the bottle. On it was a label that read, "Sun Water." He brought the bottle back to Paris and tried drinking the liquid before jumping, but it didn't seem to help his performance. Finally André took the bottle to a pharmacist who analysed the mysterious liquid and discovered its composition. The secret drink of the American jumpers was . . . water.

## 9 Mystery Liquid No. 2

Joseph Guillemot, whose heart was on the right side of his chest, smoked a pack of cigarettes a day. Before the final of the 1920 5,000 meters event, his trainer gave him a mysterious liquid concoction and said, "Swallow this and you will be unbeatable." Guillemot stayed in second place until the back stretch. Then, 200 meters from the finish, he sprinted away to win by 20 meters. The mysterious concoction turned out to be water, sugar and rum.

# 7 Big Upsets

## 1 Jim Bausch, USA, Decathlon, 1932

Akilles Järvinen, older brother of javelin gold medalist Matti Järvinen, was the strong favorite to win the decathlon. He did in fact break his own world record, but he was only able to come second. The upset winner was former University of Kansas football star Jim Bausch, whose entire decathlon career lasted less than 16 months. Fifth after the first day's events, Bausch took advantage of splendid performances in the discus and pole vault to build an insurmountable lead.

## 2 Lindy Remigino, USA, 100 Meters, 1952

The 1952 100-meter final produced one of the closest finishes in Olympic history and one of the biggest sprint upsets. Lindy Remigino had barely qualified for the US Olympic tryouts by finishing fifth in the NCAA championships. Unexpectedly, he had a clear lead at the halfway mark of the Olympic final. He held on gamely for 90 meters, but was passed by Jamaican Herb McKenley just as they reached the tape. "I was sure I had lost the race," said Remigino afterward. "I started my lean too early . . . and I saw Herb McKenley shoot past me. I was heartsick. I figured I had blown it." Lindy walked over to the delighted Jamaican and offered his congratulations. But a photo-finish showed that Remigino's right shoulder had reached the finish line an inch ahead of McKenley's chest, and the judges ruled him the winner. When someone told Remigino the results before they had been flashed on the scoreboard, he was incredulous and was sure there had been a mistake. Finally he turned to McKenley and is reputed to have said, "Gosh, Herb, it looks as though I won the darn thing." The closeness of the finish is shown by the fact that Dean Smith of the United States was only 14 inches (36 centimeters) behind the winner, yet placed only fourth.

## 3 Billy Mills, USA, 10,000 Meters, 1964

Billy Mills was born on the Pine Ridge Sioux Indian reservation in South Dakota. Orphaned at 12, he was sent to Haskell Institute, a school for Native Americans in Kansas. After attending the University of Kansas he joined the Marines. He was a motor pool officer at Camp Pendleton in California when he qualified for the Olympics by finishing second at the US Trials. In an unusually dramatic final the favorite, Ron Clarke of Australia, and Mohamed Gammoudi of Tunisia were battling for the lead on the home stretch, when Mills, fighting his way past lapped runners, suddenly sprinted past both the leaders and crossed the finish line with a three-yard lead. His winning time was 46 seconds faster than his previous best. Mills was immediately surrounded by Japanese officials, one of whom asked him, "Who are you?" During the two weeks that he had spent in the Olympic Village before the opening of the games, not one reporter had asked Billy Mills a single question.

## 4 Jon Sieben, 200-meter Butterfly, 1984

With two gold medals already under his belt, Michael Gross of West Germany entered his best event, the 200-meter butterfly, as the clear favorite. He expected stiff challenges from Pablo Morales and Rafael Vidal, and that's exactly what he got. But over in lane 6, something completely unexpected happened. Seventeen-year-old Australian Jon Sieben, seventh at the halfway mark and fourth with 50 meters to go, shot past the favorites to out-touch Gross and gain the victory, the world record, and one of the most surprising upsets in Olympic swimming history. His time of 1:57.04 was more than four seconds faster than his pre-Olympic best of 2:01.17. Sieben was so excited by his victory that it was not until an hour later that he realized that he had broken the world record. The rabidly pro-US crowd gave him a standing ovation, and the outcome was so delightful that the defeated favorites expressed pleasure more than disappointment. Gross, who had refused to appear before reporters following his two gold-medal races, and whose disdain for pomp and press had earned him the nickname "The American" in West Germany, sat beside Sieben after the 200 butterfly preferring to praise the young Australian rather than talk about himself.

## 5 Spain, Team Archery, 1992

The victory by the three-man Spanish team was the biggest upset of the Barcelona Games. In the individual competition, Antonio Vázquez had placed 29th, Alfonso Menéndez 42nd, and Juan Carlos Holgado 45th. Seeded tenth, they scored surprise victories over Denmark, the ex-Soviet Unified Team and Great Britain. In the final against Finland, Spain led by nine points after twenty arrows, and then held off a strong comeback by the Finns.

## 6 Kye Sun-hui, North Korea, Women's Extra Lightweight Judo, 1996

Since losing to France's Cécile Nowak in the 1992 Olympic final, Ryoko Tamura of Japan had gone undefeated for four years. The 4-foot 9½-inch (1.46-meter) Tamura was hugely popular in Japan, where her success had spawned an interest in women's judo; she was known as "Yawara-chan" because of her resemblance to a popular comic-book character. Tamura entered the final with an 84-match winning streak. Her opponent, 16-year-old Kye Sun-hui of North Korea, was a complete unknown. For political and economic reasons North Korea had withdrawn from international competitions of the previous three years, including all Olympic qualifying events. The International Judo Federation awarded North Korea one wild-card entry to the Olympics and the North Koreans gave that spot to Kye. Kye had never heard of Ryoko Tamura and had never seen her fight until she watched a couple of her matches on a video monitor before the final. Kye startled Tamura by attacking from the start and the double world champion was unable to establish her rhythm. With 22 seconds left, Kye scored with a leg hook and then added an insurance point when Tamura, on her knees, was penalized for "false attack."

## 7 Rulon Gardner, Super-heavyweight Greco-Roman Wrestling, 2000

By the time of the 2000 Olympics Aleksandr Karelin was 59–0 in the Olympics and world championships and had not lost a match of any kind since 1987. Although the Russian, who turned 33 during the Sydney Olympics, was starting to suffer the pain and injuries of age, he was the overwhelming favorite to become only the fourth person in Olympic history in any sport to win the same individual event four times. Any doubts about his fitness were dispelled when he qualified for the final by beating all four of his opponents without their scoring a single point amongst them. Karelin's adversary in the final was Rulon Gardner, a 29-year-old Mormon who grew up, the youngest of nine children, on a dairy farm in Afton, Wyoming. The Olympics was only Gardner's second major international tournament; the first had been the 1997 world championships, where he wrestled Karelin for the first time. Karelin had hoisted Gardner in the air with his signature reverse body lift, and the match was over. Gardner reacted good-naturedly: "I had never flown before, so I thought it was pretty cool." Gardner knew that his only chance to beat Karelin in the Olympic final was to fight a perfect match. He survived the first period 0–0. The second period began with the two wrestlers in a face-to-face clinch, their arms wrapped around each other. Thirty seconds later, the unexpected happened: Karelin's hands slipped apart. The mat referee did not see it, but the judges stopped the fight, reviewed the video and awarded a point to Gardner for Karelin's penalty. For the rest of regulation time and overtime, 5 minutes in all, Gardner resisted every attempt that Karelin made to pick him up or turn him around and the match ended with Gardner scoring one of the most surprising upsets in Olympic history. Half an hour or so after the match Gardner was asked when he had realized he could beat Karelin. "About ten minutes ago," he replied.

# 10 Incredibly Close Finishes

## 1 100-meter Freestyle Swimming, 1960

Lance Larson of the United States and John Devitt of Australia finished in a near dead heat. Devitt congratulated Larson and left the pool in disappointment. Confusion developed, however, when the judges met to discuss their verdict. Of the three judges assigned to determine who had finished first, two voted for Devitt and one for Larson. However the second-place judges also voted 2–1 for Devitt. In other words, of the six judges involved, three thought Devitt had won and three thought Larson had won. When the electronic timers were consulted, it turned out that Larson had registered 55.1 seconds and Devitt 55.2. The unofficial electronic timer also showed Larson winning—by four inches, 55.10 to 55.16. Despite this evidence, the chief judge, Hans Runströmer of Germany, who did not have any say in the matter according to the official rules, ordered Larson's time changed to 55.2 and gave the decision to Devitt. Four years of protests failed to change the result.

## 2 Cycling Road Race, 1964

Held over 194 kilometers (120 miles), the 1964 road race saw a spectacular finish in which Mario Zanin, a mechanic from Italy, emerged from the pack with 20 meters to go and won by a wheel. The finish was so close that Sture Pettersson of Sweden crossed the line only sixteen-hundredths of a second behind Zanin, yet he ended up in 52nd place.

## 3 100-meter Freestyle Swimming, 1964

A minor controversy developed over the award of the bronze medal in the 100-meter freestyle. The judges were split as to whether American Gary Ilman or German Hans-Joachim Klein had finished third. Both were clocked in the same time. The Japanese had thoughtfully provided electronic timers for the swimming events and, even though they were not used officially, they were consulted by the judges. It turned out that Ilman and Klein had stopped the clock at exactly the same hundredth of a second, but that Klein had finished one one-thousandth of a second sooner. After 35 minutes of consultation, the judges decided that, even if the electronic timing was unofficial, it had provided sufficient cause to award third place to Klein.

## 4 400-meter Individual Medley, 1972

Sweden's Gunnar Larsson and Tim McKee of the US were both credited with the Olympic record, but Larsson was declared the winner by two thousandths of a second, 4:31.981 to 4:31.983. As a result of this race, the rules were changed to declare a dead heat in any swimming contest in which the swimmers were tied to hundredths of a second, (although this rule was later changed).

## 5 Women's Pentathlon, 1976

With four events finished and only the 200 meters to be run, the top eight competitors were separated by only 95 points. All the leaders were matched against one another in the final heat. When the dust cleared 26 seconds later, officials and fans hurriedly consulted their scoring tables. It was discovered that Siegrun Siegl of East Germany, the world record holder in the long jump, and Christine Laser, also of East Germany, had finished with the exact same points total, while another East German, Burglinde Pollak, was only five points behind. Siegl was finally awarded first place, on the basis of having beaten Laser in three of the five events. Had Pollak run six hundredths of a second faster she would have won the gold medal. Instead she had to settle for her second straight bronze. While Siegl jumped from seventh to first in one event, Nadezhda Tkachenko of the Soviet Union had the misfortune of dropping from first to fifth in less than 25 seconds.

## 6 Women's 100-meter Freestyle, 1984

After the 1972 Larsson-McKee incident (see 4. above), it was decided that because of possible technical problems, hundredths of a second would have to do in future instead of thousandths. So in 1984, when Nancy Hogshead and Carrie Steinseifer, both from the United States, registered the same time in the 100-meter freestyle, a dead heat was declared, and each was awarded a gold medal—the first double gold medal in Olympic swimming history.

## 7 Kayak Singles 1,000-meter Canoeing, 1988

Greg Barton was a mechanical engineer who grew up in Homer, Michigan, a small town with more pigs than humans. In Seoul, Barton and Australia's Grant Davies crossed the finish line in a near dead heat. Barton was told by South Korean officials that he had won. Then the scoreboard flashed the news that Davies was the victor. While the Australians celebrated and Barton prepared for the final of the 1,000-meter pairs, the jury of the International Canoe Federation examined the finish-line photo. A few minutes later they announced that Barton had won by .005 seconds—less than 1 centimeter. Greg Barton had become the first US kayaker to win an Olympic gold medal. Davies was stoic. "If that's the biggest disappointment in my life," he said, "I can handle it."

## 8 100-meter Butterfly, 1988

Favorite Matt Biondi of the US led from the start. Ten meters from the finish, he was still in first place by 2 feet. But as he neared the touch pad he was caught between strokes and elected to kick in the last few feet instead of taking an extra stroke. However, he was farther away than he thought, and his miscalculation allowed 20-year-old Anthony Nesty of Suriname to slip by and win by less than an inch. After the race Biondi mused, "One one-hundredth of a second—what if I had grown my fingernails longer?" He successfully channeled his disappointment and went on to win five gold medals.

## 9 Women's 100 Meters, 1992

The 100-meter final in Barcelona was the closest track race in Olympic history. Gail Devers of the United States and Irina Privalova of Russia ran almost even most of the race, but Jamaicans Julie Cuthbert and Merlene Ottey and American Gwen Torrence all came on at the end. It was impossible to tell who had won until slow-motion replays of the finish were shown in the stadium. Even then, one couldn't be sure. The official announcement finally gave the victory to Devers. Ottey ended up in fifth place, even though she was less than one-tenth of a second behind the winner.

## 10 100-meter Butterfly, 2008

The 100-meter butterfly was the only race Michael Phelps swam at the 2008 Olympics for which he did not already hold the world record. American-born Milorad Cavic, competing for Serbia, set an Olympic record in the first round and led the field halfway through the final, with

Phelps trailing in seventh place. In a sensational finish, Phelps surged over the final 50 meters, making up a deficit of more than half a second to touch in a virtual tie with Cavic that was too close to call by the naked eye. The results of swimming races are now determined not by a photo, but by the pressure applied to touch pads. Omega, the official timekeeper of the Olympics (and one of Phelps' sponsors) announced that Phelps had won by 4.7 millimeters (one-sixth of an inch).

# 4 Especially Long Olympic Battles

## 1 Cycling, Road Time Trial, 1912
The course for the cycling road race was 320 kilometers (199 miles), the longest race of any kind in Olympic history. Starting at 2:00 a.m., competitors were sent out on the course at two-minute intervals over the next four hours. The winner was Okey Lewis of South Africa in a time of 10 hours 42 minutes and 39 seconds.

## 2 Greco-Roman Wrestling, Light Heavyweight, 1912
The light-heavyweight final was declared a draw after Anders Ahlgren of Sweden and Ivar Böling of Finland grappled for nine hours without either man giving in. Officials eventually called the contest a double loss.

## 3 Greco-Roman Wrestling, Middleweight, 1912
The longest wrestling contest in Olympic history was the 1912 middleweight semi-final bout between Martin "Max" Klein and Alfred "Alppo" Asikainen of Finland The two men struggled for hours under the hot sun, stopping every half hour for a brief refreshment break. Finally, after 11 hours, Klein, an Estonian competing for Czarist Russia, pinned his opponent. However, he was so exhausted by his ordeal that he was unable to take part in the final. Sweden's Claes Johanson was awarded first place by default.

## 4 Tennis Doubles, 2008
Sweden's Simon Aspelin and Thomas Johansson battled Arnaud Clément and Michaël Llodra of France in an epic semi-final match that lasted a record 59 games over four-and-three-quarter hours, the longest three-set match in Olympic history. Aspelin and Johansson eventually pulled ahead to win 7–6 (6), 4–6, 19–17, and went on to earn the silver medals.

# 9 Unusually Slow Olympic Competitors

### 1 John Akhwari, Tanzania, Marathon, 1968

More than one hour after Mamo Wolde of Ethiopia had won the 1968 marathon, the final runner, John Akhwari entered the stadium. He had injured his knee in a fall. Bloodied and bandaged, he struggled to the finish line. When asked by filmmaker Bud Greenspan why he had not quit despite the obvious pain he was feeling, Akhwari replied, "My country did not send me 7,000 miles away to start the race. They sent me 7,000 miles to finish it."

### 2 Olmeus Charles, Haiti, 10,000 Meters, 1976

Olmeus Charles' performance in the opening heat of the 1976 10,000 meters was the ultimate expression of the Olympic ideal that what counts is not the winning but the taking part. Charles completed the course in 42:00.11, the slowest time ever recorded in the Olympics, almost 14 minutes slower than Carlos Lopes, who won the heat, and more than eight and a half minutes slower than Chris McCubbins of Canada, who came last but one. The entire schedule had to be held up while Charles plodded the final six laps alone. In 1972 and 1976 Haitian runners consistently finished in last place. On first reflection, one might feel sympathy for the Haitians. After all, Haiti is the poorest country in the Western Hemisphere, and malnutrition is widespread. However, there is no evidence that tryouts were actually held to determine the nation's best runners. Instead, "Baby Doc" Duvalier, the dictator of Haiti, simply chose his friends and other trusted soldiers, and rewarded them with a free trip to Canada. Unfortunately, none of them were athletes.

### 3 Dieudonné Lamothe, Haiti, Marathon, 1984

The 78th and last man to cross the finish line in the 1984 Olympic marathon was Dieudonné Lamothe of Haiti. In 1976 Lamothe had competed in the 5,000-meter race, recording the slowest time in Olympic history, but insisting on finishing. While in Los Angeles in 1984 Lamothe did not speak to the press. However, after the fall of Haitian dictator "Baby Doc" Duvalier, Lamothe revealed that Haitian Olympic officials had threatened to kill him if he failed to finish. He did make it across the finish line—in 2 hours 52 minutes and 18 seconds, a much more respectable time than his 1976 performance. In 1988, under considerably less pressure, Lamothe placed 20th in 2:16:15.

## 4 Pyambuu Tuul, Mongolia, Marathon, 1992

The last finisher in the Barcelona marathon was Pyambuu Tuul of Mongolia, whose time of 4:00:44 was the slowest in 84 years. But Tuul's achievement had a touch of drama of its own. A construction worker, he was blinded by an explosion in 1978. Twelve years later he was discovered by Richard Traum, founder of the Achilles Club, a New York-based organization that helped disabled athletes. Tuul, with the help of a guide, competed in the 1990 New York Marathon. Then, in January 1991, a cornea transplant restored sight in his right eye. One and a half years later he took part in—and finished—the Olympic Marathon, not to win but "to show that a man has many possibilities."

## 5 Abdul Baser Wasigi, Afghanistan, Marathon, 1996

Abdul Baser Wasigi was a 21-year-old from Kabul, Afghanistan. Afghanistan had been so disrupted by war in 1992 that its athletes never arrived in Barcelona. Four years later, Wasigi injured his hamstring muscle shortly after his arrival in Atlanta and was forced to give up training for the two weeks before the race. He was determined to compete and finish despite his injury. Two miles into the race, he was already three-quarters of a mile behind the other runners, and when Josia Thugwane crossed the finish line, Wasigi had just passed the 25-kilometer mark. In the stadium, ground crews were already covering the track in preparation for the Closing Ceremony. Officials, who had been going to wave Wasigi aside to finish on an alternative track, let him proceed to the main stadium after all; preparations for the Closing Ceremony were halted, and volunteers cut a piece of white plastic tape, wrote "ATLANTA 96" on it, and stretched it across the finish line. When he finally arrived inside the stadium hundreds of volunteers lined the track and applauded, while the band struck up a welcoming fanfare. Wasigi's time of 4:24:17 was the slowest in Olympic history, (breaking the previous record of 4:22:45, set by George Lister of Canada in 1908), and he finished 1 hour 24 minutes and 22 seconds behind the runner in next to last place.

## 6 Zeina Mina, Lebanon, Women's 400 Meters, 1984

Of the 28 women who took part in the 400-meter competition in 1984 the slowest was Zeina Mina, who finished last in her heat with a time of 59.56. However, it is worth bearing in mind the difficulties which Mina faced training in her hometown—Beirut. Lebanon's leading heptathlete, Mina was unable to train for her specialty because shelling prevented her from reaching the stadium. So she ran on the beach, in the subway, anywhere she could find. For a year she didn't run on a track, until two weeks before the Olympics. Her performance in Los Angeles did not bother her. "It is wonderful here," she said, "away from the bombs."

## 7 Nishma Gurung, Nepal, Women's 50-meter Freestyle Swimming, 1996

The slowest swimmer in the preliminary heats was Nishma Gurung of Nepal, whose time of 41.45 was 7 seconds slower than any of the 54 other participants and was the equivalent of twenty meters behind the time of top qualifier Le Jingyi—in a fifty-meter race.

## 8 Hem Reaksmey, Cambodia, Women's 100-meter Breaststroke, 1996

In the first heat of the preliminary round, Hem Reaksmey of Cambodia finished in 1:44.68, more than 8½ seconds slower than the previous slowest time in the history of the event. It is worth noting that Hem was twelve years old.

## 9 Shizo Kaniguri, Japan, Marathon, 1912

Shizo Kaniguri dropped out of the marathon after 20 kilometers. A local family, seeing his distress, invited him in for some fruit juice. As one of Japan's two participants in the 1912 Olympics, and the nation's first Olympic entrants at that, Kaniguri was ashamed at failing to finish. Instead of contacting Japanese or Olympic authorities, he returned to Japan on his own. He did compete in the Olympics again, in 1920 and 1924. On the 50th anniversary of the Stockholm Games, Swedish journalist Oscar Söderland tracked down Kaniguri and invited him to go back to Sweden where Kaniguri, now 71 years old, symbolically completed the marathon course.

# 8 Overwhelming Victories

## 1 USA Basketball Team, 1956

Led by Bill Russell and K.C. Jones, who later became great professional stars with the Boston Celtics, the team from the United States won all eight of its games by at least 30 points and scored more than 100 points four times. Their average score was 99–46.

## 2 Kosei Inoue, Japan, Half Heavyweight Judo, 2000

The reigning world champion, Kosei Inoue put on the most dominating judo performance in Olympic history. His five victories lasted a total of only 7 minutes 43 seconds and the longest, a quarter-final defeat of Ariel Ze'evi of Israel, was over in 2 minutes 39 seconds. In the final, the score was tied 1–1 when Inoue suddenly put Canadian Nicolas Gill on his back with a right *uchi-mata*. On the victory podium, Inoue held aloft a framed photograph of his mother, who had died of a brain hemorrhage in June 1999.

## 3 Japanese Women's Volleyball Team, 1976

The Japanese team dominated the tournament so completely that only once did an opponent (South Korea) reach double figures in a single game. In the final, they defeated the Soviet team 15–7, 15–8, 15–2.

## 4 Khadr Sayed El Touni, Egypt, Middleweight Weightlifting, 1936

Twenty-one-year-old Khadr Sayed El Touni was one of the sensations of the 1936 Olympics. Not only did he outclass his opponents in the Middleweight division, he actually lifted 15 kilograms more than the winner of the Light Heavyweight division.

## 5 Ivan Yarygin, Soviet Union, Heavyweight Freestyle Wrestling, 1972

In an inspired performance, 23-year-old Ivan Yarygin pinned all seven of his opponents. Only Khorloo Baianmunkh of Mongolia was able to last more than three minutes with the Russian strong man. Yarygin spent a total of only 17 minutes and eight seconds on the mat in his seven matches. He successfully defended his Olympic title in 1976.

### 6 Argentine Football Team, 2004

The Argentinians swept through the 2004 tournament with remarkable ease, winning all six of their matches and becoming the first country in one hundred years to manage the impressive feat of going through the entire tournament without conceding a single goal. Carlos Tévez scored 8 of Argentina's 17 goals.

### 7 USA Softball Team, 2004

The US team arrived in Athens with a 70-game winning streak and having been ranked number one in the world for the past 18 years. At the Olympics they won all nine of their games and outscored their opponents 51–1.

### 8 Matt McGrath, USA, Hammer Throw, 1912

Irish-American policeman Matt McGrath was truly in a class by himself in Stockholm. The *shortest* of his six throws—173 feet 4 inches (52.8 meters)—was almost 15 feet (4.6 meters) longer than anyone else's *longest* throw. McGrath's Olympic record was not bettered for 24 years and would have earned a silver medal in the 1948 Olympics.

# 5 Underwhelming Winners

## 1 Park Si-hun, South Korea, Light Middleweight Boxing, 1988

Probably no gold-medal-winner in Olympic history has been less deserving of his prize than Park Si-hun, who benefited from five "hometown" decisions. Park's first bout, against Abdalla Ramadan of Sudan, was halted in the second round with Ramadan doubled over in pain and unable to continue after two illegal blows to the hip and kidney. The Australian referee, Ronald Mark Gregor, ruled that the injured Ramadan had "retired" and declared Park the winner.

Park's second opponent was one of the favorites, Torsten Schmitz of East Germany. Most observers thought Schmitz had won the fight; however, Park was judged the victor in a narrow but unanimous decision. While the East Germans vented their fury, Park moved on to the quarter-finals and a bout with Vincenzo Nardiello of Italy. Nardiello was ahead on the cards of all five judges after the first two rounds. Two of the judges gave Nardiello the final round as well. However, the other three decided that Park had won the round by such a wide margin that they gave him the fight. When the verdict was announced, Nardiello fell to his knees and pounded the canvas. Then he charged out of the ring and screamed at the jury until Italian team officials dragged him off to the dressing room.

In the semi-finals Park won another narrow but unanimous victory, defeating Ray Downey of Canada by the same margin by which he had beaten Schmitz. By this time he had become known as the "unbeatable Park Si-hun." Now all that stood between Park and a gold medal was 19-year-old Roy Jones, Jr., of the United States. Three days before the gold-medal bout, Jones told reporters, "I know how tough it is to get a decision against a South Korean, but it doesn't matter. If they cheat me, that's OK. I'll know if I really won it." Still, to be on the safe side, Jones announced that he would be going for a knockout. He didn't get the knockout, but he did pummel Park, dominating all three rounds. Compubox, a private company that kept track of punches thrown and connected, registered 86 hits for Jones and only 32 for Park. Incredibly, three of the five judges gave the victory to the Korean.

Veteran ring observers of all nationalities, reporters, referees and fans agreed that it was the worst decision they had ever seen. The French sports newspaper L'Equipe summed up the consensus in blunt terms: "Scandalous. To vomit." The decision was so bad that Korean fans were embarrassed, telephoning local newspapers and television stations to complain. Even Park himself apologized to Jones, telling him, through an interpreter, "I am sorry. I lost the fight. I feel very bad." On the victory stand, Park raised Jones's arm in triumph.

Sports Illustrated reported that one judge, Hiouad Larbi of Morocco, told angry journalists, "The American won easily; so easily, in fact, that I was positive my four fellow judges would score the fight for the American by a wide margin. So I voted for the Korean to make the score only 4–1 for the American and not embarrass the host country." Unfortunately, the judges from Uruguay and Uganda did the same thing.

## 2 German Women's Field Hockey Team, 2004

The Germans opened with a 2–1 upset of Australia, but were then thrashed by the Netherlands 4–1 and South Africa 3–0. However, they then edged out South Korea 3–2 to unexpectedly squeak through to the semis. The match between China and Germany was scoreless through regulation time and two extra periods, China failing to convert five penalty corners in the second half and another five in the first overtime period. Germany won the shoot-out 4–3 to register their second upset of the tournament. In the final, a rematch against the Dutch, Germany took a 2–0 lead and held on for a surprising 2–1 victory. The German team was the first in history to win an Olympic field hockey tournament despite being cumulatively outscored by their opponents (8–11).

## 3 Anatoly Parfenov, Soviet Union, Super-heavyweight Greco-Roman Wrestling, 1956

Parfenov was originally declared the loser in his opening contest with Germany's Wilfried Dietrich. However, a protest by the Soviet team was upheld by the Jury of Appeal. In the second round Parfenov lost to Bertil Antonsson of Sweden. Then he won a forfeit in the third round and received a bye in the fourth round. In the fifth round he gained his only undisputed victory, a decision over Adelmo Bulgarelli of Italy. Fortunately for Parfenov, in an era when medals were decided by penalty points rather than single elimination victories, his two wins were enough to give him first place.

## 4 Italian Épée Fencing Team, 1996

The Italian épée team fought three matches. In the first they beat the United States by one touch. In the semi-finals, after trailing by seven points, they beat Germany by winning the coin toss. In the final, the Italians were leading Russia 44–43 when Aleksandr Beketov aggressively attacked five-time Olympian Angelo Mazzoni. Beketov missed, but his handle smashed into Mazzoni's mask, twisting it into the Italian's face and cutting him on the brow and below the eye. The match was halted with six seconds left in order to clear the blood out of Mazzoni's eye. After a ten-minute break, the match resumed and three seconds later, Mazzoni scored the winning point with a quick stab.

## 5 Ian Brown and Anthony Marchant, Australia, 2000-meter Tandem Cycling, 1956

Browne and Marchant finished last in their first-round heat and lost the *repêchage* to Ladislav Foucek and Václav Machek of Czechoslovakia. However, in another *repêchage*, the Germans and Soviets crashed, leaving the Soviet riders unable to restart. In need of opponents for the German pair, the officials turned to the already-eliminated Australians and Americans. Browne and Marchant won the race, scored two more unexpected victories in the quarter-finals and semi-finals, and then upset Foucek and Machek in the final.

# 4 Notorious Olympic Disqualifications

## 1 Fred Lorz, USA, Marathon, 1904

The marathon was run in intense heat on dusty roads made dustier by the automobiles of the officials and journalists who often drove in front of the runners. The first person to cross the finish line was Fred Lorz of New York. He was immediately hailed as the winner and photographed with Alice Roosevelt, the daughter of the president of the United States. He was about to be awarded the gold medal when it was discovered that he had actually stopped running after 9 miles, hitched a ride in a car for 11 miles, and then started running again. Amateur Athletic Union (AAU) officials slapped him with a lifetime ban. However, he was reinstated well before the ban ran out and managed to win the Boston Marathon of 1905.

## 2 Borys Onyshchenko, Soviet Union, Modern Pentathlon, 1976

The favored Soviet team was fencing against the team from Great Britain when the British pentathletes noticed something odd about the defending silver medalist, Army Major Borys Onyshchenko. In his fight against Adrian Parker, the automatic light registered a hit for the Ukrainian even though he didn't appear to have touched his opponent. Veteran Jeremy Fox was next to be drawn against Onyshchenko. When he too lost a hit without being touched, it became obvious that something was wrong with Onyshchenko's épée. The weapon was taken away to be examined by the Jury of Appeal. Onyshchenko continued with a different sword, but an hour or so later the news came that he had been disqualified. Evidently Onyshchenko, desperate for victory in his final international competition, had wired his sword with a well-hidden push-button circuit breaker that enabled him to register a hit whenever he wanted. It is unknown how long Onyshchenko had been using this trick, but his fencing scores, already high, showed a marked upward surge beginning in 1970. He was spirited out of the Olympic Village almost immediately and never seen outside the USSR again. He was forever after known as Borys Dis-Onyshchenko.

## 3 Hungarian Swimmers, 1996

Like all swimmers, Attila Czene, the eventual winner of the 200-meter individual medley, was required to meet a qualifying time in order to participate in the Olympics. In Czene's case it was a 2:00.88 recorded at a meet in Budapest held June 6–8. Except, as it was revealed several weeks after the Atlanta Games, the Budapest meet never actually happened. It seems that Hungarian swimming officials had neglected to keep track of their athletes' times and had failed to arrange an official meet to allow them to meet the qualifying standards. So they did the next best thing: they invented a meet, complete with qualifying times, failed times and even disqualifications. Half of the 22-person Hungarian Olympic team qualified at this phantom meet, although Czene was the only medal-winner among them.

## 4 Kostas Kenteris and Katerina Thanou, Greece, Track and Field, 2004

On August 12, the day before the Athens Opening Ceremony, defending 200-meter Olympic champion Kostas Kenteris and defending 100-meter silver medalist Ekaterina Thanou failed to appear for a mandatory pre-competition drug test. The Greek duo, favorites in their respective events and revered by Greek fans, had been spotted in the Olympic Village just hours earlier, but vanished before they could be reached by IOC officials for the test. The pair turned up hours later in a nearby hospital, claiming that they had been involved in a motorcycle accident on the outskirts of Athens while rushing back to the Olympic Village for the drug test. Announcing that they were too badly injured to travel, the pair spent five days in the hospital and failed to appear at an IOC disciplinary tribunal. Police launched an investigation into the accident, describing it as "not natural."

As the police investigation continued, the story of the motorcycle accident unravelled. One man who claimed he had witnessed the accident was discovered to have an outstanding warrant for fraud after falsely posing as a lawyer. The man was sentenced to 14 months in prison. Twelve other people were charged with making false statements, including seven doctors at the hospital where the pair stayed. On August 17 Kenteris and Thanou left the hospital with no visible injuries, and appeared the next day before an IOC tribunal. After less than an hour of questioning, both athletes withdrew from the Olympic competition.

On August 20 the police probe concluded that the pair had faked the motor-cycle crash to avoid the drug test. The same day, Greek investigators searched the office and warehouse owned by Christos Teskos, a former nutritional supplement salesman who coached both Kenteris and Thanou. Police found 30 boxes of steroids and 1,400 boxes of food supplements containing the banned stimulant ephedrine. After an IAAF investigation, the pair were handed two-year bans. In May 2011, an Athens court found Thanou and Kenteris guilty of perjury. However, in September an appeals court acquitted them on grounds of reasonable doubt.

# 11 Especially Considerate Olympians...and 1 notable exception

### 1 Emil Zátopek, Czechoslovakia, Distance Running, 1948-1956

In 1968 the great Australian distance runner Ron Clarke visited Zátopek after failing in his last attempt to win an Olympic championship. Writing in Athletics Weekly in 1987, Clarke recalled, "As he marched me through customs and on to the plane on my way out of Prague, he shook hands and, in so doing, secretly transferred a small package into my grip. I thought I was smuggling some message to the outside world for him so did not dare open the little parcel until the plane was well outside Czechoslovakian territory. When I opened it up, it was his 1952 Olympic 10,000 meters gold medal. I thought back to the words he said as he passed it across to me, which at the time I did not understand: 'Because you deserved it,' he said. I wish I had. I do know no one cherishes any gift more than I do, my only Olympic gold medal and not because of what it is . . . but because of the man whose spirit it represents."

### 2 Bobby Pearce, Australia, Rowing, 1928-1932

The spirit of the 1928 Amsterdam Games was perhaps best exemplified by the experience of Australian single sculls rower Bobby Pearce. Midway through his quarter-final race he stopped rowing to allow a family of ducks to pass single file in front of his boat. Pearce won the race anyway and, later, the gold medal as well. He successfully defended his Olympic championship four years later.

### 3 Joe Lazarus, USA, Bantamweight Boxing, 1924

Joe Lazarus of Cornell University had the unusual misfortune of knocking out his opponent, Oscar Andrén of Sweden, and yet being declared the loser. As Andrén was being revived, the referee, Maurice Siegel of France, announced that Lazarus was disqualified for striking the knockout punch while breaking from a clinch. Siegel later apologized to US officials for his mistaken call, and Andrén and the Swedish team manager urged Lazarus to file a protest. Moved by the Swedes' good sportsmanship, Lazarus declined, as did US officials.

## 4 Kevin Barry, New Zealand, Light Heavyweight Boxing, 1984

Evander Holyfield had stopped his first three opponents in the 1984 Light Heavyweight competition and was on the verge of knocking out a fourth, when an unusual incident occurred. A few seconds before the end of the second round of his semi-final bout with Kevin Barry, Holyfield lashed out a right to the ribs and followed with a left hook that floored Barry for good. The referee, Gligorije Novicic of Yugoslavia, motioned Holyfield to a neutral corner, counted out Barry, then turned to Holyfield and disqualified him for throwing the left hook after Novicic had yelled, "Stop." Subsequent viewing of the videotapes of the fight confirmed the late hit, but also showed that Barry and Holyfield had previously thrown four late blows each. When the decision was announced, Barry turned to Holyfield and said, "You won the fight fair and square." Then he took the American's hand and raised it in the air. The crowd went berserk, raining abuse and refuse on the Yugoslavian referee. The police had to be brought in to escort Novicic from the arena. What made the incident all the more shocking was the subsequent ruling that, because Barry had been declared a knockout victim, amateur boxing regulations prevented him from fighting again for 28 days. This meant that the gold medal was awarded by default to the other semi-final winner, Anton Josipovic, who, like referee Novicic, happened to hail from Yugoslavia.

## 5 Lucien Gaudin, France, Foil Fencing, 1920-1928

Lucien Gaudin faced Giulio Gaudini in the final of the 1928 men's foil. With the score tied 2–2, Gaudini grazed Gaudin's fencing jacket. The referee called out, "No touch." The Italians were furious and began protesting vehemently. Gaudin removed his mask, walked over to the jury, and calmly announced, "I was touched." Gaudini was awarded the point and then earned another. However, Gaudin then scored three times in a row to win 5–4.

## 6/7 Bob Van Osdel (USA) and Duncan McNaughton (Canada), High Jump, 1932

Bob Van Osdel and Duncan McNaughton were good friends and fellow students at the University of Southern California in Los Angeles, but at the Olympics they competed for different countries. Before the final height, Van Osdel approached his Canadian friend and advised him on improving his technique. He concluded, "Get your kick working and you will be over." That piece of advice and encouragement did the trick. McNaughton cleared the bar while Van Osdel missed. McNaughton won the gold medal and Van Osdel the silver. In 1933 McNaughton's gold medal was stolen from his car. Van Osdel, now a dentist, made a mold from his own silver medal, poured gold into the mold, and sent the replica gold medal to McNaughton.

## 8 Judy Guinness, Great Britain, Women's Foil Fencing, 1932-1936

In the spirit of fair play, British fencer Judy Guinness gave up her hopes for a gold medal in 1932 when she pointed out to officials that they had not noticed two touches scored against her by her final opponent, Ellen Preis of Austria. This act of fair play proved to be the margin of victory.

## 9 Lawrence Lemieux, Canada, Finn Sailing, 1984-1988

In the fifth race of the 1988 Finn class contest, Lawrence Lemieux was in second place when he noticed Joseph Chan of the Singapore crew struggling in the water 25 yards from his capsized boat. Chan had injured his back and was being swept away by the powerful currents. Lemieux turned around and saved Chan, who was too exhausted to heave himself into the Canadian's boat. The International Olympic Committee gave Lemieux a special award for his act of gallantry. Lemieux, baffled by the attention he received, reminded reporters of what might have happened if he had ignored Chan. "I'm not that intense," he said.

## 10 Antal Barát Lemberkovits, Hungary, Prone Small-Bore Rifle Shooting, 1932

Antal Barát Lemberkovits hit one bull's-eye but he had unfortunately aimed at the wrong target. He called out his mistake to the officials, who ruled the shot a complete miss. Had he not made this error and had he not been so honest, Limberkovits would have won the gold medal.

## 11 Shawn Crawford, USA, 200 Meters, 2008

Shawn Crawford crossed the finish line in fifth place, but was bumped up to third when two runners ahead of him, Churandy Martina of the Netherlands Antilles and Wallace Spearman of the United States, were disqualified for running outside their lanes. Crawford gave his silver medal to Martina after the race along with a note saying, "I know this can't replace the moment, but I want you to have this because I believe it's rightfully yours."

## Notable Exception: Mohamed Ali Rashwan, Egypt, Open Class Judo, 1984

Yasuhiro Yamashita of Japan seemed as sure a bet for a gold medal as anyone in Los Angeles. But in his second match, Yamashita tore a muscle in his right calf, causing him great pain and forcing him to walk with a limp. In the final, Yamashita, described by one disgruntled opponent as "a refrigerator with a head on top," faced Mohamed Ali Rashwan, a 28-year-old building contractor from Alexandria. Yamashita scored a quick and easy victory, and was immediately overcome by his emotions. So sore was his leg that Rashwan had to help him onto the top step at the medal ceremony. Afterwards, Rashwan told reporters, "I did not attack his right side because this is against my principles. I would not want to win this way." Rashwan was applauded for his good sportsmanship and news of his deed spread far and wide. On September 26, 1985, Rashwan was awarded the Fair Play Trophy by the International Committee for Fair Play. However, this inspiring tale of the true Olympic spirit has an odd twist to it. Videotapes of the Olympic final clearly show that Rashwan did try to attack Yamashita's injured leg. In fact, it was his first move, a mere ten seconds after the match began.

# 4 Events with Two Finals

## 1 Rowing, Coxed Fours, 1900

Incompetence on the part of regatta officials resulted in the unusual development of two separate finals. At first it was declared that the winners of three heats would qualify for the final, as would the second-place finisher in heat 3, which included four of the ten entrants. When it was discovered that the losers in heats 2 and 3 had recorded faster times than the winner of heat 1, the officials announced that an extra qualifying heat would have to be run. However, they were unable to notify all of the crews, so the extra heat was cancelled. It was then decided that the three heat winners would be joined in the final by the three fastest losers. But since the course was laid out for only four boats, the heat winners protested and refused to participate in the final. So the first final was run off with only one of the original qualifiers in the water. The result was obviously ridiculous, so a second final was announced for the three heat winners. Participants in both finals were awarded prizes.

## 2 Swimming, 100-meter Freestyle, 1920

Duke Paoa Kahanamoku of the USA equaled his own world record of 1:01.4 in the semi-finals, and then set a new record of 1:00.4 in the final, to celebrate his 30th birthday. However, William Herald of Australia claimed that he had been fouled by American Norman Ross. Ross was disqualified, and the race was ordered to be reswum. The order of the finish was exactly the same the second time, except that Ross, who had won the 1,500-meter championship the day after the first 100-meter final, and the 800 meters the day before the second final, did not take part.

## 3 Sailing, Finn, 1920

The first two races were staged off Ostende, 100 kilometers from Antwerp, on July 7 and 8. The results of the second race were voided because a buoy changed position and a dispute broke out about the course. Because the only two teams entered were from the Netherlands, the final two races were rescheduled for September 3—in Holland. Other than the 1956 equestrian events, this was the only time in Olympic history that an official event was contested outside the host country.

## 4 Football, 1928

The final between Uruguay and Argentina ended in a 1–1 draw. In the days before overtimes and penalty kicks, the match had to be replayed. In the second final Hector Scarone scored with 17 minutes to play to give Uruguay a 2–1 victory.

# 3 Events with No Winner

## 1 Match Sprint Cycling, 1908

Benjamin Johnson of Great Britain suffered a punctured tire shortly after the start of the final. The other three finalists, Clarence Kingsbury and Benjamin Jones of Great Britain and Maurice Schilles of France, crawled around the track, carefully jockeying for position. At the beginning of the last bank, Kingsbury also punctured. Then the remaining two raced to the finish line, with Schilles winning by inches. However, the time limit of 1 minute 45 seconds had been exceeded, so the race was declared void. Much to the surprise of most of those present, the judges of the National Cyclists' Union refused to allow the race to be rerun.

## 2 Light Heavyweight Greco-Roman Wrestling, 1912

Anders Ahlgren of Sweden fought his way to the final match by pinning six opponents, each within 35 minutes. But in Finland's Ivar Böling he met his equal—literally. Ahlgren and Böling struggled hour after hour without either man giving in, until finally, after nine hours, officials called the contest a double loss. The rules of the Olympic competition stated that it was necessary for a first-place winner actually to defeat his adversary, so the officials decided to declare Ahlgren and Böling co-winners of the second prize.

## 3 Women's 100 Meters, 2000

In 2007 Marion Jones the winner of the 100 meters in 2000, was stripped of her medals from the Sydney Olympics after admitting to taking steroids in 2000 and 2001. In December 2009 the IOC decided to reallocate Jones' medals in the 100 meters, 200 meters and long jump events. In the 100 meters event, Jamaica's Tayna Lawrence and Merlene Ottey were awarded the silver and bronze medals, but the IOC declined to award the gold medal to Ekaterina Thanou of Greece because of her behavior at the 2004 Athens Olympics, in which she and sprinter Kostas Kenteris were accused of faking a motorcycle accident to avoid a doping test.

# 6 Disastrous Events

## 1 Marathon, 1900

This unfortunate event was held in 102° F (39° C ) heat. The course—which began in the Bois de Boulogne, followed the old city wall, and ended up back in the Bois—was poorly marked, and the runners sometimes took a wrong turn and had to double back. In addition, in certain places, the roads were filled with pedestrians, bicyclists, runners joining in for the fun of it, automobiles and animals. The local favorite was Georges Touquet-Daunis. However, twelve kilometers into the race he stopped at a café, drank a couple beers and decided it was too hot to continue. Indeed, only seven of the thirteen starters completed the course.

## 2 Marathon, 1904

The 1904 marathon ranks very high on the list of bizarre events in Olympic history. The race organizers knew almost nothing about staging such an event. The course included seven hills and was run on dusty roads, made dustier by the many automobiles that the judges, doctors and journalists used to follow—and lead—the runners. The brutal nature of the contest was made worse by the fact that it was scheduled for the middle of the afternoon in 90° F (32° C) heat. In addition, the only water available to the runners was from a well 12 miles from where the race began and ended in the stadium. With all these impediments, it is not surprising that only 14 of the 32 starters made it back to the finish line. The winner was Thomas Hicks, who lost ten pounds during the race and gladly announced his retirement. The athletes who suffered through the 1904 marathon may have received some satisfaction when they learned that two of the officials in charge of patrolling the course were badly injured as well, when their brand-new car swerved to avoid one of the runners and careered down an embankment.

## 3 Cycling Road Race, 1912

This grueling 196-mile race around Lake Mälar began at 2:00 a.m. The competitors were sent out on the course at two-minute intervals over the next four hours. "Okey" Lewis of South Africa won the race in a time of 10 hours, 42 minutes and 39 seconds. There was one terrible accident at the beginning of the race. A few hundred meters after the start, Karl Landsberg of Sweden was hit by a motor-wagon and dragged along for some distance before the wagon stopped. Another competitor, Fyodor Borisov of Russia, fell into a flooded ditch and lay there unconscious until he was discovered by a farmer.

## 4 Individual Cross-country Run, 1924

The 1924 cross-country event proved an almost total disaster, and ultimately resulted in the end of cross-country races in the Olympics. Thirty-eight runners started off in the afternoon of one of the hottest days in Parisian history. Only fifteen finished. The course was unusually difficult, including stone paths covered in knee-high thistles and weeds. The race was also run too close to an energy plant that was belching out poisonous fumes. The first man to enter the stadium and cross the finish line was the Finnish legend, Paavo Nurmi. He appeared so fresh and untroubled that the spectators had no reason to suspect that anything was wrong. But as soon as the other runners started to arrive, the horrible situation began to unfold. One after another, strong athletes staggered onto the track. José Andía of Spain collapsed, hit his head on a marker and began bleeding. Arthur Sewell of Great Britain headed the wrong way. Pointed in the right direction, he collided with another runner. Both of them fell and failed to finish. Out on the roads there had been worse scenes of carnage, as various contestants were overcome by sunstroke and vomiting. Hours later the Red Cross and Olympic officials were still searching the sides of the road for missing runners. Only 15 of the 38 starters were able to make it to the finish line.

## 5 Team Cross-country Run, 1924

The same horrible race that was the individual cross-country also counted as the team race. For Finland to win, at least three of its athletes had to cross the finish line. Paavo Nurmi and Vilho Ritola finished easily, but Heikki Liimatainen, staggering along in the oppressive heat, halted 30 meters short of his goal. Thinking he had already crossed the finish line, he turned and headed off the track. The crowd shouted at him and he stopped. After standing for a while with his back to the finish line, he finally regained control of his senses, turned around, and walked across the finish. It took him two minutes to cover the last 30 meters. Four of the seven teams failed to complete the course.

## 6 Modern Pentathlon, 1996

The riding and cross-country run took place at the Georgia International Horse Park, 37 miles (59.5 km) from the venue for the first three disciplines. Potential spectators, who had purchased tickets for the entire event, arrived to discover security roadblocks that prevented access to the Horse Park. There were no shuttle buses from the parking lot to the competition venue, and the only way to reach the venue was to walk 5 miles (8 km) in blazing heat. The situation was little better for the athletes themselves. When they reached the jumping arena, they discovered that the only shady spot where they could stand while waiting was underneath an oak tree.

# 10 Unlucky Olympic Competitors

**1** **Jules Noël, France, Discus Throw, 1932**

On his fourth attempt, Noël lofted a great throw that appeared to land just beyond the flag that marked American John Anderson's first-place effort. Unfortunately, every one of the officials in charge of the discus was, at that moment, distracted by the tense proceedings of the pole vault, taking place nearby, so none of them saw where Noël's discus had landed. Embarrassed by this blunder, they awarded Noël an extra throw in addition to the two that he still had coming. However, the Frenchman was unable to come up with another big throw and so was forced to return home without a medal.

**2** **Joe McCluskey, USA, 3,000-meter Steeplechase, 1932**

In the steeplechase final in Los Angeles, the lap-checker, a substitute for the regular man, who was ill, forgot to change the lap count the first time the runners passed by. At the end of the real regulation distance, Joe McCluskey was in second place and Tom Evenson of Great Britain in third. But during the extra lap caused by the lap checker's mistake Evenson passed McCluskey and beat him to the finish by two yards. When McCluskey pointed out to track officials what had happened, he was offered the opportunity of having the race re-run the next day. Quite exhausted, McCluskey declined, stating that anyway "a race has only one finish line."

**3** **Eduard Rapp, Soviet Union/Russia, 1,000-meter Cycling Time Trial, 1976**

One of the favorites, Eduard Rapp of the USSR was eliminated due to an unfortunate incident. He started before the gun and, assuming he would be ordered to restart, he stopped racing. But the officials ruled his start to be legal, and he was disqualified for stopping.

**4** **Michelle Chardonnet, France, Women's 100-meter Hurdles, 1984**

Originally a dead-heat was announced for third place, but, after viewing films of the race for 50 minutes, a Jury of Appeal awarded sole possession to Kim Turner of the United States. Unfortunately, Chardonnet was not informed of this decision until she was standing in the award ceremony area. When her name was not announced, she was led away in tears. Three and a half months later, the IAAF reversed the decision of the Jury of Appeal, and Chardonnet was awarded her bronze medal.

### 5/6 Yoel Sela and Eldad Amir, Israel, Flying Dutchman Sailing, 1988

Sela and Amir almost became Israel's first Olympic medalists. Unfortunately for them, the second race fell on the Jewish high holiday of Yom Kippur. Israeli Olympic officials made it clear that any of their athletes who competed on Yom Kippur would be withdrawn from competition and sent home, a punishment which they did in fact mete out to the Israeli men's 470 crew. Sela and Amir would have won medals had they taken part in the second race and placed higher than eleventh, a result which they bettered in five of their six races.

### 7 Genc Barkici, Albania, Flyweight Weightlifting, 1992

Albania made its first appearance at the Olympics in 1972. The country then set a record by boycotting the next four Olympics, returning after 20 years in 1992. Their first scheduled competitor was Genc Barkici, a weightlifter who had placed fifth at the European championships three months earlier. Unfortunately, Barkici got his finger caught in a door at the arena on the day of the competition and was forced to withdraw.

### 8 Duane Cousins, Australia, 50,000-meter Walk, 1996

Track officials miscounted Duane Cousins's laps and sent him to the finish line a lap early. He was officially recorded as "did not finish."

### 9 Natalya Shikolenko, Belarus, Women's Javelin, 1996

Reigning world champion Natalya Shikolenko was struck by an unfortunate incident on her second throw: her javelin hit an overhead camera cable. She was awarded an extra try, but was unable to match the cable shot and ended up in twelfth place.

### 10 Cary Kolat, USA, Featherweight Freestyle Wrestling, 2000

In 1997 Cary Kolat was fighting Abbas Haj Kenari in the world championship final when the Iranian, in an attempt to break Kolat's momentum, began untying and retying his shoelaces. Kolat lost the match, but the incident led to two changes in the rules, one requiring wrestlers to tape their laces and the other allowing officials to penalize wrestlers one point for stalling. At the 1998 world championships Kolat defeated Serafim Barzakov of Bulgaria, but his victory was overturned after a protest. Once again this led to a rule change, under which all protested matches would be re-wrestled. In the semi-finals of the 1999 world championships Kolat defeated Elbrus Tedeyev of Ukraine. A Ukrainian protest was upheld, the match was redone, and Kolat lost in overtime. In his opening match at the 2000 Olympics, Kolat defeated former world champion Mohammad Talaei of Iran 3–1—or so it appeared. The Iranians protested, their protest was upheld, and in the rematch . . . Kolat lost 5–4.

# 8 Olympians Who Competed While Injured

### 1 Gunnar Setterwall, Sweden, Mixed Doubles Tennis, 1912

Shortly after the final match began, Sigrid Fick inadvertently smashed her partner, Gunnar Setterwall, in the face rather severely. In the words of the Official Report for 1912: "This little accident seemed to put Setterwall off his game, for his play fell off tremendously."

### 2 Sidney Hinds, USA, Team Three-position Free Rifle Shooting, 1924

In the final, Lieutenant Sidney Hinds shot a perfect 50 for the US team, a performance that was all the more remarkable considering that he was accidentally shot in the foot in the middle of the competition, when the Belgian rifleman beside him knocked his rifle to the ground in the midst of an argument with an official.

### 3 Konrad von Wangenheim, Germany, Three-Day Event Equestrian, 1936

Lieutenant Konrad, Freiherr von Wangenheim was one of the German heroes of the Berlin Games. During the steeplechase portion of the endurance run, his horse Kurfürst stumbled at the fourth obstacle, a hurdle and pond, throwing the 26-year-old von Wangenheim to the ground and breaking his collarbone. Knowing that the German team would be disqualified if he failed to finish, von Wangenheim remounted and negotiated the remaining 32 obstacles without a fault. But the jumping competition still remained. The next day von Wangenheim appeared in the stadium with his arm in a sling. Just before he mounted Kurfürst, the sling was removed and his arm was tightly bound. However, at one of the early obstacles, a double jump, Kurfürst rushed ahead and von Wangenheim was forced to pull the reins with both hands. The horse reared up, fell backward, and landed on von Wangenheim, who managed to crawl out from underneath. Kurfürst lay still and was thought to be dead, but suddenly jumped back up. Von Wangenheim remounted and again completed the course without another fault. The stadium crowd of 100,000 gave von Wangenheim a prolonged standing ovation, as Germany won the gold medals.

## 4 Bill Roycroft, Australia, Equestrian Team Three-Day Event, 1960

Suffering from a concussion and a broken collarbone after a fall in the endurance portion of the three-day event, Bill Roycroft insisted on leaving his hospital bed to compete in the jumping test. Aided by a series of pain-killing injections and a pint of beer, he completed the course flawlessly, ensuring the gold medals for Australia. Roycroft went on to compete in four more Olympics.

## 5 Al Oerter, USA, Discus Throw, 1964

Al Oerter managed to win the 1964 discus gold medal despite suffering from a chronic cervical disc injury that forced him to wear a neck harness. If that wasn't trouble enough, Oerter had also torn the cartilage in his lower ribs a week before the competition. Oerter's gold-medal winning throw caused him so much pain he nearly had to be carried off the field.

## 6 Shun Fujimoto, Japan, Team Gymnastics, 1976

Fujimoto broke his leg at the knee while finishing his floor exercises routine. Not wanting to cause concern among his coaches or fellow team members during the tense competition with the Soviets, Fujimoto kept his injury to himself and went ahead with his side horse performance, earning a 9.5. Next up were the rings. Fujimoto completed a successful routine (9.7) and then faced a difficult moment—the dismount. Landing on his feet, he compounded his injury by dislocating his knee. The pain was intense: "My whole blood was boiling at my stomach." Fujimoto finally submitted himself to medical inspection and was convinced to withdraw from the remainder of the competition. Asked years later if he would have gone ahead on the rings if he had known how much pain he would experience, Fujimoto replied without hesitation: "No."

## 7 Károly Varga, Hungary, Prone Small-bore Rifle Shooting, 1980

Károly Varga broke his shooting hand playing soccer two days before the competition and had to wear a bandage while he shot. After winning the gold medal he explained that the injury had actually helped him, because it forced him to squeeze the trigger more delicately.

## 8 Leontien Zijlaard-van Moorsel, Netherlands, Cycling, 2004

At the age of 34 Leontien Zijlaard-van Moorsel crashed in the road race, incurring a mild concussion and putting her out of the competition. Despite bruises to her neck, hip and shoulder, she won the road time trial three days later to become the first female cyclist to earn four career gold medals and six total medals.

# 2 Athletes Who Died Competing in the Summer Olympics

*Only two athletes have died during Olympic competitions.*

**1 Francisco Lazaro, Portugal, Marathon, 1912**

The 1912 marathon was marred by a sad note. The 21-year-old Portuguese runner Francisco Lazaro collapsed from sunstroke and heart trouble toward the end of the race and was taken to a hospital, where he died the following day. The cause of his death was described as "possibly meningitis, brought on by heat exhaustion."

**2 Knut Enemark, Denmark, Cycling, 1960**

The 1960 cycling road race, which was run in 93° F (34° C) heat, was marred by the death of Danish cyclist Knut Enemark, who collapsed from sunstroke and suffered a fractured skull. It was later determined that before the race Enemark had taken Ronicol, a blood circulation stimulant.

# 12 Unauthorized Competitors

**1 James Bollinger, USA, Lightweight Boxing, 1904**

A well-known local boxer, Carroll Burton, entered the tournament and won his first match. However, it was then discovered that the victor was not Burton at all, but a man named James Bollinger posing as Burton. Bollinger was disqualified and his opponent, Peter Sturholdt, was advanced to the next round.

**2 Philip Plater, Great Britain, Prone Small-bore Rifle Shooting, 1908**

In his book *British Olympians*, Ian Buchanan related the story of the unfortunate Philip Plater of Great Britain. The rules of the competition limited each nation to 12 entries. When the entry form of George Barnes was misplaced, Plater was entered in his place. Barnes's entry form was subsequently found, but on the day of the match, confusion reigned. Thinking that only 11 British shooters had fired, Plater was allowed to start even though there were only 30 minutes remaining. Plater set a world record of 391 and was initially recognized as the Olympic champion. Then it was discovered that all 12 members of the official British team had shot before Plater. Several days later Plater was declared an illegal entrant and his performance expunged from the records.

**3/4/5 Paul Fitzgerald, Tom Gerrard and Tom Flanagan, Ireland, Cycling Road Race, 1956**

The start of the race was delayed by fifteen minutes when it was discovered that there were three "unauthorized" Irish cyclists amongst the 88 starters. After they were removed they joined 200 supporters in passing out Irish nationalist literature.

**6/7/8/9 Cycling Road Race, Northern Ireland, 1972**

Four Irish Republican Army cyclists joined the race to protest the fact that the Irish Cycling Federation competed against cyclists from Northern Ireland. One of them tried to run Irish Olympian Noel Taggart into a ditch. The four were arrested but later released without charge.

## 10 Polin Belisle, Belize, Marathon, 1992

After representing Belize at the 1988 Olympics and finishing last in the Marathon, Polin Belisle badgered the Belize Olympic Committee to send him to the Olympics again in 1992. When they refused, Belisle changed his name to Apolinario Belisle Gómez and, armed with a Honduran birth certificate, won a place on the 1992 Olympic team of Honduras. Shortly before the Marathon event some Belizean athletes recognized Belisle's name on the entry list, and he was kicked off the team. Not so easily discouraged, Belisle showed up on race day anyway, slipped into the first line of runners on the starting line and raced with the leaders for a mile before fading into the pack and disappearing.

## 11/12 Valentina Enaki, Moldova, and Virginia Gloum, Central African Federation, Women's Marathon, 1996

Enaki and Gloum were listed on the official entry list and ran the race, but as soon as it was over they were declared "unofficial competitors" because of bureaucratic blunders by their team officials, and their results were stricken from the record.

# 5 Instances of Accommodating Royalty

## 1 Marathon Distance: Marathon, 1908

The race was scheduled to conclude with 385 yards around the stadium track, so that the finish line would be directly in front of Queen Alexandra's royal box. As it happened, this random distance of 26 miles and 385 yards would later become the standardized length for marathon races.

## 2 Starting Over: Individual Sabre, 1896

The competition was almost finished when King George I and his entourage arrived. The jury decided to restart the tournament from the beginning so that the king would be better entertained. This drastically changed the outcome, as Austria's Adolf Schmal had already beaten eventual champion Ioannis Georgiadis and third-place finisher Holger Nielsen, but lost to both the second time around.

## 3 Prince's Prerogative: Gymnastics (Rings), 1896

The six judges split three for Ioannis Mitropoulos of Greece and three for Hermann Weingärtner of Germany. Prince Georgios of Greece cast the tie-breaking vote for his countryman. Mitropoulos was the first Greek winner in the Olympic stadium, and his victory was greeted with wild enthusiasm.

## 4 The Pope's Window: Canoeing, 1960

Pope John XXIII was a spectator of the 1960 Canoeing events, catching the semi-finals from a window of his summer residence overlooking Lake Albano.

## 5 One for Nawal: Women's 400-meter Hurdles, 1984

Nawal El Moutawakel was the first woman from an Islamic nation to win an Olympic medal and also the first ever gold-medal winner from Morocco. After she crossed the finish line in first place the king of Morocco decreed that all women born on the day of her victory be named Nawal.

# 15 Medal Ceremony Incidents

## 1 Black Power Salute

US sprinters Tommie Smith and John Carlos took first and third place in the 200 meters in Mexico City in 1968. Mounting the dais barefooted for the medal ceremony, they wore civil rights badges, as did Australian silver-medal winner Peter Norman, who asked to join Smith and Carlos in their protest. Smith wore a black scarf around his neck and Carlos a string of beads as a memorial to those blacks who had been lynched. When "The Star-Spangled Banner" was played, Smith and Carlos bowed their heads and each raised one black-gloved hand in the Black Power salute. They later explained that their clenched fists symbolized black strength and unity, and that their bare feet were a reminder of black poverty in the United States. They bowed their heads to express their belief that the words of freedom in the US national anthem only applied to Americans with white skin. Carlos told reporters, "White America will only give us credit for an Olympic victory. They'll say I'm an American, but if I did something bad, they'd say I was a Negro."

The pair were immediately suspended by the IOC and ordered to leave the Olympic Village by the United States Olympic Committee. The international response to the demonstration by Smith and Carlos was generally sympathetic, but back in the United States they were not so well received. They both found it difficult to make a living, and both their marriages broke up. Thirty-two years after the Mexico City protest, John Carlos reflected on Peter Norman's role, "To wear the badge as a white individual, it made the statement even more powerful. During a crucial time in our lives he was compassionate, understanding, and he showed his manhood. I'll always respect and love him for that. Pete became my brother at that moment." On October 3, 2006, Norman died of a heart attack while mowing his front lawn. Smith and Carlos both served as pallbearers at his funeral.

## 2 Jewish Athlete Gives Nazi Salute

German fencer Helene Mayer had competed at the 1928 and 1932 Olympics and planned to represent Germany at the 1936 Olympics, but in 1933 something happened that would radically change Mayer's life: Adolf Hitler and the Nazis took control of the German government. Helene Mayer was blonde, blue-eyed and stood 1.78 meters (5 feet 10 inches) tall. She was the perfect embodiment of the Nazis' conception of Aryan womanhood, except for one detail—her father, a doctor who had died before the Los Angeles Olympics, was Jewish. Mayer did not think of herself as Jewish, particularly after her father's death. But in April 1933, while she was working in California as a teacher, she learned that her membership in the Offenbach Fencing Club, her home club back in Germany, had been withdrawn for racial reasons. Under pressure from the international community, the Germans decided to allow one Jewish athlete to represent Germany at the Berlin Games. They chose Helene Mayer.

On the victory platform after winning the gold medal in the individual foil event, Helene Mayer hesitated momentarily and then raised her right arm high in the "Heil Hitler" salute. Mayer had hoped that her participation in the Olympics would allow her to regain the German citizenship that had been taken from her because of her father, but it was not to be. In 1940 Mayer took out American citizenship, and in 1943 she helped teach the German language to US soldiers on their way to World War II. She returned to Germany in 1952 and died there of cancer the following year at the age of 42.

## 3 Wrong National Gesture

Peripatetic Xeno Müller grew up in Switzerland, Germany, Spain and France (where he first took up rowing at the age of 13), before attending Brown University in the United States. By 1996 Müller had become so Americanized that after winning the gold medal in double sculls rowing, he automatically placed his hand over his heart in the American fashion during the playing of the national anthem—the Swiss national anthem.

## 4 Upside-Down Flag

As a member of the Soviet team, Erika Salumäe won the inaugural women's cycling match sprint event in Seoul in 1988. When she returned to the Estonian capital of Tallinn, where she had been raised in an orphanage, she was welcomed as a hero. At the victory parade in her honor one sign read OUR OWN TEAM IN BARCELONA IN 1992. Four years later Salumäe won the gold medal again, but this time for her newly-independent homeland. It was an emotional moment at the award ceremony when the Estonian flag was raised at the Olympics for the first time in 56 years. Unfortunately, it was raised upside down. This blunder on the part of the Spanish officials failed to dampen Salumäe's enthusiasm. "The next time," she noted with a smile, "they will get it right."

## 5 Unexpected Medal

International weightlifting competitions are separated into two sessions. In the afternoon the less-distinguished lifters take part in the "B" session and in the evening the leading contenders lift in the "A" session. The top lifter in the 100-kilogram division "B" session in 1984 was 31-year-old Pekka Niemi of Finland. Since no "B" lifter had ever won a medal in an international meet, Niemi skipped the evening session and went instead to the Los Angeles Coliseum to watch the track and field events. Niemi was playing with an Electronic Messaging System computer terminal in the press section when a German TV reporter said, "Let's see what you did." Niemi pushed some buttons and on the screen appeared the news that he had finished third. Meanwhile, back at the weightlifting venue at Loyola Marymount University, the medal ceremony was being delayed while officials unsuccessfully searched for Niemi or anyone else from the Finnish delegation. Finally they went ahead with the presentation with the bronze medal platform empty. When Niemi called home to share the good news, he found his family had learned of his good fortune on Finnish television before he himself had found out in Los Angeles. The next day he received his medal at a special ceremony, after which he patiently signed 200 autographs.

## 6 Winner Not Present

The US winner of women's flyweight weightlifting in 2000, Tara Nott, was an unlikely Olympic champion, in that she did not become interested in competitive weightlifting until she was 23 years old, and she had only placed ninth at the preceding world championships. Nott finished second in the event but was informed by cellphone that she had been elevated to Olympic champion after initial gold medalist Izabeta Dragneva tested positive for furosemide. Nott was told that a makeshift medal presentation ceremony would be held at the Olympic Village 90 minutes later. Such ceremonies were considered an embarrassment to both the IOC and the International Weightlifting Federation, so this one was scheduled to take place at the same time as the women's super-heavyweight final. Nott's friend, Cheryl Haworth, was competing in that event, and Nott chose to cheer her on rather than attend the ceremony, which thus took place without her.

## 7 Upside-Down Winner

Canadian George Lyon was an eccentric athlete who didn't pick up a golf club until he was 38 years old. Before that he had competed successfully in baseball, tennis and cricket. He caused quite a stir when he played in the 1904 St Louis Olympic golf tournament, because of his unorthodox swing. He wielded the club more like a cricket bat, provoking some newspapers to criticize his "coal-heaver's swing." His final match was a surprise victory over the 23-year-old US champion Chandler Egan which earned him the gold medal and a $1,500 sterling silver trophy—which he accepted after walking down the path to the ceremony on his hands.

## 8 Rude Hosts

Almost 40,000 French spectators watched in horror as their team was thrashed 17–3 in the 1924 rugby final by a bunch of upstart Americans. After two French players were injured the US team was booed and hissed for the remainder of the game. Fighting broke out in the stands, and Gideon Nelson, an art student from De Kalb, Illinois, was knocked unconscious after being hit in the face with a walking stick. At the awards ceremony "The Star-Spangled Banner" was drowned out by the booing of the crowd, and the US team had to be escorted from the field under police protection.

## 9 Talking and Fidgeting

After taking first and second place in the 1972 400 meters, Americans Vince Matthews and Wayne Collett showed little respect for the proceedings during the medal ceremony, talking and fidgeting during the playing of "The Star-Spangled Banner" rather than standing quietly at attention. The West German crowd booed them, and the International Olympic Committee, ignoring the US Olympic Committee, banned the two runners from further competition. Matthews and Collett denied that their actions had constituted an organized protest. "If we did have any ideas about a demonstration," Matthews said, "we could have done a better job than that." Collett added, "I couldn't stand there and sing the words [to the national anthem] because I don't believe they're true.

I wish they were. I think we have the potential to have a beautiful country, but I don't think we do."

## 10 Unintended Protest

Dave Wottle of Canton, Ohio, earned a surprise gold medal by catching favorite Yevhen Arzhanvov in the final two meters of the 1972 800 meters final. Wottle was so shocked by his victory that he forgot to take off his cap during the playing of "The Star-Spangled Banner" at the medal ceremony. He didn't realize what he had done until a reporter asked him if he had been staging a protest. Although nobody back in the United States actually held it against him, Wottle, a member of the Air Force ROTC at Bowling Green University, Ohio, was embarrassed to the point of tears and felt obliged to make a formal apology to the American people.

## 11 No National Flags

When US president Jimmy Carter called for a boycott of the 1980 Moscow Games, some nations chose a middle ground of protest: competing but refusing to display their flags. The medal-winners of individual pursuit cycling were Robert Dill-Bundi of Switzerland, Alain Bondue of France and Hans-Henrik Örsted of Denmark. The medal ceremony for the event was the first at which all three national flags were replaced by the Olympic flag.

## 12 Clowning During National Anthem

In the 4 × 100-meter relay in 2000 the US team of Jon Drummond, Bernard Williams, Brian Lewis and Maurice Greene won a clear victory. However, the four Americans offended many people with their celebrations, which included posing and clowning not only on their victory lap, but during the medal ceremony and during the playing of the "Star-Spangled Banner."

## 13 Paying the Price for Disappointment

After finishing in a three-way tie for first place in light-heavyweight weightlifting in 1992, Russian Ibragim Samadov was dropped to third place due to his higher bodyweight. Frustrated with himself and emotionally distraught, Samadov refused to lean forward during the award ceremony to allow the bronze medal to be put around his neck. When he finally took it in his hand, he dropped it onto the platform and walked away. IOC officials were outraged at this breach of protocol. They disqualified Samadov, announced that he would not be listed as the bronze-medal winner in the official results and ordered him to leave the Olympic Village. Samadov came to his senses the next day and apologized, but the IOC refused to reverse its ruling, and the International Weightlifting Federation banned him for life.

## 14 Inconsolable Runner-Up

Forty-six seconds into sudden-death overtime in the final of the 1992 middleweight freestyle wrestling tournament, Russia's Elmadi Jabrailov secured a deep leg attack on Kevin Jackson of the United States. As Jackson scrambled to counterattack, the wrestlers moved out of bounds. The referee, Todor Grudev of Bulgaria, signaled for the action to continue. Jabrailov's team coach, two-time gold-medal-winner Ivan Yarygin, immediately protested that his man had controlled Jackson and deserved a point, and with it the match and the gold medal. The match was resumed after several minutes and after another minute of fighting, Jackson won with a one-point double-leg takedown. To say that Jabrailov was disheartened would be an understatement. He cried and screamed and was inconsolable. When it came time for the medal ceremony, Jabrailov had to be pushed onto the podium. He accepted his silver medal, but refused to put it around his neck. Although Jabrailov held nothing against Jackson personally and did not hesitate to congratulate him, the Russian's supporters whipped the crowd into a frenzy and the "Star-Spangled Banner" was drowned out by whistling and booing.

## 15 Protest Denied

Defending Olympic silver medalist Ara Abrahamian of Sweden was beaten in the semi-finals of the 2008 middleweight Greco-Roman wrestling tournament by eventual gold medalist Andrea Minguzzi of Italy after having a point deducted for allegedly placing his hand on the out-of-bounds line. The Swedish team protested the result and asked that a video replay be viewed, but their request to even consider the evidence was denied. The medal ceremony was disrupted when Abrahamian dropped his bronze medal to the mat and stormed off stage to protest what he thought was biased judging. He was stripped of his medal and disqualified, but no other athletes were moved up in the rankings. The Court of Arbitration for Sport (CAS) later ruled that FILA, the international wrestling federation, had acted improperly in not allowing Abrahamian to appeal.

# 11 Notable Venues

### 1/2/3 Rome 1960, Wrestling, Gymnastics and Marathon

Fifty-four years after Italy had had to forgo hosting the Olympics following an eruption of Mt. Vesuvius, Rome finally got its chance. It made the most of its dramatic history, holding the wrestling competition in the Basilica of Maxentius, site of wrestling contests 2,000 years earlier. Among the other antique sites used were the Baths of Caracalla (gymnastics) and the Arch of Constantine (finish of the marathon).

### 4/5/6 Los Angeles 1984, Cycling Team Trial and Marathon

The site of the cycling team trial event was one of the dullest venues in Olympic history—a 15½-mile concrete stretch of the Artesia Freeway between the Harbor Freeway and the Santa Ana Freeway. During the medal ceremony, the winning teams enjoyed the rare privilege of seeing their national flags raised in front of the Regal Plastic Company and a freeway exit sign for Avalon Blvd. A three-mile stretch of the marathon event was also held on the Marina Freeway, where no spectators were allowed. Female gold medalist Joan Benoit later mused, "The one thing I'll tell my grandchildren is that one time I ran alone on an LA freeway."

### 7 Barcelona 1992, Sailing and Windsurfing

Before the Olympics there had been numerous complaints from board-sailers and other members of the yachting community that the Parc de Mar venue, which was in the harbor of Barcelona, was polluted with garbage and waste that included everything from dead rats to floating refrigerators. Under pressure from the International Yacht Racing Union, Barcelona authorities assigned four garbage vessels to collect the waste daily. Unfortunately for windsurfing silver medalist Michael Gebhardt, they didn't get it all. During the last lap of the seventh race, a plastic garbage bag got caught on his board and he was passed by six board-sailers before he could dislodge it. Had Gebhardt been able to stave off even one of those six, he would have won the gold medal.

## 8 Atlanta 1996, Whitewater Canoeing

The 1996 slalom events were staged in the Ocoee River in the state of Tennessee. The site of the 415-meter course had been dry since 1950. Water was redirected into the dry riverbed in 1994, but usually it was diverted through a tunnel to a power plant. In 1996 water was released into the course for 77 days to allow for training, a pre-Olympic event and the Olympics.

## 9/10/11 Athens 2004, Marathon, Archery and Shot Put

In 2004 the Olympic Games returned to Greece, the home of both the ancient Olympics and the first modern Olympics. The men's and women's shot put events were held in the ancient stadium in Olympia. The marathon races followed the same route as the 1896 race, beginning in Marathon and ending in Athens's Panathenaic Stadium. The archery events were also held in the Panathenaic Stadium.

# Olympians
at War

# 7 Olympic Spies

### 1 Alastair Denniston, Scotland, Field Hockey, 1908

Alastair Denniston was a member of the third-placed Scottish team. In 1914 Denniston was recruited into the British secret intelligence service because he was an expert in the German language. Over the next thirty years, he was one of the most important players in the closed world of cryptoanalysis. He was instrumental in continuing the work of code-cracking after World War I and leading operations during World War II. Despite Denniston's obsession with secrecy and security he successfully promoted the complete sharing of information with the United States.

### 2 Linn Farish, USA, Rugby, 1924

After winning the gold medal with the 1924 US rugby team, Linn Farish became a geologist and petroleum consultant. During World War II he worked for the Office of Strategic Services (OSS), the precursor to the CIA. He flew in and out of Yugoslavia, mapping potential landing strips and rescuing grounded pilots, and he died in an air crash in the Balkans in 1944. He was awarded the Distinguished Service Cross and the government's code of secrecy about secret agents was broken so that Farish's name could be released as a military hero.

### 3 Jim Thompson, USA, 6-meter Sailing, 1928

Thompson joined the Office of Strategic Services (OSS). He worked with the French resistance movement in North Africa before being sent to Bangkok. After the war he remained in Thailand, founding a textile company and hiring local weavers to revitalize the dying Thai silk industry. On Easter Sunday 1967, the 61-year-old Thompson was holidaying with friends at a Malaysian resort. At about 3:30 pm, his friends heard the sound of someone—they assumed Thompson—leaving the bungalow. He was never seen again.

### 4 Sam Hall, USA, Springboard Diving, 1960

Silver medalist Sam Hall gained dubious international fame in December 1986, when he was arrested as a freelance spy in Nicaragua. Hall, who once served in the Ohio House of Representatives, described himself as a "self-employed military advisor and counterterrorist." He was subsequently released by the Nicaraguan government, who declared him a victim of mental illness.

## 5 Jerzy Pawłowski, Poland, Sabre Fencing, 1968

Pawłowski won the gold medal in individual sabre. Considered a protégé of General Wojciech Jaruzelski, who later became premier of Poland, Pawłowski was also working as a spy for the CIA, although it is unclear whether he was motivated by ideology or money. Arrested in 1975, he was sentenced to twenty-five years in prison. Ten years later, he was exchanged for three Communist spies, but he chose to remain in Poland.

## 6 Boyan Radev, Bulgaria, Light Heavyweight Greco-Roman Wrestling, 1968

In 2010 Communist-era secret service files revealed that gold-medal-winner Boyan Radev was working as an intelligence officer for the Bulgarian State Security at the same time that he was competing at the Olympics. After the fall of communism he became a noted art collector.

## 7 Lutz Dombrowski, East Germany, Long Jump, 1980

Something of a rebel, Lutz Dombrowski kept running away from the schools to which he had been assigned by the East German government in order to return home to his family, his girlfriend and his football team. Dombrowski dominated the 1980 long jump competition, putting together a tremendous series that averaged 27 feet 3 ¼ inches. In 1991 he admitted that between 1979 and 1987 he had delivered secret reports on his teammates to the Stasi security police.

# 8 Olympians Who Fought in World War I...and one who served but didn't fight

*World War I broke out in July 1914 and lasted until November 1918. The 1916 Olympics were scheduled to be held in Berlin, but were canceled. Hundreds of athletes who took part in the Olympics between 1900 and 1912 fought in the war, as did hundreds more who competed after the Olympics resumed in 1920. Here is a sampling of noteworthy Olympic athletes who fought in "The War to End All Wars."*

## 1 Willy Dod, Great Britain, Archery, 1908

A descendant of Sir Anthony Dod of Edge, who commanded the victorious English archers at the Battle of Agincourt against the French in 1415, Willy Dod won the gold medal in York Round archery at the first London Olympics. He was born into a family so wealthy that during his 87-year life span he never attended school and never worked. In fact he never attempted anything difficult until, in a burst of patriotic enthusiasm four weeks after the outbreak of World War I, he enlisted—at the age of 47—in the Sportsman's Battalion of the Royal Fusiliers and found himself serving as a private in the trenches in France. His zeal cooled rapidly, and he managed a transfer to the navy as an administrative officer.

## 2 Wyndham Halswelle, Great Britain, Track, 1906–1908

Halswelle won three Olympic medals in the 400- and 800-meter events: one gold, one silver and one bronze. Serving as a captain during World War I, Halswelle was killed by a sniper's bullet in France on March 31, 1915.

## 3 Hanns Braun, Germany, Track, 1908–1912

A sculptor, Hanns Braun earned a bronze medal in the 800 meters in 1908 and added a silver in the 400 meters in 1912. He was also a member of the silver-medal-winning team in the 1908 relay. He served as a pilot in World War I and died in a mid-air collision a month before the war ended.

## 4 Octave Lapize, France, 100-Kilometer Cycling Track Race, 1908

Octave Lapize won the Tour de France in 1910. A fighter pilot during World War I, he was shot down over Vouziers in July 1917 and died at the age of 29.

## 5 Arnold Jackson, Great Britain, 1,500 Meters, 1912

The gold-medal-winner in the 1,500 meters event, Jackson later gained greater fame as Arnold Nugent Strode-Jackson after World War I, during which he was wounded three times. In 1918, at the age of 27, he became the youngest acting Brigadier-General in the British army. He was also a member of the British delegation to the post-war Paris Peace Conference in 1919.

## 6 Jimmy Duffy, Canada, Marathon, 1912

Jimmy Duffy, who placed fifth, went on to win the 1914 Boston Marathon, but when World War I broke out, he volunteered and was subsequently killed during a suicidal charge against the Germans on April 23, 1915.

## 7 Tony Wilding, Australia/New Zealand, Tennis, 1912

Bronze medalist Tony Wilding joined the British Army during World War I and was leading an armored car unit when he was killed during the Battle of Neuve-Chapelle on May 9, 1915.

## 8 Tommy Green, Great Britain, 50,000-meter Walk, 1932

Green had to overcome considerable adversity to make it to the Olympics. Because he had rickets as a child, he was unable to walk until he was five years old. At 12 he lied about his age and joined the army. A couple of years later he was invalided out when a horse fell on him. Recalled to service in 1914, he was wounded three times in World War I and finally sent home again in 1917, having been badly gassed while fighting in France. He did not enter his first walking contest until 1926, when he was 32 years old.

## 9 Philip Baker, Great Britain, Track and Field, 1912-1920

The 1,500 meters silver medalist in 1920, Philip Baker later changed his name to Philip Noel-Baker, adding his wife's maiden name. A Quaker pacifist, he served in the Ambulance Corps during World War I. After the war, he worked on the drafting of the Covenant of the League of Nations and after World War II he served on the sub-committee that created the preliminary agenda for the United Nations General Assembly. In 1959 Noel-Baker was awarded the Nobel Peace Prize in honor of his work in the pursuit of peace and disarmament and for his work on behalf of war refugees.

# 7 Olympians Killed During World War II

*Dozens, if not hundreds, of Olympic competitors were killed during World War II. Here are some notable examples.*

## 1 Silvano Abbà, Italy, Modern Pentathlon, 1936

Silvano Abbà, who earned the bronze medal at the Berlin Olympics, was killed at the Battle of Izbushensky near Volgograd as one of the 700 riders of the Italian Savoy Cavalry, the last recorded cavalry charge in military history.

## 2 Charley Paddock, USA, Sprints, 1920–1928

Four-time medal-winner Charley Paddock enlisted in the US Marine Corps and died in a plane crash in Alaska on July 21, 1943.

## 3 Endre Kabos, Hungary, Sabre Fencing, 1932–1936

As a student, Kabos received a fencing outfit as a birthday gift from his godfather. He hid it in his wardrobe, but his friends came across it and teased him. The next day he enrolled in a fencing club to spite them. Kabos won a total of four medals, including three golds and one bronze, at the 1932 and 1936 Olympics. He was killed during World War II when the Budapest Margaret Bridge was blown up, the day before his 38th birthday.

## 4 Takeichi Nishi, Japan, Equestrian, 1932–1936

An extremely wealthy man, Baron Takeichi Nishi was a lieutenant in the Japanese army when he won his gold medal in individual jumping at the 1932 Olympics. In Los Angeles he became friends with many celebrities, including Will Rogers, Mary Pickford, and Douglas Fairbanks. Promoted to Colonel toward the end of World War II, he was given command of a tank regiment on Iwo Jima. During the fierce fighting on that island some of the US officers learned that he was on the island and hoped to meet him. They never got a chance. Nishi refused to surrender and instead joined a mass Japanese suicide.

### 5 Luz Long, Germany, Long Jump, 1936

After defying Nazi ideology by striking up a public friendship with rival Jesse Owens at the 1936 Olympics, Luz Long served in the German Army during World War II. On July 10, 1943, Long was severely wounded during the Allied invasion of Sicily and died three days later in a British-controlled field hospital.

### 6 Farid Simaika, Egypt, Diving, 1928

Representing Egypt at the Amsterdam Olympics, Simaika earned medals in both platform and springboard diving. He became a US citizen in March 1942 and joined the United States Army Air Corps. He was shot down over New Guinea in 1944, but his body was never found.

### 7 Linn Farish, USA, Rugby, 1924

An engineer and pilot who served with the Office of Strategic Services (OSS), the predecessor of the CIA, Farish parachuted into Yugoslavia to locate and map potential landing strips to be used to rescue downed Allied airmen. On the third such trip, in September 1944, his plane crashed in the Balkan Mountains.

# 5 Olympians Held as Prisoners of War

## 1 Géo André, France, High Jump, 1908-1924

Competing in four Olympics, Géo André won two medals, a silver in the 1908 high jump and a bronze in the 1920 4 × 400-meter relay. During World War I he was badly injured and taken prisoner. After escaping at his sixth try, he rejoined the fight as an aviator. Anxious to do his part again in World War II, but too old to be a fighter pilot, André joined the infantry and was killed by the Germans near Tunis on May 4, 1943. He was 53.

## 2 Eric Liddell, Great Britain, 400 Meters, 1924

Eric Liddell was born on January 16, 1902, in Tientsin, China, where his father was a missionary. He grew up in Scotland from the age of five. His favorite sport was rugby, but he gave up a promising career in it in order to concentrate on running. After winning his 400-meters gold medal Eric Liddell returned to Scotland a hero of heroes and was paraded through the streets of Edinburgh. A year after his Olympic triumph he returned to China to join his father in missionary work. Liddell made two more trips to Scotland, but he was back in China during World War II. He died of a brain tumor in a Japanese internment camp in Weifang on February 21, 1945. Forty-five years later, his unmarked grave was located by Charles Walker, a civil engineer based in Hong Kong. On June 9, 1991, a monument of Scottish granite was erected in Liddell's honor in Weifang. On it is a quotation from the book of Isaiah: "They shall mount up with wings as eagles; they shall run and not be weary."

## 3 Louis Zamperini, USA, 5,000 Meters, 1936

Louis Zamperini, eighth in the 1936 5,000 meters, also served in World War II and was declared dead in 1944. However, he was actually still alive. A bombardier, he was flying a rescue mission when he crashed in the Pacific Ocean. He and his co-pilot spent 47 days adrift in a life raft (their tail gunner died after 33 days). Picked up by a Japanese patrol boat, Zamperini spent two years in brutal prison camps until the war ended.

## 4 Fritz Thiedemann, Germany, Equestrian, 1952

Fritz Thiedemann commanded a German cavalry unit during World War II. He was captured, and the end of the war found him in a Russian prison camp. At the Helsinki Olympics he earned bronze medals in both individual show jumping and team dressage to become the only rider in Olympic history to win medals in two equestrian disciplines at the same Games.

## 5 Helmut Bantz, Germany, Gymnastics Vault, 1956

A prisoner during World War II, Helmut Bantz helped train British gymnasts before the 1948 Olympics. He led the German team at the 1952 and 1956 Olympics and was 35 years old when he won his gold medal in the vault.

# 6 Pro-Nazi Olympians

**1 Charles Hoff, Norway, 800 Meters, 1924**
Ultimately, Hoff would become better known in Norway for his political actions than for his athletic feats. During the 1940–1945 occupation of Norway by Germany, Hoff collaborated with the Nazis. After World War II, he was convicted of treason and spent five years in prison.

**2 Sidney Leibbrandt, South Africa, Light Heavyweight Boxing, 1936**
Sidney Leibbrandt, who placed fourth, became enamored of the Nazis during his stay in Berlin. He later agreed to work as a pro-Nazi agent in South Africa. However he was arrested, convicted of treason and spent seven years in prison.

**3 Gisela Mauermayer, Germany, Women's Discus throw, 1936**
The winner of the 1936 discus throw, Gisela Mauermayer was a modest 22-year-old, a 6-foot blonde, hailed in Germany as the perfect example of Aryan womanhood. She gave the Nazi salute on the victory stand and became a top-ranking member of the Nazi women's organization. During World War II she was a teacher in Munich. After the war she lost her job because of her high-profile Nazi involvement. Starting over at the Zoological Institute of Munich University, she gained a doctor's degree by studying the social behavior of ants.

**4 Krisztián Tölgyesi, Hungary, Heavyweight Judo, 2000**
Krisztián Tölgyesi, who failed to advance out of his preliminary pool, went on to work as a car mechanic after his athletic career ended. In 2008 he was arrested in Budapest after police found several home-made bombs and detonators in his car. Tölgyesi, whose parents were members of a neo-Nazi white supremacist group, confessed to having made the bombs from instructions obtained on the Internet, intending to detonate them during Hungary's Independence Day celebrations.

## 5 Martinus Osendarp, Netherlands, 100 Meters, 1936

Bronze medalist Martinus Osendarp became the first Dutchman to win an individual track and field medal. He later joined the German SS and was imprisoned for seven years after the Nazis' defeat.

## 6 Heinz Brandt, Germany, Equestrian Team Show Jumping, 1936

After the outbreak of World War II, gold medalist Heinz Brandt served as a German staff officer and may have inadvertently saved Hitler's life during an assassination attempt. On July 20, 1944, Brandt arrived at Hitler's Prussian headquarters for a situation conference, the same meeting at which Oberst Claus von Stauffenberg attempted to assassinate Hitler with a briefcase containing a bomb. After von Stauffenberg placed the bomb next to Hitler and excused himself from the room, Brandt wanted to get a better look at a map on the table and moved the briefcase to the other side of the table. Seven minutes later the bomb exploded, killing four people, including Brandt, who died the next day. Hitler himself survived the blast after being shielded by the heavy oak conference table. The assassination attempt was later made into a movie, *Valkyrie*, starring Tom Cruise.

# 6 Anti-Nazi Heroes

### 1 Janusz Kusocinski, Poland, 10,000 meters, 1932

At the time of his Olympic triumph in the 1932 10,000 meters, Janusz Kusocinski was a gardener in a Warsaw park. After the German occupation of Poland in 1939 Kusocinski, while employed as a waiter, worked secretly for the anti-Nazi resistance. Arrested by the Gestapo on March 26, 1940, he was imprisoned, beaten and tortured. When it became clear he would not reveal the names of his colleagues, he was executed on June 21, 1940.

### 2 Werner Seelenbinder, Germany, Light Heavyweight Greco-Roman Wrestling, 1936

A member of the German Communist Party, wrestler Werner Seelenbinder was an anti-Nazi hero who was executed in 1944 because of his opposition to Adolf Hitler.

### 3 Anthonie Beijnen, Netherlands, Coxless Pairs Rowing, 1924

Twenty years after his Olympic triumph in the 1924 coxless pairs rowing event, Anthonie Beijnen played an unusual role in the Dutch resistance to the Nazis. A wealthy man, he allowed his home in Beusichem to be used by the German Wehrmacht, while secretly hiding British soldiers in his attic and helping them escape. Beijnen also listened in on the conversations of the German officers and passed on the information to the Allies.

### 4 King Olav V of Norway, Norway, 6-meter Sailing, 1928

During World War II, Crown Prince Olav became a symbol of Norwegian resistance to the Nazis. His reign as King Olav V was a popular one and lasted from 1957 until his death in 1991. As Crown Prince Olav, he had earned a gold medal in 6-meter sailing at the 1928 Olympics.

### 5 José Beyaert, France, Individual and Team Cycling Road Races, 1948

During World War II, José Beyaert, winner of the 1948 individual cycling road race, had worked with the French resistance, moving weapons on his bike. With a reputation as a street thug in his hometown of Pantin, Beyaert's arrival at the 1948 Olympics was delayed when the mayor of Pantin refused to sign his good-conduct certificate. At the London Games, Beyaert sprinted ahead with half a mile to go and won by eight lengths.

## 6 Helge Løvland, Norway, Decathlon, 1920

Norway's Helge Løvland won the decathlon in 1920. Following the Nazi occupation of Norway in 1940, Helge Løvland organized a "Sports Strike" in which Norwegian athletes refused to take part in official competitions. His letter to the various sports federations calling for the strike was intercepted by his pro-Nazi fellow Olympian Charles Hoff, and Løvland was forced to go underground.

# 12 Olympians Who Died in Nazi Concentration Camps

*Historians have identified 48 Olympic athletes who died in Nazi concentration camps, including 13 at Auschwitz, 10 at Sobibór and 8 at Mauthausen-Gusen.*

### 1/2 Alfred and Gustav Flatow, Germany, Gymnastics, 1896

When Alfred Flatow returned to Germany after winning three gymnastics events and placing second in another, he was banned from competition for two years because the Olympic Games was an unauthorized international event. In 1942 Flatow was deported by the Nazis to the concentration camp in Theresienstadt because he was Jewish; he died there on December 28. In 1987, after a 47-year battle with local residents, the Berlin street leading to the Olympic Stadium was renamed Alfred und Gustav Felix Flatow-Allee in honor of Flatow and his gymnast cousin, who also died in Theresienstadt, starving to death on January 29, 1945.

### 3 Richard Schoemaker, Netherlands, Sabre Fencing, 1908

Richard Schoemaker, who was eliminated in the second round at the first London Olympics, was an Underground commander during the German occupation of his country in World War II. Arrested by the Nazis, he was executed in the Sachenhausen concentration camp on May 3, 1942.

### 4 Julius Hirsch, Germany, Football, 1912

A noted winger, Julius Hirsch was the first Jewish athlete to play on a German national team. He was killed at Auschwitz, presumably shortly after his arrival in March 1943.

### 5 Otto Herschmann, Austria, Team Sabre Fencing, 1912

Otto Herschmann of the second-place Austrian sabre team had previously won a bronze medal in the 1896 100-meter freestyle swimming event. At the time of the 1912 Games, he was president of the Austrian Olympic Committee, making him the only sitting national Olympic committee president to win an Olympic medal. Herschmann died at the Nazi concentration camp of Izbica in Poland on June 14, 1942.

## 6 János Garay, Hungary, Sabre Fencing, 1928

Two members of the gold-medal-winning Hungarian sabre fencing team died during World War II. While fighting in Ukraine in 1943 Attila Petshauer was tortured to death by anti-Semitic Hungarian army officers. Another Jewish team member, János Garay, died at Mauthausen-Gusen in 1945.

## 7 Milutin Ivkovic, Yugoslavia, Football, 1928

The captain of the Yugoslav team at the inaugural World Cup in 1930, Ivkovic was a Communist and an active opponent of the Nazis, who arrested him and shot him to death on May 24, 1943, after taking him to the Banjica concentration camp in Serbia.

## 8 Oskar Hekš, Czechoslovakia, Marathon, 1932

Having placed eighth at the Los Angeles Olympics at the age of 24, Oskar Hekš could have been a contender in Berlin. However, he refused to take part and worked instead to help organize the alternative People's Olympics in Barcelona (cancelled at the last moment because of the outbreak of the Spanish Civil War). After the Germans occupied Czechoslovakia, Hekš was deported to the Terezín (Theresienstadt) concentration camp and killed in the gas chambers in 1944.

## 9/10/11/12 Helena Nordheim, Anna Polak, Estella Agsteribbe and Judikje Simons, Netherlands, Women's Gymnastics Team, 1928

Four of the ten members of the Dutch team were Jewish. Helena Nordheim died in a Nazi gas chamber at Sobibor on July 2, 1943, along with her husband and 10-year-old daughter; Anna Polak and her 6-year-old daughter died July 23, 1943, also at Sobibor; Estella Agsteribbe lost her life in a gas chamber at Auschwitz on September 17, 1943, along with her 6-year-old daughter and 2-year-old son. Alternate Judikje Simons also died with her son and daughter at Sobibor. The only Jewish member of the team to survive World War II was Elka de Levie.

# 3 Olympian Survivors of Nazi Concentration Camps and 1 Who Survived Japanese Internment

### 1 Otto Peltzer, Germany, 800 Meters, 1928

The 1928 800 meters was an anxiously awaited contest involving Germany's Dr. Otto Peltzer, who had broken American Ted Meredith's 14-year-old world record in a classic showdown with Douglas Lowe of Great Britain in 1926; Lloyd Hahn of the United States, who had broken Peltzer's record; and Séra Martin of France, who had broken Hahn's record. Unfortunately, Peltzer became ill and was eliminated in the semi-finals. Peltzer endured hard times during the reign of the Nazis. First he was imprisoned for homosexuality. He was out of Germany when World War II broke out but was extradited by the Swedish government. The Nazis put him in the Mauthausen concentration camp and kept him there for four years. After the war, Peltzer served as a popular coach in India.

### 2 Károly Kárpáti, Hungary, Lightweight Freestyle Wrestling, 1936

Kárpáti was born Károly Klein, but changed his name to Kárpáti to hide the fact that he was Jewish. Because he was an Olympic champion he was not sent to a Nazi concentration camp until 1943. At the camp in Nadvirna, Poland, he threw a German soldier off a bridge and into a stream. The commanding officer did not punish him on that occasion, however when he resisted again at a different camp, he was beaten badly. Kárpáti survived the war, changed his name back to Klein and became a successful coach in Hungary.

### 3 Viktor Chukarin, Ukraine, Gymnastics, 1952

Chukarin, a Ukrainian who had spent four years in a concentration camp during World War II, earned six medals at Helsinki—four gold and two silver. Of his years in the camp, Chukarin said, "I had gone through a most severe ordeal, but I emerged with an enlightened soul cleansed of pettiness, conceit and uncertainty."

### 4 Martin Gison, Philippines, Prone Small-bore Rifle Shooting, 1936

Fourth place finisher Gison was captured by the Japanese during World War II and forced to take part in the infamous Bataan death march. He survived and was able to compete in the 1948 Olympics in London.

# 4 North American Olympians Killed in Warfare Since World War II

### 1 Ron Zinn, USA, 20,000-meter Walk, 1964

Sixth-place finisher Ron Zinn was a graduate of the US Military Academy and was sent to fight in Vietnam in late 1964. On July 7, 1965, he was presumed killed in a firefight near Saigon, although he was listed as missing in action for many years.

### 2 Cliff Cushman, USA, 400-meter Hurdles, 1960

Silver medalist Cliff Cushman was a career soldier and a pilot. In 1966 his plane was shot down over Vietnam, and he was officially listed as missing in action. His body was never found, and he was declared dead on November 6, 1975.

### 3 Bob Carmody, USA, Flyweight Boxing, 1964

Bronze-medal-winner Bob Carmody joined the Army in 1957 and trained several military boxing teams. In June 1967 he was called to fight in Vietnam with the 17th Cavalry Regiment. Several weeks after arriving, while on a routine foot patrol north of Saigon, he and the rest of his six-man squad were ambushed. All but one were killed, including Carmody, who was posthumously awarded the Bronze Star.

### 4 Mark Graham, Canada, 4 x 400-meter Relay, 1992

After competing at the 1992 Olympics, Mark Graham joined the Canadian military. Serving in Afghanistan in 2006, he was killed in a friendly-fire incident when two US aircraft fired on his platoon, mistaking them for Taliban insurgents

# After the
# Olympics

# 4 Olympic Myths

## 1 Original Marathon Race

The idea for a marathon race was inspired by the legend of Pheidippides, a professional runner who allegedly carried the news of the Greek victory over the Persians at the Battle of Marathon in 490 BC. On his arrival in Athens he called out, "Be joyful, we win!" and then dropped dead of exhaustion. Actually there is no evidence that this dramatic incident ever took place. The fifth-century-BC historian Herodotus wrote about the Battle of Marathon, and made mention of a professional runner named Pheidippides. However, Herodotus, who thrived on such juicy titbits, said nothing about a run from Marathon to Athens. The story didn't appear in print until the second century AD—more than 600 years after it was alleged to have occurred. However, Herodotus did write about an earlier incident in which a runner was sent from Athens to Sparta—a distance of about 230 kilometers—to ask that soldiers from Sparta be sent to help in the battle of Marathon. The longest race to be included in the ancient Greek Olympics was only 4,614 meters.

## 2 1908 US Flag Dip

One of the most enduring Olympic myths is that the US flag-bearer at the 1908 Opening Ceremony infuriated the English spectators by refusing to dip the US flag to the King of England, stating that "this flag dips to no earthly king." This story became so embedded in American culture that in 1942 the US Congress actually passed a law stipulating that "the flag of the United States of America . . . should not be dipped to any person or thing." The quotation, "this flag dips to no earthly king," is usually attributed to the discus-thrower Martin Sheridan, and so it has been assumed that it was also Sheridan who carried—and refused to dip—the flag. In fact it was shot-putter Ralph Rose who carried the flag. Contemporaneous accounts make it clear that Rose did in fact refuse to dip the flag, although the English spectators appear not to have cared or even noticed. As for the famous "earthly king" quote, there is no evidence that Martin Sheridan or anyone else said this.

## 3 Running with a Bible

There is an enduring anecdote that Forrest Smithson, while winning the final of the 1908 110-meter hurdles, carried a Bible in one hand as a protest against Sunday competition. There is no evidence to support this otherwise admirable story. It is not mentioned in any contemporary newspaper accounts, and none of Smithson's races were held on a Sunday. A much-reprinted photograph of Smithson clearing a hurdle while holding a Bible is clearly a posed shot not taken during competition.

## 4 Jesse Owens Snubbed by Hitler

The most famous Olympic myth is that after African-American Jesse Owens won the 100 meters in Berlin he was snubbed by Adolf Hitler, who refused to meet Owens after he had personally congratulated three earlier gold-medal-winners. Actually, if such a snub did occur, the recipients were not Jesse Owens, but Cornelius Johnson and David Albritton, black Americans who had finished one-two in the high jump the previous day. At first, Owens tried to set the record straight and repeatedly denied that the incident had happened. But the persistence of the Hitler snub story was so great that Owens finally stopped denying it and actually incorporated it into his motivational speeches.

# 5 Olympians Who Used Their Sport Skills in Real Life

## 1 Sumner Paine, USA, Free Pistol Shooting, 1896

Two years after winning the gold medal in the free pistol event, Sumner Paine returned home early one day and discovered his wife with his daughter's music teacher, who was in "a state of partial undress." Paine chased the teacher out of the house and, using the .32 caliber pistol that he usually carried with him, fired four shots. He was jailed and charged with assault. However, he was released when it was determined that, as he was after all an expert marksman, he could easily have killed the music teacher if he had wanted to.

## 2 Duke Paoa Kahanamoku, USA, Swimming and Water Polo, 1912-1924

Duke Paoa Kahinu Mokoe Hulikohola Kahanamoku was born in Honolulu on August 24, 1890. He was named after his father, who in turn was named after the Duke of Edinburgh, who visited Hawaii in 1869. Kahanamoku eventually competed in three Olympics, winning three gold medals and two silvers. He later appeared in minor roles in 28 Hollywood films and also played a major role in introducing the sport of surfing around the world. On June 14, 1925, Kahanamoku was relaxing on the beach in Corona del Mar, California, when a luxury yacht capsized, killing 17 people. The death toll would have been higher, but Duke used his surfboard to save the lives of eight of the passengers.

## 3 Giorgio Santelli, Italy, Team Sabre Fencing, 1920

When the French and Italian foil teams met in the final pool, it was assumed that the winners would go on to take the gold medals. France took a 3–1 lead. In the fifth assault, Lucien Gaudin and Aldo Boni were tied at four touches each when the jury awarded a decisive, and questionable, fifth touch to Gaudin. Boni was incensed and launched a verbal attack against György Kovács, the Hungarian judge. Kovács approached the Jury of Appeal and demanded an apology, whereupon Boni denied everything. Kovács then produced a witness, the Italian-born Hungarian fencing master Italo Santelli, who reluctantly supported

Kovács' allegations of abusive language. The Italian team withdrew in protest, singing the Fascist hymn as they left, and their remaining matches were declared forfeited. Back in Italy, the Italian foil team issued a statement which accused Santelli of testifying against them because he feared the Italians would defeat the Hungarian team, which he had coached. When he heard about this insult, Santelli, who was 58 years old, challenged Adolfo Contronei, the Italian captain, to a real duel. Before the two men could meet, Santelli's 26-year-old son Giorgio invoked the code duello and demanded that he fight in his father's place. Giorgio had earned a gold medal at the 1920 Olympics. In the small town of Abazzia near the Hungarian border, Giorgio and Contronei met and fought with heavy sabres. After two minutes the younger Santelli slashed Contronei deeply on the side of the head, drawing blood. Doctors rushed in and halted the duel. Giorgio Santelli later moved to the United States, where he became the coach of the US team. He taught fencing to 8,000 people and spent more than 100,000 hours with a sword in his hand, but he never again engaged in a real duel.

## 4 Oreste Puliti, Italy, Men's Sabre Fencing, 1924

After leading Italy to the gold medal in the team sabre event, Oreste Puliti seemed certain to compete for the gold medal in the individual event, until the Italians were accused by Hungarian judge György Kovács of throwing their matches against Puliti to increase his chances of a gold medal. An outraged Puliti threatened to cane Kovács and was disqualified, and his teammates walked out in protest. Two days later Puliti and Kovács ran into each other at a music hall and renewed their argument. When Kovács haughtily told Puliti that he couldn't understand the furious fencer because he didn't speak Italian, Puliti hit the Hungarian in the face and said that Kovács surely couldn't fail to understand that. The two men were pulled apart, but further words were exchanged and a formal duel was proposed. Four months later Puliti and Kovács met again, at Nagykanizsa on the Yugoslav–Hungarian border. This time they were accompanied by seconds, swords and spectators. After slashing away at each other for an hour, the two were finally separated by spectators, who had become concerned about the wounds which both men had received. Their honor restored, Puliti and Kovács shook hands and made up.

## 5 Hugh Edwards, Great Britain, Rowing, 1932

Hugh "Jumbo" Edwards won two gold medals in one day, following up his victory in the coxless pairs with another in the coxless fours. During World War II Edwards used his rowing ability to save his life. While serving as a squadron leader with the Royal Air Force's Coastal Command in 1943, he was forced to ditch his plane in the Atlantic Ocean. He rowed a dinghy four miles through a minefield to safety. He was the only member of the plane's crew to survive.

# 18 Unusual Olympic Celebrations

### 1 Jamaican 4 x 400-meter Relay Team, 1952

The night of their victory, the Jamaican foursome of Arthur Wint, Leslie Laing, Herb McKenley and George Rhoden celebrated in their quarters by drinking whisky with the Duke of Edinburgh out of the only available vessel—a toothbrush tumbler.

### 2 Michelle Ostermeyer, France, Women's Shot Put, 1948

Three months before the Olympics, pianist Micheline Ostermeyer had graduated with high honors from the Paris Conservatory of Music. In London she used the hands that so delicately played the piano to win gold medals in both the shot put and discus. She also placed third in the high jump. She celebrated her shot-put victory by performing an impromptu Beethoven recital back at the French team headquarters.

### 3 Chris Brasher, Great Britain, 3,000-meter Steeplechase, 1956

Gold-medal-winner Chris Brasher (whose previous claim to fame had been pacing Roger Bannister when he broke the four-minute mile) spent the next 19 hours celebrating. This included sharing a "liquid lunch" with thirteen members of the British press. He arrived, in his own words, "blind drunk, totally blotto, on the Olympic podium. I have an asinine grin on my face and nearly fall flat on my face as I lean forward, breathing gin fumes all over an IOC Frenchman as he attempts to hang a medal around my neck."

### 4 Michael Carruth, Ireland, Welterweight Boxing, 1992

Michael Carruth was Ireland's first Olympic champion in any sport since Ron Delany won the 1,500 meters in 1956. When his victory was announced the arena reverberated with the cheers of the Irish supporters. But the celebration in Barcelona was nothing compared to what went on back in Dublin. Army helicopters flew over Carruth's house to salute his victory. And, most incredible of all, on the day of his return to Ireland, local pubs dropped the price of beer to that of 1956. For one day in 1992 a pint of Guinness could be bought for four pence.

### 5 Dick McTaggart, Great Britain, Lightweight Boxing, 1956

After earning the gold medal in Melbourne, McTaggart found his return to Dundee, Scotland, almost as dangerous as his Olympic bouts. He was met at the railway station by members of his boxing club, who lifted him onto their shoulders, carried him up the stairs . . . and banged his head on the ceiling.

### 6 Jefferson Pérez, Ecuador, 50,000-meter Walk, 1996

As Ecuador's first Olympic champion, Jefferson Pérez was instantly transformed into a national hero and was flooded with gifts, including cash, a car, free vacations and a lifetime supply of yogurt. To celebrate his victory, Pérez spent 17 days walking 460 kilometers (285 miles) from Quito to Cuenca as the public came out to applaud him and join him.

### 7 Khashaba Jadav, India, Bantamweight Freestyle Wrestling, 1952

Khashaba Jadav was India's first medal-winner in an individual event. In fact, until 1996 Jadav was the only individual medalist from the world's second most populous nation. When he returned to India Jadav was accompanied for the final 40 kilometers of his journey to his home village of Goleshwar by his fellow villagers and a procession of 151 bullock carts. However he was soon forgotten by his nation and died in humble obscurity.

### 8 Liu Xiang, China, 110-meter Hurdles, 2004

Liu was the first Chinese man ever to win an Olympic track gold medal. Asked how he planned to celebrate his victory, Liu responded, "Karaoke! I love karaoke. That is how I celebrate after all my medals at big championships."

### 9 Manus Boonjumnong, Thailand, Welterweight Boxing, 2004

After Boonjumnong's gold medal victory, he received a phone call from Thailand's King Bhumibol Adulyadej, and was rewarded with more than 20 million baht (US $480,000) in prizes, not to mention the chance to see, for the first time, his six-week-old son, named Athens. Within two years Boonjumnong had spent his prize money and earned a reputation as a big-spending playboy. In an attempt to straighten him out for the 2008 Olympics, the Thai amateur boxing association sent him to train in Cuba—without any money. The lesson appeared to have worked: when

Boonjumnong won a gold medal at the Asian Games in 2006, he celebrated by shaving his head and spending two weeks in a Buddhist monastery. He returned to the Olympics in 2008 and earned a silver medal.

## 10 Štepánka Hilgertová, Czech Republic, Women's Kayak Slalom Singles Canoeing, 2000

Defending champion Štepánka Hilgertová paddled two flawless runs in both the qualifying round and final. When asked if she had been motivated by the $24,000 bonus she earned for winning, she replied, "I would compete even if there were no bonus. First, I like winning, and second, like any woman, I am vain and I like to be the center of attention." Back in Prague she celebrated by taking a bath in a tub filled with 160 bottles of champagne.

## 11 George Hungerford and Roger Jackson, Canada, Coxless Pairs Rowing, 1964

Given only six weeks to get used to each other, George Hungerford and Roger Jackson had their first race together ever in the opening round of the Olympics. In the final they built a one-and-a-half-length lead at the 1,500-meter mark and then hung on desperately to win Canada's only victory of the 1964 Olympics. they were considered such long shots that no Canadian journalists were present for their race. The two young men celebrated their victory by drinking seven Cokes each.

## 12 Luciano Giovannetti, Italy, Trap Shooting, 1980

The 34-year-old Giovannetti celebrated his victory in the trap event by tossing his cap into the air and shooting a hole through it.

## 13 West German 4 x 100-Meter Swimming Relay Team, 1988

The West German team celebrated the end of the Olympic meet by walking to the blocks dressed in lederhosen. At the 1986 world championships they had appeared in togas made of bed sheets.

## 14 Susi Susanti and Allan Budi Kusuma, Indonesia, Badminton, 1992

Before the victories by Susanti and Kusuma in the women's and men's badminton singles events, Indonesia, the fourth most populous nation in the world, had never earned a gold medal, despite taking part in the

Olympics since 1952. Not surprisingly, the pair became national heroes, and their return to Jakarta was cause for an enormous celebration that included a two-hour parade led by a car carrying a gigantic shuttlecock.

## 15 Claudia Poll, Costa Rica, Women's 200-meter Freestyle, 1996

After winning the gold medal Poll was mobbed by the small but emotional Costa Rican contingent that included her sister, her mother and two aunts who had traveled from Germany to support their niece. But this was nothing compared to the celebration that took place when Costa Rica's first Olympic champion returned to San José. The entire nation shut down, and an estimated 1,500,000 people—almost half the population—thronged the streets to honor their heroine.

## 16 Rolf Sørensen, Denmark, Cycling Road Race, 1996

Sørensen was passed just before the finish line by Pascal Richard of Switzerland and lost by less than a wheel. Sørensen slammed his handlebars in frustration. By the early hours of the next morning, however, he had recovered his spirits sufficiently to be found in a local nightclub dancing on a table wearing his silver medal and little else.

## 17 Fernanda Ribeiro, Portugal, Women's 10,000 Meters, 1996

During a dark period when she was hobbled by injury Fernanda Ribeiro vowed that if she won the gold medal at the 1996 Olympics she would walk 175 kilometers (110 miles) from Oporto to the shrine of Fatima and give thanks to the Virgin Mary. She did win the gold medal. Back in Portugal, she completed the walk in two days.

## 18 Harald Abrahams, Great Britain and Arthur Porritt, New Zealand, 100 meters, 1924

Abrahams and Porritt won the gold and bronze medals at the Paris Olympics. Until Abrahams' death in 1978, he and Porritt and their wives had dinner every year at 7.00 pm on July 7—the day and the hour of the 1924 100-meter final.

# 9 Medals Lost and Then Recovered (and 1 stolen wallet)

**1/2 Otis Davis, USA, 400 Meters and 4 x 400-meter Relay, 1960**

In 1994 Otis Davis's two gold medals were stolen from his home. After an intensive "medal hunt" the Jersey City, New Jersey, police received an anonymous call and found Davis' prizes in a paper bag on the front steps of the police station.

**3/4 Jim Hines, USA, 100 Meters and 4 x 100-meter Relay, 1968**

One night after his return from Mexico City, Jim Hines came home to his Houston apartment to discover that burglars had stolen his television and stereo, his wife's jewelry and his two gold medals. Hines placed an ad in his local newspaper asking the thieves to return the gold medals. Eventually they arrived by mail in a plain brown envelope.

**5 Howard Davis, USA, Lightweight Boxing, 1976**

Howard Davis's gold medal took as strange a journey as any ever awarded. In 1981 it was stolen from Davis' home on Long Island, New York. Apparently the robber threw it out the window of his car while being chased by police. Ten years later, a landscaper named Jake Fiesel was trimming the long grass beside the Long Island Freeway when he came upon a heavy piece of round metal. Fiesel took it home, cleaned it up and, for the next four years, used it as a paperweight. In 1995 a visitor studying the paperweight realized that it was actually an Olympic gold medal, and Howard Davis's gold medal at that. Fourteen years after his Olympic medal was stolen Davis received a phone call from Jake Fiesel, who then presented him with the medal.

**6 Davide Tizzano, Italy, Quadruple Sculls Rowing, 1988**

During the Italian team's celebration, team member Davide Tizzano was thrown into the water and lost his gold medal on the muddy bottom of the Han River. A South Korean diver, working as a security guard at the regatta course, retrieved it after a 50-minute search.

## 7 Rachael Taylor, Australia, Women's Coxless Pairs, 2000

During a rowdy late-night celebration Rachael Taylor lost her silver medal in a taxi cab. Fortunately, when her plight was publicized a Sydney taxi driver found the medal underneath his back seat.

## 8/9 Nicolás Massú, Chile, Singles and Doubles Tennis, 2004

Massú accidentally left both his gold medals behind in his room at the Olympic Village when he left Athens. Luckily, they were found by Chile's swimming coach, Rodrigo Banados, who called Massú immediately.

## And... Oscar De La Hoya, USA, Lightweight Boxing, 1992

Boxing star and Olympic gold medalist Oscar De La Hoya was regarded as a hero in his native East Los Angeles. One night he was surrounded on the street by five hoodlums with guns who stole his wallet, which contained $150 in cash. Two hours later De La Hoya found the wallet on his front porch. When the thieves had opened it and discovered whom they had robbed, they returned it. The $150 was still inside.

# 8 Medal-winners Who Sold or Donated Their Medals

### 1 Lauri Lehtinen, Finland, 5,000 Meters, 1936

Gunnar Höckert, Finnish gold-medal-winner in the 1936 5,000 meters, died fighting on the Karelian Isthmus on February 11, 1940. In his honor Lauri Lehtinen donated his own gold medal, from the same event in 1932, to be awarded to a Finnish soldier who fought with distinction on the Isthmus.

### 2 Hendrika "Rie" Mastenbroek, Netherlands, Women's 400-meter Freestyle Swimming, 1936

Mastenbroek was the first woman to win four medals in one Olympics. She donated one of her gold medals to raise funds for the construction of a village for disabled people.

### 3 Shirley de la Hunty (Strickland), Australia, Women's 100-meter Hurdles, 1948-1956

By 1956 Shirley de la Hunty, competing in her third Olympics, had become a mother and was employed as an assistant lecturer in physics and mathematics at Perth Technical College. Her decisive two-yard victory in the 80-meter hurdles and her gold medal in the relay gave her a total of seven Olympic medals: three gold, one silver, three bronze. In 2001 she sold a huge collection of her sporting memorabilia, including her Olympic medals, in order to raise money for her grandchildren's education and to support environmental causes.

### 4 Raelene Boyle, Australia, Women's 100 Meters, 1968-1972

In 1997 Raelene Boyle auctioned one of her three silver medals to raise money to rebuild her life after surviving treatment for breast cancer.

### 5 Lukáš Pollert, Czech Republic, Canadian Slalom Singles Canoeing, 1992-1996

A gold-medal-winner in 1992, Lukáš Pollert earned a silver medal four years later at the Atlanta Games. He then sold his medals to a Czech brokerage firm. He told some journalists he did so to protest the commercialization and politicization of the Olympics, but to others he said he needed the money to buy an apartment. Pollert had taken part in the demonstrations that led to the overthrow of communism in Czechoslovakia in 1989. He later said that taking part in the "Velvet Revolution," as it came to be known, was more important to him than winning the Olympic gold medal.

## 6 Anthony Ervin (USA), 100-meter Freestyle Swimming, 2000

In May 2005 Ervin sold his gold medal on eBay for $17,100, which he donated to UNICEF to help the victims of the 2004 Asian tsunami.

## 7 Hadi Saei, Iran, Featherweight Taekwondo, 2000

Three years after finishing third at the Sydney Olympics, Saei donated his Olympic bronze, as well as other medals, to be auctioned in aid of the survivors of the earthquake of December 26, 2003, that devastated his hometown of Bam. Saei went on to win a gold medal in 2004.

## 8 Otylia Jedrzejczak, Poland, Women's 200-meter Butterfly, 2004

World-record-holder and reigning world champion Otylia Jedrzejczak was the favorite in the event, but needed to come from behind in the final lap to take the gold. After the race Jedrzejczak auctioned her gold medal on the Internet, donating the proceeds ($82,000) to a children's hospital in Warsaw.

# 11 Olympians Who Acted in Movies...and one near miss

*Olympic success has turned out to be a common springboard to acting in movies. Dozens of athletes from different sports and nations have attracted the attention of film producers. Here are some of the most famous or most unusual. In two of these cases, the athletes competed in the Olympics after they had performed in movies.*

## 1 Norman Pritchard, Great Britain/India, Sprint and Hurdles, 1900

Norman Pritchard's parents were English, but he was born in a suburb of Calcutta, India, on June 23, 1875. Pritchard visited England in 1900 and in competitions that he entered he was listed as representing both the Bengal Presidency Athletic Club of India and the London Athletic Club, which has led to disputes as to his true nationality when he took part in the 1900 Olympics. At the Paris Games, he took part in five events and finished second in two, the 200 meters and the 200-meter hurdles. Pritchard returned to India and served as secretary of the Indian Football Association. After being involved in the jute business, he turned to acting. He moved to the United States in 1913 and, as Norman Trevor, achieved success on the stage. He is known to have appeared in at least 28 plays on Broadway between 1914 and 1926. He also acted in 27 movies, most notably *Dancing Mothers* (1926) with Clara Bow, *Beau Geste* (1926) with Ronald Colman, and *The Love Trap* (1929), which was directed by William Wyler. He died penniless in California, after being in and out of mental asylums.

## 2 Nat Pendleton, USA, Super-heavyweight Freestyle Wrestling, 1920

Silver medalist Nat Pendleton became a well-known actor. Between 1924 and 1947 he appeared in 109 films including *Horse Feathers* (1932) and *The Thin Man* (1934). He also played the part of hospital attendant Joe Wayman nine times in the Dr Kildare and Dr Gillespie movie series.

## 3 Herman Brix, USA, Shot Put, 1928

Silver medalist Herman Brix later became a well-known movie actor, appearing in more than 100 films. Among his early roles was Tarzan in

*The New Adventures of Tarzan* (1935). Unfortunately, Brix became so associated with the role of Tarzan that in 1939 he had to change his name to Bruce Bennett in order to continue his career. Although he appeared in such critically acclaimed features as *Mildred Pierce* (1945) and *The Treasure of Sierra Madre* (1948), Bennett also acted in clunkers like The *Alligator People* (1959) and *The Fiend of Dope Island* (1961).

## 4 Johnny Weissmuller, USA, Freestyle Swimming and Water Polo, 1924-1928

On July 9, 1922, Johnny Weissmuller made swimming history by becoming the first person to swim 100 meters in less than one minute. On February 17, 1924, he lowered his time from 58.6 seconds to 57.4, establishing a world record that would last for ten years. At the 1924 Olympics in Paris he won three swimming gold medals plus a bronze in water polo. He added two more gold medals in 1928. Back in Hollywood he was noticed while swimming at a club on Sunset Boulevard and was invited to try out for the part of Tarzan. Needless to say, he got the part, and in 1932 Weissmuller made his film debut in *Tarzan, the Ape Man*. The first of four Olympic medalists to play the part of Tarzan in the movies (the others being Buster Crabbe, Herman Brix, and Glenn Morris), Weissmuller acted in 11 more Tarzan films in the next 16 years.

In 1958 he was taking part in a celebrity golf tournament in Havana at a time when Fidel Castro's guerrilla troops were fighting the soldiers of the Batista government. Weissmuller was on his way to the golf course with some friends and a couple of bodyguards when rebel soldiers suddenly appeared out of the bushes and surrounded their car. They disarmed the guards and pointed their rifles at the decadent Yankee imperialists. But Weissmuller had the solution to a difficult situation: slowly raising himself to his full height, he beat his chest with his fists and let out an enormous yell. After a moment of stunned silence, the revolutionaries broke into smiles of delight and began calling out, "Tarzan! Tarzan! *Bienvenido!* Welcome to Cuba!" Dropping their weapons, they crowded around Johnny, shaking his hand and asking for his autograph. After a few minutes Weissmuller and his party were not only not kidnapped, but they were actually given a rebel escort to the golf course.

## 5 Buster Crabbe, USA, 400- and 1,500-meter Freestyle, 1928-1932

Paramount Studios, jealous of MGM's success with Johnny Weissmuller, wanted an Olympic star of its own. So scouts visited the Olympic Village at the 1932 Los Angeles Games, rounded up twenty likely candidates, and brought them to the studio for a screen test. As Buster Crabbe described it later, "They take the twenty of us to wardrobe and issue each guy a G-string, and put us in front of a camera. Nobody knew what to do. The director said, 'Here, throw a spear.' So we each threw a spear. 'Here, throw this big rock.' So we each picked up this papier-mâché rock and tried to make our muscles bulge throwing it. Then we went back to the Olympic Village and forgot about it." Seven days later, Crabbe came from behind to win the gold medal in the 400-meter freestyle by one-tenth of a second. Three days after that the Paramount scouts reappeared and brought him back to the studio. "That one-tenth of a second changed my life," Crabbe later recalled. "It was then that [the Hollywood producers] discovered latent histrionic abilities in me." Crabbe went on to great fame as an actor; he was best known for his roles as Tarzan, Buck Rogers and Flash Gordon.

## 6 Eleanor Holm, USA, Women's 100-meter Backstroke, 1928-1932

Eleanor Holm competed in her first Olympics at the age of 14, placing fifth. Four years later she won a gold medal at the 1932 Los Angeles Olympics and soon thereafter married singer Art Jarrett. Scheduled to compete for a third time in 1936, Holm was overtaken by a scandal on the ship to Berlin and dropped from the team by the American Olympic Committee for drinking and partying. Despite the expulsion, Holm became more popular than ever. In 1938 she divorced Art Jarrett and also acted in her only film, co-starring as Jane in *Tarzan's Revenge* with 1936 decathlon champion Glenn Morris. The following year she married impresario Billy Rose. The pair divorced in 1954 following a spicy case which became known as "The War of the Roses" and which was filled with titillating accusations of sexual "misbehavior" on both sides. In 1999 Holm was invited to the White House for a reception in honor of Women in Sports. Standing beside President Bill Clinton, who had just survived a sex-related scandal of his own, the 85-year-old Holm looked up at him and said, "Mr. President, you're really a good-looking dude."

## 7 Harold Sakata, USA, Light Heavyweight Weightlifting, 1948

Gold-medal-winner Stanley Stanczyk of the United States was a well-known figure in weightlifting circles, but the man who really achieved fame was silver medalist Harold Sakata. After a successful career as a professional wrestler (using the name Tosh Togo), Sakata became an actor. He reached international stardom in the role of Oddjob in the James Bond film *Goldfinger*.

## 8 Ken Richmond, Great Britain, Super-heavyweight Freestyle Wrestling, 1948-1960

When Ken Richmond entered the ring, he was one of the most recognized men in the world, even though no one knew his name. Richmond's muscular body was famous because he was the one who struck the gong at the beginning of J. Arthur Rank films. Richmond earned a bronze medal in 1952.

## 9 Cornishman V, Great Britain, Equestrian Three-Day Eventing, 1968-1972

Many Olympic gold-medal-winners have exploited their success by pursuing movie careers. All but one have been humans. The exception was Cornishman V, the British horse who helped two different riders win gold medals in the three-day event: Richard Meade in 1968 and Mary Gordon-Watson in 1972. Cornishman V appeared in *Dead Cert* (1974) and *International Velvet* (1978).

## 10 Mark Breland, USA, Welterweight Boxing, 1984

At 6 feet 2 inches with a 78-inch reach, Brooklyn's Mark Breland towered over his fellow welterweights. Entering the tournament, Breland was the overwhelming favorite, having won the 1982 world amateur championship and having beaten everyone in his division including those from boycotting nations. His pre-Olympic record was 104 wins and 1 loss. A well-composed student of yoga, the 20-year-old Breland had also gained fame outside the world of boxing by appearing in the 1983 film *The Lords of Discipline*. He won the Olympic championship with ease.

## 11 Hillary Wolf, USA, Women's Extra Lightweight Judo, 1996-2000

Before she competed in the first of her two Olympics, Hillary Wolf had already gained a degree of fame for playing Macaulay Culkin's sister in *Home Alone*.

## 12 Donald Bragg, USA, Pole Vault, 1960

Don "Tarzan" Bragg won the pole vault competition at the Rome Olympics. Bragg, whose dream it was to play Tarzan in the movies, then delighted the crowd by celebrating with a Tarzan yell. He never did get to play Tarzan, although he did come close. Shooting had already begun for *Tarzan and the Jewels of Opar* in 1964, and Bragg was in front of the cameras, happily swinging from vines, when a court order halted the production because of copyright infringement. Forced to become a salesman of drug supplies, Bragg later opened a boys' camp in New Jersey.

# 6 Olympian Film Stunt Doubles

### 1 Robert Anderson, Great Britain, Sabre Fencing, 1952

Bob Anderson represented Great Britain in both the Team and Individual events at the 1952 Olympics. He went on to become the British national fencing coach and worked as a stunt performer and fight choreographer for a number of action films. His most famous role was playing Darth Vader in the light saber scenes in the Star Wars movies *The Empire Strikes Back* and *Return of the Jedi*. Anderson's participation was kept secret until 1983 when Mark Hamill, who played Luke Skywalker, revealed it during an interview.

### 2 Reginald "Snowy" Baker, Australia, Middleweight Boxing, 1908

Silver-medal-winning boxer Reginald "Snowy" Baker also took part in the springboard diving competition and the 4 × 200-meter freestyle swimming relay at the 1908 Olympics. In fact, Baker was probably the greatest all-round athlete ever produced by Australia. He competed in twenty-nine different sports and represented Australia in international competition in five of them. In later years Baker moved to Hollywood and starred in several silent films, most notably *The Fighting Breed* (1921), and performed stunts in *National Velvet* (1944). He also taught fencing, riding and swimming to stars such as Greta Garbo, Douglas Fairbanks, Shirley Temple, Rudolph Valentino and Elizabeth Taylor.

### 3 Steven Paul, Great Britain, Épée Fencing, 1980-1984, 1992

Ten years after competing in his third Olympics, Steven Paul trained Pierce Brosnan for his fencing scenes in the James Bond film *Die Another Day* and served as Brosnan's double for the more technical shots.

### 4 Dean Smith, USA, 100 Meters, 1952

Fourth place in the 1952 100 meters event went to Texan Dean Smith, who also competed in rodeos. Smith later became a stuntman in hundreds of television shows and films, including *Stagecoach* and *True Grit*, and doubled for Robert Redford three times in the early 1970s.

## 5 Pete Mehringer, USA, Light Heavyweight Freestyle Wrestling, 1932

Pete Mehringer of Kinsley, Kansas, first learned how to wrestle from a correspondence course: the Frank Gotch and Farmer Burns School of Wrestling and Physical Culture Course. After the Olympics he played professional football for eight years and then worked as a stuntman in Hollywood. His credits included *Knute Rockne, All-American* (1940) and *Road to Zanzibar* (1941).

## 6 Lee Barnes, USA, Pole Vault, 1924

Barnes was a 17-year-old student at Hollywood High School when he won the gold medal at the Paris Olympics. Three years later he appeared in the film *College*, as a stand-in for Buster Keaton in a scene that required him to pole vault into a second-story window.

# 17 Olympians Who Pursued Political Careers

*It is actually relatively easy for Olympic athletes to move on to politics, because they have gained high name recognition in a positive, non-controversial pursuit.*

### 1 Albert Hill, Great Britain, Middle-Distance Running, 1920

The winner of the 800 meters and the 1,500 meters at the Antwerp Olympics, Albert Hill served as a Member of Parliament for 36 years, but was considered so boring that he earned the nickname, "the chambermaid," because he always cleaned out the chamber whenever he spoke.

### 2 David Burghley, Great Britain, Hurdles, 1924-1932

David George Brownlow Cecil, Lord Burghley, was an extremely colorful character, who once set an unusual record by racing around the upper promenade deck of the ocean liner *Queen Mary* in 57 seconds, dressed in street clothes. Burghley was elected to Parliament in 1931, but was granted a leave of absence to compete in the 1932 Olympics in Los Angeles. He later served as governor of Bermuda for three years, as well as president of the British Amateur Athletic Association for 10 years, president of the International Amateur Athletic Federation for 30 years, and as a member of the International Olympic Committee for 48 years.

### 3 Grigorios Lambrakis, Greece, Track and Field, 1936

Although he failed to qualify for the Olympic final, Greek long jumper Grigorios Lambrakis went on to lead an unusually eventful life. He was an active member of the Greek resistance movement during the Axis occupation, then graduated from medical school after World War II and opened a gynecology clinic to treat indigent patients. An avowed pacifist, he later joined the United Democratic Left party and was elected to the Greek Parliament. On May 22, 1963, Lambrakis was attacked by two right-wing extremists while giving a speech at a pacifist rally. He sustained a serious brain injury and died five days later. His funeral sparked a demonstration of half a million people against the right-wing government. Lambrakis' life was the basis of the political novel Z, and in the later movie version Lambrakis was played by Yves Montand.

## 4 Bob Mathias, USA, Decathlon, 1948-1952

Robert Mathias was the first of only two men to win successive Olympic decathlon titles. Mathias also acted in four films (including The Bob Mathias Story) and was elected to the US House of Representatives in 1966, serving until 1975.

## 5 Yuri Vlasov, Soviet Union, Super-heavyweight Weightlifting, 1960-1964

Vlasov won a gold medal in 1960 and a silver medal in 1964. In 1989, by then an outspoken critic of the Soviet sports system, he was elected to the Council of People's Deputies. On May 30 of that year he stunned the Communist government when he attacked the KGB in a speech that was broadcast live throughout the nation. Vlasov was elected to the State Duma in 1993, but lost a bid for re-election two years later. In 1996 he ran for president of Russia on an anti-Semitic nationalist platform, but received only 220,000 votes.

## 6 Ben Nighthorse Campbell, USA, Open Class Judo, 1964

Ben Nighthorse Campbell served in the US House of Representatives from 1987 to 1993 and the US Senate from 1993 to 2005. A member of the Northern Cheyenne nation, in 1998 he became the first Native American to chair the Indian Affairs Committee of the US Senate.

## 7 Pál Schmitt, Hungary, Épée Fencing, 1968-1976

Pál Schmitt competed in three Olympics and won two gold medals in team épée. After the fall of communism in Hungary in 1990 he became a diplomat and served as his nation's ambassador to Spain from 1993 to 1997 and to Switzerland from 1999 to 2002. He was elected to the European Parliament in 2009 and then was chosen by the National Assembly to be President of Hungary in July 2010. However he resigned in April 2012 when it was revealed that he had plagiarized his university thesis.

## 8 Guy Drut, France, 110-meter Hurdles, 1972-1976

The son of a French father and an English mother, Guy Drut was an excellent all-around athlete who, in 1976, became the first person from a non-English-speaking country to win the 110-meter hurdles. He had previously earned a silver medal in 1972. Drut served in the National Assembly from 1986 to 2002 and was Minister of Youth and Sport between 1995 and 1997. In 2005, however, he was convicted of corruption and receiving misused funds, after it was discovered that in the early 1990s he had held a fictitious job at a construction company, for which he was paid 3,000 Euros per month. Drut was given a 15-month suspended sentence and a 50,000 Euro fine but was pardoned by French president Jacques Chirac in 2006.

## 9 Taro Aso, Japan, Skeet Shooting, 1976

Three years after he tied for 41st place at the Montréal Olympics Taro Aso was elected to the Japanese House of Representatives, and he has remained in the legislature ever since. He served as the head of three different ministries when his party, the Liberal Democrats (LDP), was in power and was chosen to be Japan's prime minister in September 2008. He lasted one year in the position before the LDP was driven from power.

## 10 Lasse Virén, Finland, Long-Distance Running, 1972-1980

Lasse Virén earned four Olympic gold medals and was the first repeat winner of the 5,000 meters event. He went on to serve in Finland's parliament from 1999 to 2007 and again from 2010 to 2011.

## 11 Vladimir Parfenovich, Belarus, Kayak Canoeing, 1980

Vladimir Parfenovich, a 21-year-old physical education instructor from Minsk, won three gold medals at the Moscow Olympics. In 2000 he was elected to the national legislature of Belarus and became a spokesman for the movement to bring democracy to his nation, a goal which has not yet been achieved.

## 12 Sebastian Coe, Great Britain, Middle-Distance Running, 1980-1984

After winning two Olympic gold medals and two silver medals and retiring from athletics, Sebastian Coe threw his energies into politics. In 1980 he had defied the Conservative government of Margaret Thatcher and competed in the Moscow Olympics. Twelve years later, running as a Conservative, he was elected to parliament. Driven from office at the next election, he became chief of staff for Conservative Party leader, William Hague. Later he became chairman of the organizing committee for the 2012 Olympics.

## 13 Seiko Hashimoto, Japan, Women's Cycling and Speed Skating, 1984-1996

Born just before the Tokyo Games, Seiko Hashimoto was named after the Olympic flame (*seika*). She ended up competing in seven Olympics: four as a speed skater in the Winter Games and three as a cyclist, winning one bronze medal at the 1992 Winter Olympics. Hashimoto's training was no doubt disrupted by the demands of her profession: in 1995 she was elected to Japan's parliament, the House of Councillors, a position she continues to hold. In 2008–2009 she served as vice-minister of foreign affairs in the cabinet of prime minister Taro Aso, himself a former Olympian.

## 14 María Isabel Urrutia, Colombia, Throwing and Weightlifting, 1988-2000

Maria Isabel Urrutia first competed in the Olympics in 1988 as a discus-thrower and shot-putter. When women's weightlifting was added to the Olympic program in 2000 Urrutia, already 35 years old, won the heavyweight division. As the first South American woman to win an Olympic championship and the first Colombian champion of either sex to do so, she became a major celebrity back home, particularly as she came from a poor family. A year later she was suspended when she tested positive for both the anabolic steroid nandrolone and the stimulant ephedrine. Yet her popularity was unaffected, and only five months later she was elected to the Chamber of Representatives. She was re-elected in 2006.

## 15 Aleksandr Karelin, Russia, Super-heavyweight Greco-Roman Wrestling, 1988-2000

Aleksandr Karelin dominated Greco-Roman wrestling for 12 years, going undefeated from 1987 to 2000—in fact between 1993 and 1999 he didn't give up a single point. He won gold medals in 1988, 1992 and 1996, but was upset in the 2000 final by American Rulon Gardner. A supporter of Vladimir Putin, Karelin was elected to the Russian State Duma in 1999 and has been re-elected three times since then, most recently in December 2011.

## 16 Marcus Stephen, Nauru, Weightlifting, 1992-2000

Marcus Samuel was definitely one of the top ten lifters in his weight category in 1992 and a legitimate qualifier for the Olympics. Unfortunately, he hailed from the Pacific island of Nauru, a nation so small (population: 9,000) that it didn't have a national Olympic committee. So Samuel did what he had to do: he acquired citizenship in a "big" country—Western Samoa (population: 195,000). At the 1992 Barcelona Games he placed a creditable ninth. In 1994, thanks to his accomplishments, Nauru was admitted as the 196th—and smallest—nation in the Olympic movement. In 2003 Stephen was elected to the Nauru parliament. He also served for less than a year as Minister of Education and Finance. In December 2007, when the sitting President lost a no-confidence vote in the parliament, Stephen was sworn in as his nation's President. He served until November 2011. He was the first non-royal Olympic athlete to go on to lead a nation.

## 17 Erki Nool, Estonia, Decathlon, 1992-2004

Erki Nool won the 2000 decathlon gold medal despite a controversial final discus throw that was initially ruled a foul. Back in Estonia, he became so popular that he had to trademark his name to protect it from being used on a wide range of products. In response to the controversy about his discus throw the Czech Athletic Federation hired a Czech firm, Euro G.V., to perform a computer analysis of it; in February 2001 the firm issued a 30-page report concluding that Nool had avoided overstepping the edge of the rink by 9 millimeters, and that the validation of his throw was correct after all. In 2007 Nool was elected to the Estonian Parliament.

# 7 Sailing Medalists Who Found Fame in Other Fields (and 1 who became infamous)

### 1 Jacques Lebrun, France, Finn Class, 1932

During World War II Lebrun distinguished himself by helping to hide the treasures of the Louvre from the Nazis.

### 2 Peter Scott, Great Britain, Finn Class, 1936

In 1941 Scott created the camouflage scheme that was eventually used by most of the Allied forces during World War II. After the war, Scott, who had previously been an ardent hunter of geese and ducks, renounced his former ways and became a wildfowl protection activist. Co-founder of the World Wildlife Fund, he was known as "the patron saint of conservation."

### 3 Paul Cote, Canada, Soling Class, 1972

In 1971 Cote was part of a group of five people who formed the "Don't Make a Wave Committee," whose purpose was to sail a boat to Amchitka Island in Alaska where the United States military was planning to test a 5.2-megaton nuclear bomb. As the committee grew a new name was chosen for the group: Greenpeace. A Greenpeace boat, the Phyllis Cormack, did sail into the zone, although Cote, who was training for the Olympics, was not a member of the crew.

### 4 Britton Chance, USA, 5.5-meter Class, 1952

Britton Chance was an extremely well respected professor of biophysics and physical biochemistry, most noted for his research into how oxygen is used by the body to provide energy.

### 5 Crown Prince Olav, Norway, 6-meter Class, 1928

During World War II, Crown Prince Olav became a symbol of Norwegian resistance to the Nazis. His reign as King Olav V was a popular one and lasted from 1957 until his death in 1991.

### 6 Stewart Morris, Great Britain, Swallow Class, 1948

During World War II, Morris helped design an air defense system for aircraft carriers that was later adopted as the standard for British carriers.

## 7 Owen Churchill, USA, 8-meter Class, 1932

In 1940 Churchill patented the first rubber swim fin. His fins were used by American and British frogmen during World War II, and he continued to collect royalties on his invention until his death in 1985.

## 8 Alfred Krupp, Germany, 8-meter Class, 1936

Alfred Krupp was the owner and director of the infamous Krupp armaments works. He was convicted as a war criminal at the Nuremberg trials after World War II.

# 7 Non-Sailors Achieving Fame and Fortune in Other Fields

## 1 A.C. Gilbert, USA, Pole Vault, 1908

Gold medalist A.C. Gilbert worked his way through Yale Medical School as a magician. He is best known today as the inventor of the Erector Set, one of the most popular toys of all time. In 1918 Gilbert was involved in an incident that caused a sensation. During World War I, the US government's Council of National Defense demanded that all segments of the American population make sacrifices for the war effort—including children. To this end, they proposed a ban on toy sales for Christmas. Gilbert led a group of toy makers to a meeting with the Council to argue in favor of toys. After making a stirring speech in support of toys Gilbert pulled out a toy submarine, a toy steam engine, tin soldiers, wire puzzles and other items. The Secretary of the Navy, the Secretary of Commerce and the other Council members tried out the toys and then withdrew their proposed ban. When word of the meeting reached journalists A.C. Gilbert became known as "The Man Who Saved Christmas for Children."

## 2 George Patton, USA, Modern Pentathlon, 1912

The fifth-place finisher was a 26-year-old army lieutenant, George S. Patton, Jr. who later went on to considerable fame as a general during World War II. Ironically, Patton might have won the event had he not been such a poor marksman, placing a mediocre 21st (of 32) in the shooting competition. Patton claimed that he was penalized for missing the target completely when in fact the bullet had gone through a previously-made hole. Had he been able to prove his case, he would have won the gold medal; however, there is no evidence at all to support his contention.

## 3 René Lacoste, France, Tennis Doubles, 1924

René Lacoste won an Olympic bronze medal and was the world's number one ranked tennis player in 1926 and 1927, but is now better known for the clothing brand that carries his name. Once, while playing in the United States, Lacoste coveted an alligator skin bag. His coach offered to buy it for him—if he won the tournament. Lacoste lost in the final, but the story made its way back to France, where the alligator was transformed into a crocodile. Lacoste himself became known as the "crocodile," and it was the crocodile that would become the emblem of the clothing line that he created.

## 4 Arthur Porritt, New Zealand, Sprints, 1924

Arthur Porritt took the bronze medal in the 100 meters behind Harold Abrahams and Jackson Scholz. A surgeon, in 1960 he became the first person to serve as president of the British Medical Association and the Royal College of Surgeons of England at the same time. In 1967 he became the first New Zealand-born Governor-General of New Zealand. For more than 30 years he was surgeon to members of the British royal family.

## 5/6 Arthur Wint, Jamaica, and David Bolen, USA, 400 Meters, 1948

The 400-meter final in London turned out to be an unusually diplomatic race. Arthur Wint, who won the gold medal, interrupted his medical career to serve as Jamaica's High Commissioner to Great Britain from 1974 to 1978. Dave Bolen, who finished fourth, served as US ambassador to Botswana, Lesotho, and Swaziland from 1974 to 1976, and then as ambassador to East Germany from 1977 to 1980.

## 7 James Wolfensohn, Australia, Team Épée Fencing, 1956

After moving to New York and working as a banking executive, Wolfensohn became a US citizen in 1980. He served as president of the World Bank from 1995 to 2005. He regained his Australian citizenship in 2010.

# 8 Olympian Authors of Books Not About Sport

### 1 James Connolly, USA, Triple Jump, 1896

The first Olympic champion of the modern era, James Connolly later became a noted journalist and war correspondent, and also authored 25 novels and 200 short stories. Connolly covered the 1908 London Olympics as a journalist and responded to the numerous judging controversies by producing an unpublished manuscript entitled "The English as Poor Losers."

### 2 Ellery Clark, USA, High Jump and Long Jump, 1896

Ellery Clark was a 22-year-old Harvard undergraduate who was granted leave of absence for the Olympics because of his high grade-point average—but only on the condition that he should not bring attention to the fact that he was associated with Harvard. He gained two victories. Clark returned to the Olympics in 1904, placing fifth in the decathlon. He eventually authored nineteen books including a novel, *Loaded Dice*, which was made into a 1952 film entitled *Caribbean* that starred John Payne and Arlene Dahl.

### 3 Jean-Joseph Renaud, France, Team Sabre Fencing, 1900-1908

After competing in two Olympics, Jean-Joseph Renaud went on to write more than sixty novels and several plays. However, he was best known as the organizer and director of several hundred illegal private duels. He justified his role in these clandestine encounters by explaining that "generally both parties are so nervous that nobody gets hurt, the offended hero soothes his honor, and everyone goes away happy."

### 4 Joshua "Jerry" Millner, Great Britain, Free Rifle Shooting, 1908

At 61 Colonel Millner remains the oldest winner of an individual event in any sport in Olympic history. Millner devoted much of his life to breeding red setters and in 1924 published the book *The Irish Setter: Its History and Training*.

## 5 Benjamin Spock, USA, Coxed Eights Rowing, 1924

Twenty years after his Olympic victory, Spock wrote *The Common Sense Book of Baby and Child Care*, which eventually sold more than 35 million copies.

## 6 Jesse Owens, USA, Sprints, 1936

In 1968 Owens took the side of the US Olympic Committee in its struggle with militant black athletes, and two years later he wrote a book called *Blackthink*, which criticized racial militancy. However in 1972 he published another book, *I Have Changed*, retracting his earlier criticisms.

## 7 Valery Brumel, Soviet Union, High Jump, 1960-1964

One year after winning the gold medal in 1964 Valery Brumel's athletic career was upended when a motorcycle accident left him with an open tibia fracture of his right leg. Remarkably, after more than twenty operations Brumel did jump again. Although he never made it back to international competition, in 1970 he actually cleared 6 feet 11¾ inches. He was also able to channel his energy into other directions, earning a doctorate in sports psychology and publishing a novel, a play and an opera libretto.

## 8 Dick Roth, USA, 400-meter Individual Medley Swimming, 1964

Three days before the competition, world record holder Dick Roth was stricken with an acute attack of appendicitis. Japanese doctors recommended an immediate operation, but Roth refused. Since he also refused to take drugs, they packed him in ice instead. The 17-year-old Californian took the lead 70 meters from the finish and won the final in world record time. After successful careers as a rancher and entrepreneur, Roth wrote the 1999 book *No, It's Not Hot in Here: A Husband's Guide to Understanding Menopause*.

# 5 Olympian Circus Performers

### 1 Alberto Braglia, Italy, All-Around Gymnastics, 1908-1912

After winning the all-around gymnastics title in 1908, Alberto Braglia of Modena found it difficult to earn a living and took to performing as "The Human Torpedo." He was declared a professional and drummed out of the Italian national gymnastics federation. However he regained his amateur status in time for the 1912 Olympics and successfully defended his championship. Afterwards he became a popular circus performer. In 1932 Braglia coached the Italian gymnastics team to a surprise victory at the Los Angeles Olympics.

### 2 Haig "Harry" Prieste, USA, Platform Diving, 1920

Harry Prieste, the winner of the bronze medal in platform diving in Antwerp, was apparently the first of a long line of Olympic athletes to steal official Olympic flags, climbing a 15-foot flagpole to snatch his souvenir. After keeping the flag in a suitcase for 80 years, Prieste returned it to the IOC's president, Juan Antonio Samaranch, at a ceremony at the Sydney Olympics. (In return Samaranch presented the 103-year-old Olympian with a box containing a commemorative Olympic medal; the hard-of-hearing Prieste responded, "What is it? Kleenex?") After competing in the Olympics Prieste acted in Mack Sennett's Keystone Kops series. He also worked vaudeville and performed in the Ice Follies and with the Ringling Brothers and Barnum & Bailey Circus. He died on April 19, 2001, at the age of 104.

### 3 Heinz Schattner, West Germany, Super-heavyweight Weightlifting, 1952

Fourth-place finisher Schattner was a circus performer. He began his act by hoisting a weightlifting bar attached to two enormous globes. Once they were above his head, the globes opened to reveal his wife and son.

### 4 Ymer Pampuri, Albania, Featherweight Weightlifting, 1972

Ymer Pampuri, a circus clown, broke the Olympic record in the press and actually led the competition after the first round, due to his lower bodyweight. However, the snatch and the jerk were not practiced in Albania, and he could do no better than 12th and tenth in those disciplines. He wound up in ninth place.

## 5 Emma George, Australia, Women's Pole Vault, 2000

Australian Emma George had performed as a circus acrobat until the age of thirteen. Between 1995 and 1999 the glamorous George broke the outdoor pole vault world record twelve times. On December 17, 1995, she became the first woman to clear 14 feet (4.28 meters) and on February 21, 1998, the first to clear 15 feet (4.57 meters). George had a disappointing result in the 2000 Olympics, failing to advance out of the qualifying round.

# 20 Olympians Who Did Time in Prison

*Unfortunately, it is not uncommon for Olympic athletes to go on to criminal careers. What follows is a sampling of the more colorful or notorious cases.*

## 1 James Snook, USA, Free Pistol Shooting, 1920

Dr. James H. Snook of the gold-medal-winning US team gained national notoriety in June 1929 after being arrested for first-degree murder. Snook, then a 48- year-old professor of veterinary medicine at Ohio State University, confessed to killing his 25-year-old mistress, Theora Hix, by beating her with a hammer after an over-violent sexual act that took place at the local rifle range. He was put to death in an electric chair eight months later.

## 2 Humberto Mariles, Mexico, Equestrian, 1948-1952

The winner of two gold medals and one bronze at the 1948 Olympics, General Humberto Mariles was driving home from a party in his honor in Mexico City on the night of August 14, 1964, when another motorist attempted to force him off the road. At the next traffic light Mariles pulled out a gun and shot the man. He was sent to prison, but was later released by presidential pardon. In 1972 Mariles was arrested in Paris during a raid in which 132 pounds of pure heroin were seized. He died in prison before coming to trial.

## 3 Gazanfer Bilge, Turkey, Featherweight Freestyle Wrestling, 1948

Gold-medal-winner Gazanfer Bilge was rewarded by the Turkish government with a house and 20,000 liras ($7,142). This made him ineligible for the 1952 Olympics, but he was able to parlay his rewards into a fortune as a bus mogul. In 1963 Bilge was imprisoned for a year after he shot Adil Atan, a business rival, who had won a bronze medal as a light heavyweight wrestler in 1952.

## 4 Murray Riley, Australia, Double Sculls Rowing, 1952-1956

Murray Riley earned a bronze medal in double sculls at the Melbourne

Games. An ex-policeman, he went on to become one of Sydney's most notorious criminals. Beginning in 1966 he was convicted of various charges of fraud, counterfeiting and drug-related offenses. The Sydney 2000 Olympics found him in prison in England.

Riley's partner in the double sculls, Mervyn Woods, never served time in prison, but he was a dubious character nonetheless. He rose to the position of New South Wales police commissioner in 1977, but in 1989 he was charged with two counts of "perverting the course of justice." The charges were eventually dropped, although Wood's reputation was sufficiently controversial that in 2000 he was one of only a handful of Australian Olympians who was not invited to carry the Olympic torch. Needless to say, Riley was another.

## 5 Brian Phelps, Great Britain, Platform Diving, 1960-1964

Bronze medalist Brian Phelps went on to found a gymnastics and trampoline club in the south of England. In 2008 he was arrested and charged with sexually abusing three young girls whom he trained in the 1970s and 1980s. Phelps pleaded guilty and was sent to prison for nine years.

## 6 Bob Hayes, USA, 100 Meters, 1964

One of the stars of the Tokyo Olympics, Hayes graduated to a successful career in American football. However, when he retired he plunged into alcoholism and drug use. In 1978 he was arrested by undercover narcotics agents, and the following year he pleaded guilty to selling cocaine and methaqualone. He served ten months.

## 7 Mamo Wolde, Ethiopia, Marathon, 1968

Twenty-four years after winning the 1968 Marathon in Mexico City, Mamo Wolde was arrested in his home country, Ethiopia, for unspecified crimes committed by a previous government known as the Derguc. Twice he was released and then rearrested, definitively in April 1993. For years Wolde languished in prison without being charged. Meanwhile the IOC sent financial assistance to his wife and children and hired a lawyer on his behalf. In March 1999, after more than six years in prison, Wolde finally went on trial. He was accused of shooting to death, on March 22, 1978, a teenager who belonged to an anti-government organization. On January 18, 2002, Wolde was finally convicted of murder and sentenced to six years. Since he had already spent nine years in prison, he was immediately released. However he enjoyed only four months of freedom. He died, aged 69, on May 26, 2002, and was buried at St Joseph's Cemetery in Addis Ababa next to his idol, Abebe Bikila.

### 8 George Tajirian, Iraq, Cycling, Road Race, 1968

Thirty years after his Olympic appearance, George Tajirian was convicted in one of the largest immigrant smuggling cases in United States history. He admitted to smuggling more than 1,000 people, mostly from the Middle East, and was sentenced to thirteen years in prison.

### 9 Warren Richards, Australia, Lightweight Judo, 1976

When the Olympics came to Sydney in 2000 Warren Richards, as one of Australia's 1,800 living Olympians, was invited to carry the torch as part of the Torch Relay. He accepted and sent in money to pay for a torch replica to keep as a souvenir. It was then discovered that Richards resided in the maximum security section of Sydney's Long Bay Jail, where his was serving a 12-year sentence for smuggling heroin. His invitation was withdrawn and his payment returned.

### 10 David Jenkins, Great Britain, 400 Meters, 1972-1980

The winner of a silver medal as the anchor of the British 4 × 400-meter relay team in 1972, Jenkins was sent to prison in 1987 after pleading guilty to charges related to the manufacture and smuggling of anabolic steroids. He served nine months and then went into the dietary supplement business.

### 11 Wolfgang Schmidt, East Germany, Discus Throw, 1976

In 1982, East Germany's Wolfgang Schmidt was sentenced to 15 months imprisonment for "antisocial behavior" because of his opposition to communism and his friendships with Western athletes. He was unable to return to competition until 1988, after he was permitted to emigrate to West Germany.

### 12 Henry Tillman, USA, Heavyweight Boxing, 1984

The winner of the gold medal at the Los Angeles Olympics, Henry Tillman had learned to box while serving time for armed robbery. He was not the cleverest of criminals. In 1994 he pleaded no contest to a charge of using a credit card not in his name; the judge gave him probation and community service. Then he was videotaped at a casino in Inglewood, California, trying to use a counterfeit credit card with a fake name, even though he was wearing a jacket with "TILLMAN" stenciled across the back. He pleaded guilty and in 1996 was sentenced to at least two years in prison. But even before the sentencing, he had got himself into worse trouble. This time he was charged with murdering one man outside a nightclub and shooting another. Eventually, Tillman pleaded no contest to charges of attempted murder and voluntary manslaughter. Released from prison in 2002, he returned in 2004 after pleading guilty in another case involving counterfeit checks and credit cards.

## 13 Bruce Kimball, USA, Platform Diving, 1984

In 1981 Kimball was struck head-on by a drunken driver. Every bone in his face was broken, his skull was fractured, his left leg broken, the ligaments in his knee torn, his liver was lacerated, and his spleen had to be removed. When he returned to diving nine months later, he earned the nickname "The Comeback Kid." On August 1, 1988, two weeks before the US Olympic diving trials, Kimball, himself drunk, struck a crowd of teenagers while driving 75 miles per hour, killing two boys and injuring six others. Despite the tragedy, Kimball took part in the trials but failed to make the team. He subsequently pleaded guilty to vehicular manslaughter and was sentenced to 17 years in prison. He was released on November 24, 1993, after serving less than five.

## 14 Pernell Whitaker, USA, Lightweight Boxing, 1984

After he stopped fighting, 1984 Olympic champion Pernell Whitaker built up a record of alcohol- and drug-related arrests. The most colorful occurred on August 10, 2001, when he was sentenced to four days in jail after pleading guilty to speeding and driving without a license. While sheriff's deputies were taking an inventory of his possessions before taking him away to jail, a packet of cocaine fell out of his money roll. This indiscretion led to a new sentence of one year's probation. Whitaker violated this probation by driving drunk and in 2003 was sentenced to 27 months in prison. After his release, he was inducted into the International Boxing Hall of Fame.

## 15 James Waithe, Barbados, Middleweight Judo, 1988

One of the Olympics' nastier competitors, Waithe was arrested in October

2009 after police stumbled upon a massive cocaine production facility at an apartment he owned. Waithe had been the drug gang's "enforcer," torturing its debtors with a variety of sadistic techniques, including putting a man's hand in an electric toaster. In December 2009 he was given an indefinite prison sentence with a minimum of nine years.

## 16 Angel Genchev, Bulgaria, Lightweight Weightlifting, 1988

Genchev was awarded the gold medal in the lightweight division at the Seoul Olympics; however, he tested positive for a diuretic used as a masking agent for steroids and was stripped of his medal. In 1992 he was convicted of rape and sent to prison for two years. However he was released early, not for good behavior but so that he could represent Bulgaria at the 1994 world championships, where he won a bronze medal.

## 17 Péter Farkas, Hungary, Middleweight Greco-Roman Wrestling, 1992

The winner of the gold medal at the Barcelona Olympics, Péter Farkas became a popular heart-throb singer in Hungary. However, in 2004 he and his brother Karoly were arrested after police discovered more than 3,000 marijuana plants growing in their mother's basement in Budapest. They both escaped from police custody in November 2008 shortly before being sentenced to five years in prison. Karoly pretended to be ill, and during the break between the announcement of the verdict and sentencing the two left the courtroom and did not return. Karoly was recaptured almost immediately, but Péter was not rearrested until a year later in Andorra. Their sentences were subsequently extended to seven years.

## 18 Ludovit Plachetka, Czech Republic, Middleweight Boxing, 1996

Less than a year after his Olympic appearance, Plachetka, who worked as a bouncer at a disco, was arrested for shooting to death the mother of his former girlfriend, following a dispute over child visitation rights. He would have shot his girlfriend too, but his pistol jammed. Plachetka was sentenced to thirteen years in prison.

## 19 Tim Montgomery, USA, Sprint Relay, 1996–2000

A double medal-winner in the 4 × 100-meter relay, Tim Montgomery was arrested in April 2006 for involvement in a New York-based multi-million-dollar money-laundering and check-fraud scheme. In April 2007 he pleaded guilty to depositing bogus checks totaling $775,000. In May 2008, two weeks before being sentenced in the fraud case, a Virginia court also indicted him for dealing 111 grams of heroin while he was out on bond. He was handed a 46-month sentence for the first charge and five years for the second.

## 20 Marion Jones, USA, Sprints and Long Jump, 2000-2004

Marion Jones won five medals at the 2000 Olympics, including three golds. However she later admitted to taking steroids, and the IOC stripped her of all her medals. In October 2007 she confessed to lying to a grand jury and was sentenced to six months in prison for perjury.

# 14 Murdered Olympians...
# and one who nearly was

**1** **Marcello Nizzola, Italy, Bantamweight Greco-Roman Wrestling, 1932**

A member of Benito Mussolini's Republican Fascist Party (P.F.R.), Nizzola was assassinated on February 22, 1947, almost two years after the end of World War II.

**2** **Jorge Agostini, Cuba, Foil Fencing, 1948**

After competing in the 1948 Olympics, Cuban fencer Jorge Agostini joined Castro's revolutionary forces in the fight against the country's president Fulgencio Batista. In June 1955 Agostini was found by Batista's forces and brutally killed; an autopsy revealed 21 bullet holes scattered throughout his body.

**3** **Olivér Halassy, Hungary, Water Polo, 1928-1936**

Olivér Halassy played on three Hungarian Olympic water polo teams, winning three medals (two golds and a silver). On September 10, 1946, at the age of 37, Halassy was murdered by a Soviet soldier while walking down the street in Budapest.

**4** **Boughèra El Ouafi, France, Marathon, 1928**

The winner of the 1928 marathon, El Ouafi was an Algerian who represented France before Algeria achieved independence. On October 18, 1959, he was shot to death while sitting in a café in Paris on his 61st birthday.

**5/6/7/8/9** **Yossef Romano, Ze'ev Friedman, David Berger, Eliezer Halfin, Mark Slavin, Israel, Wrestling and Weightlifting, 1972**

Weightlifters Romano, Friedman and Berger, and wrestlers Halfin and Slavin were among the eleven Israelis killed during the Palestinian terrorist attack against the Israeli team at the 1972 Olympics. Romano was shot to death in the Athletes Village while fighting back against the terrorists. The others were killed by the kidnappers during the bungled rescue attempt by the Germans.

## 10 Stella Walsh, Poland, Women's 100 Meters and Discus Throw, 1932-1936

The winner of the 100 meters in 1932, Stella Walsh (a.k.a. Stanisława Wałasiewicz) added a silver medal in 1936. She grew up in Cleveland in the United States but was a Polish citizen. On December 4, 1980, Walsh went to a discount store in Cleveland to buy ribbons for a reception for the Polish national basketball team. In the parking lot she was shot to death during a robbery attempt.

## 11 Josef Odložil, Czech Republic, 1,500 Meters, 1964-1968

The 1964 1,500 meters silver medalist, Josef Odložil married the famous Czech gymnast Vera Cáslavská at the 1968 Olympics. The couple divorced in 1992. The following year, their teenage son, Martin, killed Odložil during a fight in a pub.

## 12 Dave Schultz, USA, Welterweight Freestyle Wrestling, 1984

Winner of the Olympic title in 1984, Schultz retired three years later, but staged a successful comeback beginning in 1993. When the Olympic year of 1996 began he was ranked first in the United States. However, on January 26, he was shot to death by John du Pont, one of the major sponsors of the US freestyle wrestling team.

## 13 Matija Ljubek, Croatia, Canadian Singles Canoeing 1,000 Meters, 1976

An Olympic champion in 1976, Ljubek went on to become vice-president of the Croatian Olympic Committee and *chef de mission* of the Croatian Olympic team. Six days after returning to Zagreb from the 2000 Olympics he was shot to death while trying to defend his mother from an estranged brother-in-law.

## 14 Tamás Bujkó, Hungary, Half-lightweight Judo, 1988

In 2008 Hungarian judoka Bujkó was gruesomely murdered outside a tube station in north-west London. The attacker, a waiter at a five-star hotel near Buckingham Palace, threw acid in his face, then stabbed and beat him to death in front of a crowd of horrified bystanders. The two men had clashed six months earlier at the attacker's former home, which

Bujkó had moved into. The killer was sentenced to life in prison.

---

## And... Denis Horgan, Great Britain/Ireland, Shot Put, 1908

Denis Horgan was 37 years old and past his prime. His second-place performance at the 1908 Olympics was particularly noteworthy considering that he had almost been killed the year before. On duty as a New York City policeman, Horgan tried to break up a brawl and was severely attacked with sticks and shovels. After his surprising recovery, he was given a pension and allowed to return to Ireland.

# 8 Unusual Deaths

### 1 Jacky Boxberger, France, Running, 1968-1976, 1984

Jacky Boxberger, who placed sixth in the 1,500 meters at the 1968 Mexico City Games, eventually represented France in four Olympics at distances ranging up to the marathon. In 2001, when he was 52 years old, Boxberger was on vacation with his family in Kenya. He was filming an elephant when it suddenly turned round, picked him up with his trunk, slammed him against a tree, threw him to the ground and stamped him to death.

### 2 Fereidoun Esfandiary, Iran, Basketball, 1948

Fereidoun Esfandiary later became a well-known futurist, changing his name to FM-2030 and predicting that humans would become "post-biological organisms" possessing limitless resources and would achieve eventual immortality. When he died in 2000, at the age of 69, his body was placed in cryogenic suspension.

### 3 Ken Sitzberger, USA, Springboard Diving, 1964

Gold-medal-winner Ken Sitzberger died on January 2, 1984, from a traumatic head injury. He had been involved in the murky world of cocaine trafficking. Because he was due to testify in six weeks as a federal witness in a drug trial, there was speculation that his death might have been related to the case. However, his wife, fellow 1964 diving medalist Jeanne Collier, told authorities that Sitzberger had hit his head on a table during a New Year's party.

### 4 Larry Andreasen, USA, Springboard Diving, 1964

In 1988, towards the end of the Seoul Olympics, Larry Andreasen, then 42 years old, dived 160 feet from the center of the Gerald Desmond Bridge in Long Beach, California. Andreasen was under the mistaken impression that he was breaking the record for the highest dive. In fact, the record was 174 feet 8 inches. He survived the dive uninjured but was arrested. Andreasen then became obsessed with another, higher bridge: the Vincent Thomas Bridge in Los Angeles Harbor, in particular its 385-

foot west tower. Three times police removed him from the bridge tower. Finally, on October 26, 1990, he took the plunge and died of multiple injuries. His death was ruled not a suicide but an accident.

## 5 Samuel Wanjiru, Kenya, Marathon, 2008

Despite his Olympic success, earning a gold medal in Beijing, Wanjiru's life soon began to unravel. In December 2010 he was arrested after threatening his wife, a maid and a security guard with an AK-47 assault rifle. Five months later he died in a bizarre home accident. After his wife caught him in bed with another woman and locked the pair of them inside the bedroom, Wanjiru apparently fell from the first-floor balcony of his home while trying to stop his wife leaving the house; he later died of his injuries. However, two of the three pathologists who studied his body reportedly said that the injuries were not consistent with an accident.

## 6 Tapio Rautavaara, Finland, Javelin, 1948

Gold-medal-winner Tapio Rautavaara later became a successful folk singer and film actor. While posing for a photograph, he fell and hit his head on a concrete floor; he died on September 25, 1979, at the age of 64.

## 7 Rod Milburn, USA, 110-meter Hurdles, 1972

On November 11, 1997, Olympic champion Rod Milburn was unloading a hopper car filled with hot water and crystallized sodium chlorate at a paper plant in Port Hudson, Louisiana, when he fell in and died from burns caused by the scalding liquid. He was 46 years old.

## 8 Volodymyr Smirnov, Soviet Union, Foil Fencing, 1980

Two years after winning the Olympic gold medal in Moscow, Smirnov was defending his world championship in Rome when the foil of his opponent, Matthias Behr of West Germany, snapped, pierced Smirnov's mask, penetrated his eyeball and entered his brain. The 28-year-old Ukrainian fencer died nine days later.

# Nations at
# the Olympics

# 20 Winners of Their Nation's Only Medal

**1** **Rohullah Nikpai, Afghanistan, Flyweight Taekwondo, 2008**
After 21-year-old Rohullah Nikpai won his bronze medal match, he said, "I hope this will send a message of peace to my country after 30 years of war."

**2** **Jan Boersma, Netherlands Antilles, Windsurfer Sailing, 1988**
Silver medal.

**3** **Obadele Thompson, Barbados, 100 Meters, 2000**
Bronze medal. In 1960 Barbadian quarter-miler Jim Wedderburn had won a bronze medal as a member of the relay team of the British West Indies.

**4** **Vénuste Niyongabo, Burundi, 5,000 Meters, 1996**
Gold medal. Niyongabo was a medal favorite at 1,500 meters, but withdrew from that race to make way for his friend, Dieudonné Kwizera, who had spearheaded the drive to enter Burundi in the Olympics, but had not qualified for an event himself. Niyongabo entered the 5,000 meters instead, even though he had competed at that distance only twice before.

**5** **Clarence Hill, Bermuda, Super-heavyweight Boxing, 1976**
Hill's bronze gave Bermuda the honor of being the least populous nation (53,500) ever to win a medal in the Summer Olympics.

**6** **Gabriel Tiacoh, Ivory Coast, 400 Meters, 1984**
Silver medal. Tiacoh, who improved his personal best by seven-tenths of a second in the final, died of viral meningitis eight years later, at the age of 28.

**7** **Ahmed Salah, Djibouti, Marathon, 1988**
Bronze medal.

**8** **Zersenay Tadesse Eritrea, 10,000 Meters, 2004**
Bronze medal.

**9** Michael Anthony, Guyana, Bantamweight Boxing, 1980

Bronze medal. Guyana's James Gilkes had been one of the favorites in the 200 meters in 1976, but was prevented from competing when his government boycotted the Montréal Games.

**10** Abdul Wahid Aziz, Iraq, Lightweight Weightlifting, 1960

Bronze medal.

**11** Peter Holmberg, Virgin Islands, Finn Class Sailing, 1988

Silver medal.

**12** Fehaid Al-Deehani, Kuwait, Double Trap Shooting, 2000

Bronze medal.

**13** Magamed Ibragimov, Macedonia, Light-heavyweight Freestyle Wrestling, 2000

Bronze medal. Two Macedonian boxers and two wrestlers had earned medals while representing Yugoslavia.

**14** Bruno Julie, Mauritius, Bantamweight Boxing, 2008

Bronze medal.

**15** Issaka Daborg, Niger, Light-welterweight Boxing, 1972

Bronze medal.

**16** Amadou Dia Bâ, Senegal, 400-meter Hurdles, 1988

Silver medal. In 1960 Senegalese Abdoulaye Seye had won a bronze medal in the 200 meters while competing for France.

**17** Ismail Ahmed Ismail, Sudan, 800 Meters, 2008

Silver medal. Ismail and his teammate Abubaker Kaki endured facilities so poor that they used paint cans filled with cement for weight training. A donation from the British embassy helped pay for their trip to Beijing.

**18** Paea Wolfgramm, Tonga, Super-heavyweight Boxing, 1996

Silver medal. One of the most unlikely medalists ever, Wolfgramm stunned Cuban favorite Alexis Rubalcaba in the quarter-finals and then qualified for the final with a last-second punch. Back in Tonga, the least populous independent nation ever to win an Olympic medal, King Taufa'ahou Topou IV ordered a national day of fasting and prayer. Later Wolfgramm was asked if he himself ever fasted. He pointed to his 309-pound (140 kg) frame and replied, "Do I look like I've fasted a lot?" Wolfgramm was outpointed 7-3 in the final by none other than Wladimir Klitschko.

## 19 Benjamin Boukpeti, Togo, Kayak Slalom Singles Canoeing, 2008

Boukpeti was born in France to a French mother and a Togolese father. Ranked 56th in the world, he was so excited after winning his bronze that he snapped his paddle in half in celebration.

## 20 Sheikh Ahmed Al-Maktoum, United Arab Emirates, Double Trap Shooting, 2004

Gold medal. A member of Dubai's ruling family, Al-Maktoum did not take up shooting as a sport until the age of 34.

# 6 Least Populous Nations to Win a Summer Olympics Medal

**1 Bermuda (Population 53,500), 1976**

Clarence Hill's bronze in boxing's Super-heavyweight division brought Bermuda the honor of being the least populous nation ever to win a medal in the Summer Olympics.

**2 Tonga (Population 97,784), 1996**

Before each match in boxing's Super-heavyweight division, Paea Wolfgramm recited a traditional Tongan chant: "Tonga mounga kihe loto—"Your mountains are your hearts." When Wolfgramm returned home with his silver medal, the king declared a national holiday and a local rugby team carried him on a chair through his home village of Utungako (population 500). Wolfgramm let anyone who asked wear his medal. "I felt like it was national property," he explained.

**3 Iceland (Population 161,000), 1956**

When Vilhjálmur Einarsson earned a silver medal in the long jump at the 1956 Melbourne Olympics, Iceland had a population of only 161,000. By the time the men's handball team earned the nation's second podium in 2008, the figure had jumped to 317,000.

**4 Netherlands Antilles (Population 185,900), 1988**

Nineteen-year-old windsurfer Jans Boersma earned a silver medal at the 1988 Olympics. The Netherlands Antilles—consisting of the Caribbean islands of Curacao, St Maarten, St Eustatius, Bonaire and Saba—was dissolved as a political entity in October 2010 and lost IOC recognition three months later.

**5 Barbados (Population 268,792), 2000**

Sprinter Obadele Thompson earned the bronze medal at 100 meters at the Sydney 2000 Olympics.

**6 Bahamas (Population 294,982), 2000**

By winning the women's 4 × 100-meter relay, the Bahamian quartet made their nation the smallest country to win a team event in any sport.

*Athletes from Liechtenstein, with a current population of 36,000, have earned nine medals in Alpine skiing at the Winter Olympics.*

# 13 Longest National Winning Streaks in One Event (excluding boycotts and bannings)

| | | | | |
|---|---|---|---|---|
| 1 | 16 | USA | Pole Vault | 1896-1968 |
| 2 | 12 | USA | Swimming Medley Relay | 1960-2008 |
| 3 | 11 | Hungary | Sabre Fencing | 1908-1964 |
| 4 | 11 | USA | Springboard Diving | 1920-1968 |
| 5 | 10 | Soviet Union | Women's Team Gymnastics | 1952-1992 |
| 6 | 9 | Kenya | 3,000-meter Steeplechase | 1968-2008 |
| 7 | 8 | USA | High Jump | 1896-1928 |
| 8 | 8 | USA | Women's Springboard Diving | 1920-1956 |
| 9 | 8 | USA | Coxed Eights Rowing | 1920-1956 |
| 10 | 8 | USA | 4 x 100-meter Relay | 1920-1956 |
| 11 | 8 | USA | Long Jump | 1924-1960 |
| 12 | 8 | USA | 4 x 400-meter Relay | 1976-2008 |
| 13 | 8 | Germany | Equestrian Team Dressage | 1976-2008 |

*Having been on the losing side of World War I, Hungary was not allowed to compete in the 1920 Olympics. Kenya boycotted the 1976 and 1980 Olympics, the United States and West Germany boycotted the 1980 Olympics, and the Soviet Union boycotted the 1984 Games.*

# 10 Most Populous Nations Never to Win an Olympic Medal

| | | CURRENT POPULATION |
|---|---|---|
| 1 | Bangladesh | 142,319,000 |
| 2 | Democratic Republic of Congo | 67,758,000 |
| 3 | Burma (Myanmar) | 48,337,000 |
| 4 | Nepal | 26,620,000 |
| 5 | Yemen | 23,833,000 |
| 6 | Madagascar | 20,696,000 |
| 7 | Angola | 19,618,000 |
| 8 | Burkina Faso | 15,730,000 |
| 9 | Guatemala | 14,713,000 |
| 10 | Mali | 14,517,176 |

# 7 Examples of Home Nation Advantage

## 1 Athens, 1896

At the first modern Olympics in Athens in 1896 the Greek hosts made sure of coming away with at least one champion by creating a special event: the 100-meter freestyle swimming race for members of the Greek navy.

## 2 St Louis, 1904

At the 1904 St Louis Games the United States ensured victory in the men's team gymnastics competition by banning the only foreign team that entered, the Germans, on the grounds that its members were not from the same club.

## 3 Berlin, 1936

The German three-day event equestrian team spent 18 months practicing full-time on a replica of the Olympic course that had been built on a private estate.

## 4 Moscow, 1980

In the men's 100 meters, four of the nine first-round winners were placed in the same quarter-final heat, along with defending Olympic champion Hasely Crawford. On the other hand, heat number three saw local favorite Aleksandr Aksinin unchallenged by any other first-round winners. Aksinin won his quarter-final in a time that would have placed him only seventh in the other heat. In the javelin throw, Soviet officials were accused of opening a tunnel gate whenever their athletes threw, in order to take advantage of a following wind.

## 5 Los Angeles, 1984

At the 1984 women's gymnastics competition in Los Angeles, Ellen Berger, the head of the International Gymnastics Federation technical committee, warned the United States that points would be deducted from the score of Mary Lou Retton if her personal coach, Béla Károlyi, stepped onto the competition floor, because he was not a member of the US team coaching staff. Károlyi replied, "She [Berger] doesn't have the guts to do it here with 10,000 screaming Americans." When Retton completed the vault that gave her the gold medal, Károlyi jumped over a barrier onto the floor, a violation whose penalty should have cost Retton the gold. But Károlyi was right: Retton's score was allowed to stand unpenalized.

## 6 Barcelona, 1992

José Manuel Moreno of Spain was the defending world champion in the 1000-meter time trial and very familiar with the Olympic Velodrome. But the Spanish team decided to take no chances in securing their nation's first gold medal of the Barcelona Games. Moreno warmed up at a track a few kilometers away and was then airlifted by helicopter to the Velodrome just in time for his ride. He won the gold medal by almost a full second.

## 7 Sydney, 1996

Many observers were shocked when the two pools for the women's soccer tournament were announced, because the three medalists from the 1996 Olympics, the United States, China and Norway were put in one pool, while host nation Australia was put in the other. Similar lopsided seedings occurred in indoor volleyball. In beach volleyball, the teams were seeded according to their world rankings—except the Australians, who were moved ahead.

# 3 Olympic Triumphs that Led to National Holidays

## 1 Jamaica, 1952

The day after the Jamaican 4 × 400-meter relay team edged the United States at the Helsinki Olympics, the Governor of Jamaica declared a national holiday, which led to many arrests for drunkenness. When brought to court and asked their plea, most replied, "Helsinki," and received unusually mild sentences.

## 2 Tonga, 1996

When boxer Paea Wolfgramm unexpectedly returned home with a silver medal, King Taufa'ahou Topou IV declared a national holiday.

## 3 Cameroon, 2004

Lightly regarded Cameroon won the football final against Spain with a penalty shoot-out. Back in Cameroon, dictator Paul Biya declared a national holiday to add to the informal one already celebrated by many Cameroonians in preparation for the final, which began at 2 a.m. local time.

# 6 Olympic Boycotts

## 1 Melbourne, 1956

The 1956 Olympics were affected by two boycotts. Egypt, Iraq and Lebanon withdrew in protest at the Israeli-led invasion of the Suez Canal, and the Netherlands, Spain and Switzerland boycotted to protest the Soviet invasion of Hungary.

## 2 Tokyo, 1964

In 1962 Indonesia hosted the Asian Games in Jakarta. When the Indonesian government refused to allow athletes from Israel and Taiwan to participate, the IOC suspended the Indonesian Olympic Committee until it agreed to abide by the rules of the IOC. Indonesia withdrew its team from the 1964 Olympics, as did North Korea.

## 3 Montréal, 1976

The 1976 games faced a major political obstacle when the dictator of Tanzania, Julius Nyerere, called for a boycott of the Olympics because the national rugby team of New Zealand had toured South Africa, and New Zealand was scheduled to compete in the Olympics. The fact that South Africa had been banned from the Olympics for twelve years because of its racial policies did not seem to faze Nyerere. Nor did the fact that rugby was not affiliated with the Olympic movement. Still, 22 African governments ended up boycotting the Montréal Games, as did the South American nation of Guyana. Guyanese sprinter James Gilkes asked to be allowed to compete as an independent participant, but the International Olympic Committee rejected his appeal.

## 4 Moscow, 1980

The 1980 Moscow Olympics were disrupted by another, even larger boycott, this one led by US president Jimmy Carter, part of a package of actions to protest the December 1979 Soviet invasion of Afghanistan. With his eyes on the impending presidential election, Carter engaged in extensive arm-twisting to gain support from other nations. Some governments, like those of Great Britain and Australia, supported the boycott but allowed the athletes to decide for themselves whether to go to Moscow. No such freedom of choice was allowed to US athletes; Carter threatened to revoke the passport of any athlete who tried to travel to the USSR. In the end, 65 nations turned down their invitations to the Olympics; probably 45 to 50 did so because of the US-led boycott. Eighty nations did participate—the lowest number since 1956.

## 5 Los Angeles, 1984

With the Olympics being held in the United States only four years after the US-led boycott of the Moscow Games, it was not surprising that the Soviet Union organized a revenge boycott in 1984. This time only fourteen nations stayed away—but those nations accounted for 58% of the gold medals at the 1976 Olympics.

## 6 Seoul, 1988

The 1988 Olympics were held in Seoul, South Korea, a nation that turned democratic in order to welcome the world to the Summer Games. North Korea boycotted, and was joined by Cuba, Ethiopia and Nicaragua. Still, records were set with 159 nations participating, 52 winning medals and 31 taking home gold medals.

# 4 Nations Boycotting the Olympics 3 Times or More

| | | | |
|---|---|---|---|
| 1 | 4 | Albania | 1976-1988 |
| 2 | 3 | Egypt | 1956, 1976-1980 |
| 3 | 3 | North Korea | 1964, 1984-1988 |
| 4 | 3 | Ethiopia | 1976, 1984-1988 |

# 19 Olympic Favorites Boycotts Prevented from Competing

**1 Atie Voorbij, Netherlands, Women's 100-meter Butterfly, 1956**

The reigning world record holder, Voorbij was prevented from competing in the inaugural women's butterfly event because of the Dutch boycott.

**2 John Akii-Bua, Uganda, 400-meter Hurdles, 1976**

The African boycott prevented a potentially historic showdown in the 400-meter hurdles, between defending Olympic champion and world-record-holder John Akii-Bua and rising star Edwin Moses of the United States. No matter how sympathetic one might have been to the movement to bring self-determination for blacks in South Africa, it is hard to not be cynical when you realize John Akii-Bua was not allowed to compete in Montréal because his country's leader, the notorious Idi Amin, who caused the deaths of hundreds of thousands of his own citizens, was offended by human-rights violations in another country.

**3 Edwin Moses, USA, 400-meter Hurdles, 1980**

This time is was Moses's turn to be sidelined by a boycott. The defending Olympic champion, he set a world record of 47.13 seconds three weeks before the Olympics.; the winning time in the Olympic final was 48.70. Moses regained his Olympic title in 1984.

**4 Yasuhiro Yamashita, Japan, Open Category Judo, 1980**

Between 1977 and 1984 Yamashita fought 194 matches without a loss and won four world championships. When Japan joined the US-led boycott of the 1980 Moscow Olympics, Yamashita appeared on national television pleading, with tears in his eyes, for a reversal of that decision. It was not to be, but he did win the Olympic title in 1984.

**5 Shozo Fujii, Japan, Half-middleweight Judo, 1980**

Fujii had won the last four world championships dating back to 1971.

**6 Mary T. Meagher, USA, Women's Butterfly, 1980**

Fifteen-year-old Mary T. Meagher was the world-record-holder in both butterfly events and the favorite to win two gold medals in Moscow until the anti-Soviet boycott forced her to stay at home. She went on to win both events in 1984.

## 7 Greg Louganis, USA, Diving, 1980

Favored to win two gold medals at the 1980 Olympics, Louganis was shut out by the US boycott, but accomplished the feat instead at the 1982 world championships, the 1984 Olympics and the 1988 Olympics.

## 8 Evelyn Ashford, USA, Women's Sprints, 1980

At a World Cup meet in Montréal in 1979 Evelyn Ashford defeated East German world-record-holder Marita Koch in the 200 meters, 21.83 to 22.02, and then beat the 100-meters world record holder, Marlies Göhr, 11.06 to 11.17. Ashford seemed right on track to fulfill her dreams of Olympic glory—until US President Jimmy Carter announced that US athletes would not be allowed to go to Moscow. When the boycott was made official, Ashford was again competing in Canada. She and her coach and a teammate went to a bar, where Evelyn, completely out of character, "got sloppy drunk," stood up and fell on her face. She went on to earn gold medals in the next three Olympics.

## 9 Mary Decker, USA, Women's Middle-Distance Running, 1980

Mary Decker discovered running at the age of 11, during a period when her life was in turmoil. Her family had just moved from New Jersey to California, and her parents were on the road to divorce. Decker missed competing at the 1976 Olympics due to physical problems stemming from Compartment Syndrome (in which the sheaths of tissues surrounding muscles fail to expand with the muscles' growth). An operation on her calf relieved the pain. After surviving two automobile accidents and then another operation, her times began improving again. In 1980 she set her first world record, running the mile in 4:21.7, and she qualified easily for the US Olympic team, but the anti-Soviet boycott prevented her from competing. Again she watched the Olympics on television. In 1984 Decker finally got her chance to compete in the Olympics. Trailing Great Britain's Zola Budd in the 3,000 meters final, Decker hit one of Budd's legs, throwing Budd off balance just a bit. Five strides later, they bumped again. This time Budd landed awkwardly, her left leg shooting out in search of balance. Decker, running straight and hard, tripped on

Budd's right leg, her spikes cutting deeply into Budd's heel. Decker lost her balance and pitched forward onto the infield. As the runners zipped by, she attempted to rise, but her hard landing had caused her to pull a left hip stabilizer muscle. "It was like I was tied to the ground," she said later. As the race continued Decker was left writhing in agony and weeping in frustration.

## 10 Rowdy Gaines, USA, Swimming, 1980

In 1980, Rowdy Gaines, then at the peak of his career, had been expected to win four gold medals. His dreams of triumph and glory were shattered by the US boycott. He decided to stick it out until 1984 and qualified for the 100-meter freestyle by finishing second to Mike Heath at the US trials. This time Gaines felt much less confident of victory. He even prepared a loser's speech in which he would graciously praise those swimmers who had beaten him. As it turned out, he was first off the starting block and maintained his lead for the entire race, earning the first of his three gold medals.

## 11 Birgit Fischer, East Germany, Women's Kayak Pairs Canoeing, 1984

In 1980 Birgit Fischer, then 18 years old, defeated Vania Gesheva to become the youngest-ever winner of an Olympic canoeing event. If East Germany had not boycotted the 1984 Games, she would have been favored to win all three women's kayak events, just as she did in the world championships of 1981, 1982, 1983, 1985 and 1987. She took 1986 out to have a baby but then, undeterred, competed in the next five Olympics, winning 7 more gold medals and 4 silvers.

## 12 Dmitri Bilozerchev, Soviet Union, Gymnastics, 1984

Dmitri Bilozerchev caused a sensation in 1983 when he became world champion at the tender age of 16. The following year he was kept out of the Olympics by the Soviet boycott. In 1985 his career was again derailed, this time by a car accident. Bilozerchev, on unauthorized leave from training camp, drank too much champagne and, only ten days after receiving his driver's license, borrowed his father's car and went driving in a rainstorm. On the slippery Moscow streets he turned in front of a truck and lost control. His left leg was shattered into more than 40 pieces. He was injured so badly that amputation was seriously considered. Abandoned by the Soviet sports community, Bilozerchev was determined to regain his world-class form. Unfortunately he renewed his training too early. Overcompensating for his still tender left leg, he injured his right leg and required surgery on his ankle in December 1986. Despite these setbacks he was selected for the 1988 Soviet Olympic team and won 3 gold medals and one bronze.

### 13 Serhei Bubka, Soviet Union, Pole Vault, 1984

The definite pre-boycott favorite, Bubka set a world record of 19 feet 4¼ inches (5.90 meters) two weeks before the Olympics began. However, nine days after the Olympic final, he was beaten at the Friendship Games by Soviet teammate Konstantin Volkov. He did gain the gold medal at the 1992 Olympics.

### 14 Yuri Sedykh, Soviet Union, Hammer Throw, 1984

A month before the Los Angeles Olympics, two-time defending champion Yuri Sedykh broke countryman Sergei Litvinov's world record; Litvinov had finished second to Sedykh at the 1980 Olympics. Boycotted out of the 1984 Games, the two returned in 1988 and finished 1–2 again, with Litvinov gaining the victory this time.

### 15 Sylvia Gerasch, East Germany, Women's 100-meter Breaststroke, 1984

In eighth place at the 2000 Games was Sylvia Gerasch, competing in her first Olympics at the age of 31. When she was 15 years old Gerasch had been one of the favorites for the 1984 Olympics, but East Germany boycotted the Games. Three weeks after the Olympic final Gerasch broke the world record. She broke it again in winning the 1986 world championships. But then she failed to qualify for the next three Olympics, most painfully in 1992, when she missed by only three hundredths of a second. In the meantime her swimming club expelled her for being too old, and she took a job in a bank. Then in 2000 she won the German Olympic trials. She made it to the 100-meter breaststroke in Sydney and also placed fourth in the medley relay.

### 16 Javier Sotomayor, Cuba, High Jump, 1988

Javier Sotomayor set a world record of 7 feet 11½ inches (2.42 meters) only 17 days before the Olympic final. However, he was kept out of the Seoul Games by the Cuban boycott. He did earn a gold medal at the 1992 Olympics.

## 17 Ana Quirot, Cuba, Women's 800 Meters, 1988

Quirot won all 13 of her 800-meter races in 1988, including victories over the Olympic gold- and silver-medal-winners, Sigrun Wodars and Christine Wachtel of East Germany, both of whom, it was later revealed, were taking steroids at the time.

## 18 Félix Savón, Cuba, Heavyweight Boxing, 1988

World champion Savon would have been the overwhelming favorite had he been allowed to compete. He did win the next three Olympic championships.

## 19 Li Jae-sik, North Korea, Light Flyweight Freestyle Wrestling, 1988

Li was the two-time defending world champion, but North Korea boycotted the Seoul Olympics just across their border.

## Special Note No. 1: 1984 Weightlifting

No sport was as hard-hit by the 1984 Soviet-bloc boycott as weightlifting. Missing from the competition in the ten weight categories were all ten defending world champions, 29 of the 30 medalists at the last world championships, and 94 of the top 100 ranked lifters.

## Special Note No. 2: 1984 Freestyle Wrestling

Freestyle wrestling was also hard hit by the Soviet-bloc boycott. Of the 30 medal-winners at the 1983 world championships 23 were from boycotting nations, including nine of the ten champions. The light flyweight division was so depleted that there were only seven entrants—the smallest wrestling competition since 1932.

# 4 Medal-winners Forced to Compete under Foreign Flags

## 1 Peter O'Connor, Ireland, Long Jump, 1906

When Peter O'Connor and his Irish teammates Con Leahy and John Daly arrived in Athens, they were outraged to discover that they were described in the athletics program as "British" rather than Irish. O'Connor filed a protest with the Greek Olympic Organizing Committee. But the Committee voted to support the British claim that because Ireland was part of the United Kingdom, they should compete for the British team. When three flags were required to indicate the nationality of the medal-winners, the British Union Jack was flown to represent silver medalist O'Connor. This was too much for the proud Irish nationalist. He climbed the flagpole, unfurled a green Irish flag and waved it vigorously while Con Leahy stood guard at the foot of the pole. O'Connor recalled that this flag incident took place after the long jump; however some newspaper accounts suggest it happened after the triple jump, in which he won the gold medal.

## 2 Sohn Kee-chung, Korea, Marathon, 1936

On November 3, 1935, Sohn Kee-chung of Korea set a world marathon record of 2:26:42.0. Because Korea was, at the time, occupied by Japanese forces, Sohn's hopes of competing in the Olympics depended on his ability to qualify for the Japanese team. This he accomplished, as did fellow Korean Nam Seung-yong. Both young men were forced to endure the further insult of adopting Japanese names. Sohn, a fervent nationalist, always signed his Korean name in Berlin, and whenever he was asked where he was from, made it a point to explain that Korea was a separate nation which was currently a victim of Japanese imperialism. After winning the gold medal, Sohn was forced to suffer the humiliation of having his victory celebrated by the raising of the Japanese flag and the playing of the Japanese national anthem. Both Sohn and bronze-medal-winner Nam registered a silent protest by bowing their heads. In 1948 Sohn was given the honor of carrying the South Korean flag in the Opening Ceremony of the London Olympics, the first attended by an independent Korea. Forty years later, in a moment that brought tears to an entire nation, he entered the Seoul Olympic Stadium bearing the Olympic torch. The 76-year-old Sohn bounded around the track, leaping for joy and bursting with pride for himself and for his country.

### 3 Indian Field Hockey Team, 1936

As India was a British colony, its athletes had to march behind the flag of Great Britain. But in the dressing room before their final match against Germany, the Indian team saluted the tricolor flag of the Indian National Congress. The team went on to win 8–1, with Dhyan Chand scoring six goals while playing barefoot.

### 4 Lithuanian Basketball Team, 1988

Lithuanians had traditionally played a significant role in Soviet basketball. However, for 52 years Lithuania had been a reluctant member of the Soviet Union, and support for independence ran high. In 1988 the Soviet players posed for a team photo after winning the Olympic championship. After the session was over the four Lithuanian members of the team gathered for their own "team" photo. Four years later, in Barcelona, those four players were back in the Olympics representing an independent Lithuania.

# Record Book: Medals

# 10 Who Won the Most Gold Medals

| | | | | | |
|---|---|---|---|---|---|
| **1** | 14 | Michael Phelps | USA | Swimming | 2004-2008 |
| **2** | 9 | Paavo Nurmi | Finland | Track and Field | 1920-1928 |
| **3** | 9 | Larysa Latynina | Soviet Union | Gymnastics | 1956-1964 |
| **4** | 9 | Mark Spitz | USA | Swimming | 1968-1972 |
| **5** | 9 | Carl Lewis | USA | Track and Field | 1984-1996 |
| **6** | 8 | Ray Ewry | USA | Track and Field | 1900-1908 |
| **7** | 8 | Sawao Kato | Japan | Gymnastics | 1968-1976 |
| **8** | 8 | Matt Biondi | USA | Swimming | 1984-1992 |
| **9** | 8 | Birgit Fischer (Schmidt) East Germany/Germany | | Canoeing | 1980-2004 |
| **10** | 8 | Jenny Thompson | USA | Swimming | 1992-2004 |

*In the Winter Olympics, cross-country skier Bjørn Dæhlie of Norway earned 8 gold medals between 1992 and 1998.*

# 8 Winners of the Most Gold Medals in Individual Events

| | | | | | |
|---|---|---|---|---|---|
| **1** | 9 | Michael Phelps | USA | Swimming | 2004-2008 |
| **2** | 8 | Ray Ewry | USA | Track and Field | 1900-1908 |
| **3** | 7 | Vera Cáslavská | Czechoslovakia | Gymnastics | 1964-1968 |
| **4** | 7 | Carl Lewis | USA | Track and Field | 1984-1996 |
| **5** | 6 | Paavo Nurmi | Finland | Track and Field | 1956-1964 |
| **6** | 6 | Larysa Latynina | Soviet Union | Gymnastics | 1956-1964 |
| **7** | 6 | Boris Shakhlin | Soviet Union | Gymnastics | 1956-1964 |
| **8** | 6 | Nikolay Andrianov | Soviet Union | Gymnastics | 1972-1980 |

*In the Winter Olympics, Soviet speed skater Lidiya Skoblikova earned six gold medals in individual events in 1960 and 1964, as did Norwegian cross-country skier Bjørn Dæhlie between 1992 and 1998.*

# 6 Gold-medal-winners in 5 or 6 Olympics

| | | | | | |
|---|---|---|---|---|---|
| **1** | 6 | Aladár Gerevich | Hungary | Fencing | 1932-1960 |
| **2** | 6 | Birgit Fischer (Schmidt) | East Germany/Germany | | |
| | | | | Canoeing | 1980-2004 |
| **3** | 5 | Pál Kovács | Hungary | Fencing | 1936-1960 |
| **4** | 5 | Reiner Klimke | West Germany | | |
| | | | | Equestrian | 1964-1988 |
| **5** | 5 | Steven Redgrave | Great Britain | | |
| | | | | Rowing | 1984-2000 |
| **6** | 5 | Elisabeta Lipa (Oleniuc) | Romania | Rowing | 1984-2004 |

# 10 Athletes Winning Gold Medals 20 or More Years Apart

| | | | | | |
|---|---|---|---|---|---|
| **1** | 28 | Aladár Gerevich | Hungary | Fencing | 1932-1960 |
| **2** | 24 | Pál Kovács | Hungary | Fencing | 1936-1960 |
| **3** | 24 | Edoardo Mangiarotti | Italy | Fencing | 1936-1960 |
| **4** | 24 | Reiner Klimke | West Germany | Equestrian | 1964-1988 |
| **5** | 24 | Birgit Fischer-Schmidt | East Germany/Germany | Canoeing | 1980-2004 |
| **6** | 20 | Lars Jørgen Madsen | Denmark | Shooting | 1900-1920 |
| **7** | 20 | Hubert Van Innis | Belgium | Archery | 1900-1920 |
| **8** | 20 | Manlio Di Rosa | Italy | Fencing | 1936-1956 |
| **9** | 20 | Jochen Schümann | East Germany/Germany | Sailing | 1976-1996 |
| **10** | 20 | Elisabeta Lipa (Oleniuc) | Romania | Rowing | 1984-2004 |

# 7 Winners of 7 or 8 Gold Medals at One Olympics

| | | | | | |
|---|---|---|---|---|---|
| **1** | 8 | Michael Phelps | USA | Swimming | 2008 |
| **2** | 7 | Willis Lee | USA | Shooting | 1920 |
| **3** | 7 | Lloyd Spooner | USA | Shooting | 1920 |
| **4** | 7 | Borys Shakhlin | Soviet Union | Gymnastics | 1960 |
| **5** | 7 | Mark Spitz | USA | Swimming | 1972 |
| **6** | 7 | Nikolay Andrianov | Soviet Union | Gymnastics | 1976 |
| **7** | 7 | Matt Biondi | USA | Swimming | 1988 |

# 10 Winners of 4 or 5 Gold Medals in Individual Events at One Olympics (including one who did it twice)

| | | | | | |
|---|---|---|---|---|---|
| **1** | 5 | Vitaly Shcherbo | Soviet Union | Gymnastics | 1992 |
| **2** | 5 | Michael Phelps | USA | Swimming | 2008 |
| **3** | 4 | Alvin Kraenzlein | USA | Track & Field | 1900 |
| **4** | 4 | Anton Heida | USA | Gymnastics | 1904 |
| **5** | 4 | Marcus Hurley | USA | Cycling | 1904 |
| **6** | 4 | Boris Shakhlin | Soviet Union | Gymnastics | 1960 |
| **7** | 4 | Vera Cáslavská | Czechoslovakia | Gymnastics | 1968 |
| **8** | 7 | Mark Spitz | USA | Swimming | 1972 |
| **9** | 4 | Nikolay Andrianov | Soviet Union | Gymnastics | 1976 |
| **10** | 4 | Kristin Otto | East Germany | Swimming | 1988 |
| **11** | 5 | Michael Phelps | USA | Swimming | 2004 |

*In the Winter Olympics, speed skater Eric Heiden of the United States earned five individual gold medals in 1980, and Soviet speed skater Lidiya Skoblikova earned four in 1964.*

# 3 Who Won the Same Individual Event 4 Times

| 1 | Paul Elvstrøm | Denmark | Sailing, Finn Class | 1948-1960 |
|---|---|---|---|---|
| 2 | Al Oerter | USA | Discus Throw | 1956-1968 |
| 3 | Carl Lewis | USA | Long Jump | 1984-1996 |

# 10 Who Won the Same Team Event 4 Times or More

| 1 | 6 | Aladár Gerevich<br>Fencing, Team Sabre | Hungary<br>1932-1960 |
|---|---|---|---|
| 2 | 5 | Pál Kovács<br>Fencing, Team Sabre | Hungary<br>1936-1960 |
| 3 | 5 | Reiner Klimke<br>Equestrian, Team Dressage | West Germany<br>1964-1968, 1976, 1984-1988 |
| 4 | 4 | Rudolf Kárpáti<br>Fencing, Team Sabre | Hungary<br>1948-1960 |
| 5 | 4 | Edoardo Mangiarotti<br>Fencing, Team Épée | Italy<br>1936, 1952-1960 |
| 6 | 4 | Hans Günter Winkler<br>Equestrian, Team Jumping | West Germany<br>1956-1964, 1972 |
| 7 | 4 | Teresa Edwards<br>Basketball | USA<br>1984-1988, 1996-2000 |
| 8 | 4 | Birgit Fischer (Schmidt)<br>Canoeing, Kayak Fours | East Germany/Germany<br>1988, 1996-2004 |
| 9 | 4 | Lisa Leslie<br>Basketball | USA<br>1996-2008 |
| 10 | 4 | Isabell Werth<br>Equestrian, Team Dressage | Germany<br>1992-2000, 2008 |

*In the Winter Olympics, Aleksandr Tikhonov of the Soviet Union won the biathlon relay 4 times (1968–1980), as did Ricco Gross of Germany (1992–1998, 2006).*

# 12 Who Won the Most Medals

**1**   18   **Larysa Latynina**     **Soviet Union**
**Gymnastics**     **1956-1964**

**2**   15   **Michael Phelps**     **USA**
**Swimming**     **2004-2008**

**3**   14   **Nikolay Andrianov**     **Soviet Union**
**Gymnastics**     **1972-1980**

**4**   13   **Edoardo Mangiarotti**     **Italy**
**Fencing**     **1936-1960**

**5**   13   **Takashi Ono**     **Japan**
**Gymnastics**     **1952-1964**

**6**   13   **Borys Shakhlin**     **Soviet Union**
**Gymnastics**     **1956-1964**

**7**   12   **Paavo Nurmi**     **Finland**
**Track and Field**     **1920-1928**

**8**   12   **Sawao Kato**     **Japan**
**Gymnastics**     **1968-1976**

**9**   12   **Aleksey Nemov**     **Russia**
**Gymnastics**     **1996-2000**

**10**   12   **Jenny Thompson**     **USA**
**Swimming**     **1992-2004**

**11**   12   **Birgit Fischer (Schmidt)**     **East Germany/Germany**
**Canoeing**     **1980-2004**

**12**   12   **Dara Torres**     **USA**
**Swimming**     **1984-2008**

*Competing in the Winter Olympics, cross-country skier Bjørn Dæhlie of Norway earned 12 medals between 1992 and 1998.*

# 10 Who Won the Most Medals in Individual Events

| # | | | | | |
|---|---|---|---|---|---|
| 1 | 14 | Larysa Latynina | Soviet Union | Gymnastics | 1956-1964 |
| 2 | 12 | Nikolay Andrianov | Soviet Union | Gymnastics | 1972-1980 |
| 3 | 10 | Takashi Ono | Japan | Gymnastics | 1952-1964 |
| 4 | 10 | Borys Shakhlin | Soviet Union | Gymnastics | 1956-1964 |
| 5 | 10 | Aleksey Nemov | Russia | Gymnastics | 1996-2000 |
| 6 | 10 | Michael Phelps | USA | Swimming | 2004-2008 |
| 7 | 9 | Paavo Nurmi | Finland | Track & Field | 1920-1928 |
| 8 | 9 | Viktor Chukarin | Soviet Union | Gymnastics | 1952-1956 |
| 9 | 9 | Sawao Kato | Japan | Gymnastics | 1968-1976 |
| 10 | 9 | Vitaly Shcherbo | Belarus | Gymnastics | 1992-1996 |

*In the Winter Olympics, cross-country skier Bjørn Dæhlie of Norway earned nine individual medals between 1992 and 1998.*

# 6 Who Won 6 or More Medals in Individual Events at One Olympics

| # | | | | | |
|---|---|---|---|---|---|
| 1 | 7 | Aleksandr Dityatin | Soviet Union | Gymnastics | 1980 |
| 2 | 6 | Burton Downing | USA | Cycling | 1904 |
| 3 | 6 | George Eyser | USA | Gymnastics | 1904 |
| 4 | 6 | Boris Shakhlin | Soviet Union | Gymnastics | 1960 |
| 5 | 6 | Mikhail Voronin | Soviet Union | Gymnastics | 1968 |
| 6 | 6 | Nikolay Andrianov | Soviet Union | Gymnastics | 1976 |

# 10 Who Won 7 or 8 Medals in One Olympics (including one who did it twice)

| | | | | | |
|---|---|---|---|---|---|
| 1 | 8 | Aleksandr Dityatin | Soviet Union | Gymnastics | 1980 |
| 2 | 8 | Michael Phelps | USA | Swimming | 2004 |
| 3 | 8 | Michael Phelps | USA | Swimming | 2008 |
| 4 | 7 | Willis Lee | USA | Shooting | 1920 |
| 5 | 7 | Lloyd Spooner | USA | Shooting | 1920 |
| 6 | 7 | Mariya Horokhovska | Soviet Union | Gymnastics | 1952 |
| 7 | 7 | Borys Shakhlin | Soviet Union | Gymnastics | 1960 |
| 8 | 7 | Mikhail Voronin | Soviet Union | Gymnastics | 1968 |
| 9 | 7 | Mark Spitz | USA | Swimming | 1972 |
| 10 | 7 | Nikolay Andrianov | Soviet Union | Gymnastics | 1976 |
| 11 | 7 | Matt Biondi | USA | Swimming | 1988 |

# 5 Women Winning 5 Medals in Individual Events at One Olympics (including one who did it twice)

| | | | | |
|---|---|---|---|---|
| 1 | Mariya Horokhovska | Soviet Union | Gymnastics | 1952 |
| 2 | Larysa Latynina | Soviet Union | Gymnastics | 1960 |
| 3 | Larysa Latynina | Soviet Union | Gymnastics | 1964 |
| 4 | Vera Cáslavská | Czechoslovakia | Gymnastics | 1968 |
| 5 | Shane Gould | Australia | Swimming | 1972 |
| 6 | Daniela Silivas | Romania | Gymnastics | 1988 |

# 4 Who Won Medals in 6 Different Olympics

| | | | | |
|---|---|---|---|---|
| **1** | Aladár Gerevich | Hungary | Fencing | 1932-1960 |
| **2** | Hans Günter Winkler | West Germany Equestrian | | 1956-1976 |
| **3** | Birgit Fischer (Schmidt) | East Germany/Germany Canoeing | | 1980-2004 |
| **4** | Elisabeta Lipa (Oleniuc) | Romania | Rowing | 1984-2004 |

# 3 Who Won 6 Silver Medals

| | | | | |
|---|---|---|---|---|
| **1** | Mikhail Voronin | Soviet Union | Gymnastics | 1968-1972 |
| **2** | Shirley Babashoff | USA | Swimming | 1972-1976 |
| **3** | Aleksandr Dityatin | Soviet Union | Gymnastics | 1976-1980 |

*Four of Babashoff's six silver medals were earned behind chemically augmented East German swimmers. Fourteen athletes have earned five silver medals· five gymnasts, three swimmers, two fencers, one equestrian and three winter athletes.*

# 4 Who Won 6 Bronze Medals

| | | | | |
|---|---|---|---|---|
| **1** | Heikki Savolainen | Finland | Gymnastics | 1928-1952 |
| **2** | Merlene Ottey | Jamaica | Track and Field | 1980-2000 |
| **3** | Aleksey Nemov | Russia | Gymnastics | 1996-2000 |
| **4** | Franziska van Almsick | Germany | Swimming | 1992-2004 |

*In the Winter Olympics, cross-country skier Harri Kirvesniemi of Finland earned six bronze medals between 1980 and 1998.*

# 14 Who Won Medals
# More Than 20 Years Apart

1  28 Tore Holm               Sweden        Sailing      1920-1948
2  28 Aladár Gerevich         Hungary       Fencing      1932-1960
3  24 Magnus Konow            Norway        Sailing      1912-1936
4  24 Heikki Savolainen       Finland       Gymnastics   1928-1952
5  24 Gustaf Adolf Boltenstern, Jr.
                              Sweden        Equestrian   1932-1956
6  24 Pál Kovács              Hungary       Fencing      1936-1960
7  24 Edoardo Mangiarotti     Italy         Fencing      1936-1960
8  24 Hans Fogh               Denmark       Sailing      1960-1984
9  24 Reiner Klimke           West Germany
                                            Equestrian   1964-1988
10 24 Bruce Davidson          USA           Equestrian   1972-1996
11 24 Jochen Schümann         East Germany/Germany
                                            Sailing      1976-2000
12 24 Birgit Fischer (Schmidt) East Germany/Germany
                                            Canoeing     1980-2004
13 24 Josefa Idem             West Germany/Italy
                                            Canoeing     1984-2008
14 24 Dara Torres             USA           Swimming     1984-2008

# 3 Who Won Medals in Summer and Winter Olympics

## 1 Eddie Eagan, USA, Boxing and Bobsleigh, 1920-1932

Eddie Eagan is the only person to have won a gold medal in both Summer and Winter Olympics sports. He grew up in a poor family in Denver but made his way through Yale, Harvard Law School and Oxford, became a successful lawyer and married an automobile heiress. He lived his life according to the precepts of Frank Merriwell, the fictional hero of dime novels. In 1932 he wrote, "To this day I have never used tobacco, because Frank didn't. My first glass of wine, which I do not care for, was taken under social compulsion in Europe. Frank never drank." Twelve years after winning the Light-heavyweight boxing division at the 1920 Antwerp Olympics, he reappeared as a member of the four-man bobsled team led by Billy Fiske that finished first at the 1932 Lake Placid Winter Games.

## 2 Jacob Tullin Thams, Norway, Ski Jumping and Sailing, 1924-1936

Jacob Tullin Thams won the ski jumping event at the first Winter Olympics in 1924; he also competed in the same event in 1928. Switching to sailing, he gained a silver medal in the 8-meter class at the 1936 Berlin Games.

## 3 Christa Luding-Rothenburger, Germany, Speed Skating and Cycling, 1980-1992

In 1984 Christa Rothenburger of East Germany won a gold medal in the 500-meter speed-skating event in Sarajevo. In 1988 in Calgary she missed another gold in the 500 by two hundredths of a second, but came back three days later to win the 1,000-meter event.

Eight years earlier her coach, Ernst Luding, had persuaded her to take up cycling in the off-season. When she saw her first match sprint race she was terrified. "I was convinced that as soon as I tried to ride I would undoubtedly topple right over." Rothenburger learned quickly. But when asked to be allowed to enter competitions, East German sports officials turned her down and told her to stick to skating. She went over their heads and petitioned the president of East Germany's sports federation, Manfred Ewald, who gave her permission. At the 1986 world championships, her first international competition, she upset Estonian Erika Salumäe for the gold medal, although Salumäe turned the tables in 1987.

In 1988 Rothenburger, with her Calgary speed-skating gold under her belt, was on target to become the first person to win medals in the Winter and Summer Olympics in the same year. She married Luding and then in Seoul ensured her place in sports history by defeating Isabelle Gautheron of France in the semi-finals of the 1,000-meter cycling sprint. She won the first race of the final, and it looked like she might match Eddie Eagan's feat of winning Olympic gold in both winter and summer sports. But Salumäe outmaneuvered her twice in a row, and Luding-Rothenburger ended up instead like Jacob Tullin Thams: gold in winter, silver in summer.

# Record Book:
# Oldest
# and Youngest

# 10 Oldest Competitors

**1** 72 years, 281 days    Oscar Swahn    Sweden
Single-shot Shooting    1920

**2** 72 years, 59 days    Arthur von Pongracz    Austria
Equestrian, Dressage    1936

**3** 71 years, 260 days    Thomas Scott    USA
Double York Round Archery    1904

**4** 71 years, 207 days    William Martin    France
Sailing, Open Class    1900

**5** 70 years, 330 days    Durward Knowles    Bahamas
Sailing, Star Class    1988

**6** 70 years, 201 days    Krasimir Krastev    Bulgaria
Sailing, Tornado Class    1980

**7** 70 years, 11 days    Owen Phillips    Belize
Small-bore Rifle Shooting, Prone    1976

**8** 70 years, 6 days    Lorna Johnstone    Great Britain
Equestrian, Dressage    1972

**9** 69 years, 96 days    Louis, Comte du Douet de Graville    France
Equestrian, Four-in-Hand    1900

**10** 68 years, 229 days    Roberto Soundy    El Salvador
Trap Shooting    1968

# 5 Oldest Female Competitors

**1** 70 years, 6 days    Lorna Johnstone    Great Britain
Equestrian, Dressage    1972

**2** 59 years, 184 days    Marjory Saunders    Canada
Archery    1972

**3** 58 years, 268 days    Ulla Håkansson    Sweden
Equestrian, Dressage    1996

**4** 58 years, 155 days    Emily Woodruff    USA
Double National Round Archery    1904

**5** 58 years, 72 days    Mieko Yagi    Japan
Equestrian, Dressage    2008

# 10 Oldest Gold-medal-winners

**1** 64 years, 258 days    Oscar Swahn        Sweden
Team Single-shot Running Target Shooting   1912

**2** 64 years, 2 days    Galen Spencer        USA
Team Archery        1904

**3** 63 years, 240 days    Robert Williams        USA
Team Archery        1904

**4** 61 years, 4 days    Joshua Millner        Great Britain
Free Rifle Shooting, 1,000 yards        1908

**5** 60 years, 264 days    Oscar Swahn        Sweden
Team Single-shot Running Target Shooting   1908

**6** 59 years, 112 days    Everard Endt        USA
Sailing, 6 Meters        1952

**7** 59 years, 35 days    William Northam        Australia
Sailing, 5.5 Meters        1964

**8** 58 years, 160 days    Charles Winder        USA
Team Military Rifle Shooting        1908

**9** 57 years, 77 days    Allen Whitty        Great Britain
Team Double-shot Running Target Shooting   1924

**10** 57 years, 44 days    Johan Anker        Norway
Sailing, 6 Meters        1928

# 5 Oldest Female Gold-medal-winners

**1** 53 years, 274 days    Sybil "Queenie" Newall    Great Britain
Double National Round Archery        1908

**2** 46 years, 112 days    Heike Kemmer        Germany
Equestrian, Team Dressage        2008

**3** 46 years, 16 days    Ulla Salzgeber        Germany
Equestrian, Team Dressage        2004

**4** 45 years, 23 days    Lida Howell        USA
Double National Round Archery        1904

**5** 45 years, 13 days    Liselott Linsenhoff    West Germany
Equestrian, Dressage        1972

# 10 Oldest Gold-medal-winners in an Individual Event

**1** 61 years, 4 days — Joshua Millner — Great Britain
Free Rifle Shooting, 1,000 yards — 1908

**2** 60 years, 263 days — Oscar Swahn — Sweden
Team Single-shot Running Target Shooting — 1908

**3** 56 years, 96 days — Walter Winans — USA
Double-shot Running Target Shooting — 1908

**4** 56 years, 91 days — Ernst Linder — Sweden
Equestrian, Dressage — 1924

**5** 54 years, 343 days — Georges Nagelmackers — Belgium
Equestrian, Four-in-Hand — 1900

**6** 54 years, 162 days — Hubert Van Innis — Belgium
Archery, 28 Meters — 1920

**7** 54 years, 93 days — Henri Saint Cyr — Sweden
Equestrian, Dressage — 1956

**8** 53 years, 274 days — Sybil "Queenie" Newall — Great Britain
Double National Round Archery — 1908

**9** 50 years, 136 days — Henri Saint Cyr — Sweden
Equestrian, Dressage — 1952

**10** 49 years, 251 days — Cornelius van Oyen — Germany
Rapid-fire Pistol Shooting — 1936

*In the Winter Olympics, cross-country skier Nikolay Zimyatov of the Soviet Union earned a gold medal in the 30-kilometer event in 1980 at the age of 50 years 273 days, another in the 50-kilometer event nine days later, and one in the 30-kilometer event in 1984 at the age of 54 years 269 days.*

# 10 Oldest Female Gold-medal-winners in an Individual Event

**1**   53 years, 274 days    Sybil "Queenie" Newall    Great Britain
Double National Round Archery    1908

**2**   45 years, 23 days    Lida Howell    USA
Double National Round Archery    1904

**3**   45 years, 13 days    Liselott Linsenhoff    West Germany
Equestrian, Dressage    1972

**4**   43 years, 224 days    Silvia Sperber    West Germany
Small-bore Rifle Shooting, Three Positions    1988

**5**   42 years, 40 days    Doreen Wilber    USA
Archery    1972

**6**   41 years, 77 days    Ilona Elek-Schacherer    Hungary
Foil Fencing    1948

**7**   40 years, 230 days    Anky van Grunsven    Netherlands
Equestrian, Dressage    2008

**8**   40 years, 212 days    Linda Thom    Canada
Sporting Pistol Shooting    1984

**9**   39 years, 315 days    Ellina "Elya" Zvereva    Belarus
Discus Throw    2000

**10**   39 years, 200 days    Diana Igaly    Hungary
Skeet Shooting    2004

# 10 Oldest Medal-winners in an Individual Event

**1** 64 years, 257 days    Oscar Swahn    Sweden
Double-shot Running Target Shooting    1912

**2** 63 years, 262 days    Jean "Jessie" Pollock    USA
Double National Round Archery    1904

**3** 63 years, 239 days    Robert Williams    USA
Double York Round Archery    1904

**4** 61 years, 4 days    Joshua Millner    Great Britain
Free Rifle Shooting, 1,000 yards    1908

**5** 60 years, 264 days    Oscar Swahn    Sweden
Double-shot Running Target Shooting    1908

**6** 60 years, 103 days    William Milne    Great Britain
Small-Bore Rifle Shooting, 50 Meters    1912

**7** 60 years, 96 days    Josef Neckermann    West Germany
Equestrian, Dressage    1972

**8** 59 years, 191 days    George Barnes    Great Britain
Small-Bore Rifle Shooting, Prone    1908

**9** 58 years, 48 days    Ragnar Skanåker    Sweden
Free Pistol Shooting, 50 Meters    1992

**10** 58 years, 2 days    André Jousseaumé    France
Equestrian, Dressage    1952

# 10 Oldest Female Medal-winners in an Individual Event

**1**   63 years, 262 days    Jean "Jessie" Pollock     USA
Double National Round Archery    1904

**2**   56 years, 13 days    Emma Cooke     USA
Double National Round Archery    1904

**3**   53 years, 274 days    Sybil "Queenie" Newall     Great Britain
Double National Round Archery    1908

**4**   52 years, 143 days    Patricia Dench     Australia
Sporting Pistol Shooting    1984

**5**   46 years, 174 days    Irada Asumova     Azerbaijan
Sporting Pistol Shooting    2004

**6**   46 years, 117 days    Heike Kemmer     Germany
Equestrian, Dressage    2008

**7**   46 years, 20 days    Ulla Salzgeber     Germany
Equestrian, Dressage    2004

**8**   45 years, 71 days    Ilona Elek-Schacherer     Hungary
Foil Fencing    1952

**9**   45 years, 23 days    Lida Howell     USA
Double National Round Archery    1904

**10**   45 years, 13 days    Liselott Linsenhoff     West Germany
Equestrian, Dressage    1972

# 11 Medal-winners Over 61

**1** 72 years, 280 days | Oscar Swahn — Sweden
Team Double-shot Running Target Shooting 1920

**2** 68 years, 194 days | Samuel Duvall — USA
Team Archery 1904

**3** 66 years, 164 days | Louis Noverraz — Switzerland
Sailing, 5.5 Meters 1968

**4** 64 years, 258 days | Oscar Swahn — Sweden
Team Single-shot Running Target Shooting 1912

**5** 64 years, 2 days | Galen Spencer — USA
Team Archery 1904

**6** 63 years, 262 days | Jean "Jessie" Pollock — USA
Double National Round Archery 1904

**7** 63 years, 240 days | Robert Williams — USA
Team Archery 1904

**8** 61 years, 244 days | John Butt — Great Britain
Team Trap Shooting 1912

**9** 61 years, 224 days | Ian Millar — Canada
Equestrian, Team Jumping 2008

**10** 61 years, 130 days | Bill Roycroft — Australia
Equestrian, Team Three-Day Event 1976

**11** 61 years, 4 days | Joshua Millner — Great Britain
Free Rifle Shooting, 1,000 yards 1908

# 5 Women Medal-winners Over 50

**1** 63 years, 262 days | Jean "Jessie" Pollock — USA
Double National Round Archery 1904

**2** 56 years, 13 days | Emma Cooke — USA
Double National Round Archery 1904

**3** 53 years, 274 days | Sybil "Queenie" Newall — Great Britain
Double National Round Archery 1908

**4** 52 years, 143 days | Patricia Dench — Australia
Shooting, Sporting Pistol, 25 Meters 1984

**5** 51 years, 88 days | Eva-Maria Pracht — Canada
Equestrian, Team Dressage 1988

# 10 Youngest Competitors in the Summer Olympics

| 1 | 10 years, 216 days | Dimitrios Loundras | Greece |
| | | Team Gymnastics, Parallel Bars | 1896 |
| 2 | 11 years, 250 days | Carlos Front | Spain |
| | | Coxed Eights Rowing | 1992 |
| 3 | 11 years, 297 days | Yip Tsz Wa | Hong Kong |
| | | 100-meter Breaststroke | 2004 |
| 4 | 11 years, 300 days | Luigina Giavotti | Italy |
| | | Team Gymnastics | 1928 |
| 5 | 11 years, 326 days | Liana Vicens | Puerto Rico |
| | | 4 x 100-meter Medley Relay | 1968 |
| 6 | 12 years, 21 days | Inge Sørensen | Denmark |
| | | 200-meter Breaststroke | 1936 |
| 7 | 12 years, 64 days | Chin Say "Molly" Tay | Malaysia |
| | | 100-meter Butterfly | 1964 |
| 8 | 12 years, 183 days | Judit Kiss | Hungary |
| | | 400-meter Freestyle | 1992 |
| 9 | 12 years, 187 days | Werner Grieshofer | Austria |
| | | Coxed Pairs Rowing | 1972 |
| 10 | 12 years, 217 days | Ines Vercesi | Italy |
| | | Team Gymnastics | 1928 |

*Six 11-year-old girls have taken part in the figure-skating competitions at the Winter Olympics: Sonja Henie of Norway in 1924, Cecilia Colledge and Megan Taylor of Great Britain in 1932, Marcelle Matthews of South Africa in 1960, Beatrice Hustiu of Romania in 1968 and Liu Luyang of China in 1988. Colledge was the youngest, at 11 years 73 days.*

# 10 Youngest Gold-medal-winners

**1** 13 years, 267 days    Marjorie Gestring    USA
   Springboard Diving    1936

**2** 13 years, 282 days    Klaus Zerta    Germany
   Coxed Pairs Rowing    1960

**3** 13 years, 298 days    Hans Bourquin    Switzerland
   Coxed Pairs Rowing    1928

**4** 13 years, 345 days    Fu Mingxia    China
   Platform Diving    1992

**5** 14 years, 6 days    Kyoko Iwasaki    Japan
   200-Meter Breaststroke    1992

**6** 14 years, 40 days    Krisztina Egerszegi    Hungary
   200-meter Backstroke    1988

**7** 14 years, 94 days    Bernard Malivoire    France
   Coxed Pairs Rowing    1952

**8** 14 years, 96 days    Lillian "Pokey" Watson    USA
   4 x 100-meter Freestyle Relay    1964

**9** 14 years, 119 days    Aileen Riggin    USA
   Springboard Diving    1920

**10** 14 years, 172 days    Gunther Tiersch    West Germany
   Coxed Eights Rowing    1968

At the 1900 Paris Olympics, Dutch rowers François Antoine Brandt and Roelof Klein needed a lightweight coxswain for the final of the coxed pairs and picked a local Parisian boy. They won the race. The boy stayed around long enough to have his photo taken with his new Dutch friends, but then he disappeared into the city. His name and age are still unknown.

In the Winter Olympics, Kim Yoon-mi, a short-track speed skater from South Korea, earned a gold medal in the 3,000-meter relay in 1994 at the age of 13 years 84 days. Another member of the same relay team, Won Hye-kyung, was 14 years and 133 days old.

# 10 Youngest Gold-medal-winners in an Individual Event

**1** 13 years, 267 days — Marjorie Gestring — USA
Springboard Diving — 1936

**2** 13 years, 345 days — Fu Mingxia — China
Platform Diving — 1992

**3** 14 years, 6 days — Kyoko Iwasaki — Japan
200-Meter Breaststroke — 1992

**4** 14 years, 40 days — Krisztina Egerszegi — Hungary
200-meter Backstroke — 1988

**5** 14 years, 119 days — Aileen Riggin — USA
Springboard Diving — 1920

**6** 14 years, 251 days — Nadia Comaneci — Romania
Gymnastics, All-Around — 1976

**7** 14 years, 320 days — Simona Pauca — Romania
Gymnastics, Balance Beam — 1984

**8** 15 years, 62 days — Beth Botsford — USA
100-meter Backstroke — 1996

**9** 15 years, 72 days — Andrea Pollack — East Germany
200-meter Butterfly — 1976

**10** 15 years, 108 days — Rica Reinisch — East Germany
100-meter Backstroke — 1980

# 10 Youngest Male Gold-medal-winners in an Individual Event

**1**   14 years, 308 days    Kuzuo Kitamura      Japan
                                          1,500-meter Freestyle      1932

**2**   15 years, 296 days    Yasuji Miyazaki      Japan
     100-meter Freestyle      1932

**3**   16 years, 101 days    Ioannis Malokinis      Greece
     100-meter Freestyle for Greek Sailors      1896

**4**   16 years, 162 days    Jackie Fields      USA
     Featherweight Boxing      1924

**5**   16 years, 173 days    Warren Paoa Kealoha      USA
     100-metre Breaststroke      1920

**6**   16 years, 195 days    Sun Shuwei      China
     Platform Diving      1992

**7**   16 years, 288 days    Ramón Fonst      Cuba
     Épée Fencing      1900

**8**   16 years, 312 days    Konstantin Lukashik      Soviet Union
     Free Pistol Shooting      1992

**9**   16 years, 338 days    Andrew "Boy" Charlton      Australia
     1,500-meter Freestyle      1924

**10**   17 years, 7 days    Sándor Wládár      Hungary
     200-meter Breaststroke      1980

*In the Winter Olympics, Toni Nieminen of Finland won the Large Hill Ski Jump in 1992 at the age of 16 years 261 days.*

# 10 Youngest Medal-winners

**1** 10 years, 215 days     Dimitrios Loundras     Greece
       Gymnastics Team, Parallel Bars     1896

**2** 11 years, 301 days     Luigina Giavotti     Italy
       Gymnastics, Team All-Around     1928

**3** 12 years, 24 days     Inge Sørensen     Denmark
       200-meter Breaststroke     1936

**4** 12 years, 217 days     Ines Vercesi     Italy
       Gymnastics, Team All-Around     1928

**5** 12 years, 233 days     Noël Vandernotte     France
       Rowing: Coxed Pairs, Coxed Fours     1936

**6** 12 years, 270 days     Clara Marangoni     Italy
       Gymnastics, Team All-Around     1928

**7** 13 years, 23 days     Dorothy Poynton-Hill     USA
       Springboard Diving     1928

**8** 13 years, 267 days     Marjorie Gestring     USA
       Springboard Diving     1936

**9** 13 years, 282 days     Klaus Zerta     Germany
       Coxed Pairs Rowing     1960

**10** 13 years, 286 days     Nian Yun     China
       4 x 100-meter freestyle relay     1996

*Dimitrios Loundras grew up to be an admiral in the Greek navy and served in both world wars.*

*In the Winter Olympics, South Korean short-track speed skater Kim Yoon-mi won a gold medal in the 3,000-meter relay in 1994 at the age of 13 years, 84 days.*

# 10 Youngest Medal-winners in an Individual Event

| | | | | |
|---|---|---|---|---|
| **1** | 12 years, 24 days | Inge Sørensen<br>200-meter Breaststroke | | Denmark<br>1936 |
| **2** | 13 years, 23 days | Dorothy Poynton-Hill<br>Springboard Diving | | USA<br>1928 |
| **3** | 13 years, 267 days | Marjorie Gestring<br>Springboard Diving | | USA<br>1936 |
| **4** | 13 years, 307 days | Kornelia Ender<br>200-meter Individual Medley | East Germany<br>1972 | |
| **5** | 13 years, 345 days | Fu Mingxia<br>Platform Diving | | China<br>1992 |
| **6** | 14 years, 6 days | Kyoko Iwasaki<br>200-meter Breaststroke | | Japan<br>1992 |
| **7** | 14 years, 10 days | Nils Skoglund<br>Plain High Diving | | Sweden<br>1920 |
| **8** | 14 years, 37 days | Krisztina Egerszegi<br>100-meter Breaststroke | | Hungary<br>1988 |
| **9** | 14 years, 51 days | Silva Emirzyan<br>Platform Diving | Soviet Union<br>1980 | |
| **10** | 14 years, 57 days | Katherine Rawls<br>Springboard Diving | | USA<br>1932 |

# 5 Youngest Male Medal-winners in an Individual Event

**1** 14 years, 10 days  | Nils Skoglund | Sweden
Plain High Diving | 1920

**2** 14 years, 246 days | Xiong Ni | China
Platform Diving | 1988

**3** 14 years, 308 days | Kuzuo Kitamura | Japan
1,500-meter Freestyle | 1932

**4** 15 years, 106 days | Dániel Gyurta | Hungary
200-meter Breaststroke | 2004

**5** 15 years, 296 days | Yasuji Miyazaki | Japan
100-meter Freestyle | 1932

*In the Winter Olympics, figure skater Scotty Allen of the United States earned a bronze medal in 1964 at the age of 14 years 362 days.*

# Record Book: Miscellaneous

# 7 Who Competed in 8 or More Olympics

| | | | | |
|---|---|---|---|---|
| **1** | 9 | Hubert Raudaschl | Austria<br>Sailing | 1964-1996 |
| **2** | 9 | Ian Millar | Canada<br>Equestrian | 1972-2008 |
| **3** | 8 | Piero D'Inzeo | Italy<br>Equestrian | 1948-1976 |
| **4** | 8 | Raimondo D'Inzeo | Italy<br>Equestrian | 1948-1976 |
| **5** | 8 | Paul Elvstrøm | Denmark<br>Sailing | 1948-1988 |
| **6** | 8 | Durward Knowles | Bahamas/Great Britain<br>Sailing | 1948-1988 |
| **7** | 8 | Afanasijs Kuzmins | Latvia/Soviet Union<br>Shooting | 1976-2008 |

# 4 Women Competing in 7 Olympics

| | | | | |
|---|---|---|---|---|
| **1** | 7 | Kerstin Palm | Sweden<br>Fencing | 1964-1988 |
| **2** | 7 | Merlene Ottey | Jamaica/Slovenia<br>Track and Field | 1980-2004 |
| **3** | 7 | Josefa Idem-Guerrini | West Germany/Italy<br>Canoeing | 1984-2008 |
| **4** | 7 | Jeannie Longo-Ciprelli | France<br>Cycling | 1984-2008 |

# 10 Athletes with the Longest Olympic Careers

**1** 44 years   Hiroshi Hoketsu   Japan
  Equestrian   1964-2008

**2** 40 years   Ivan Osiier   Denmark
  Fencing   1908-1948

**3** 40 years   Magnus Konow   Norway
  Sailing   1908-1948

**4** 40 years   Paul Elvstrøm   Denmark
  Sailing   1948-1988

**5** 40 years   Durward Knowles   Bahamas/Great Britain
  Sailing   1948-1988

**6** 36 years   Paul Van Asbroeck   Belgium
  Shooting   1900-1936

**7** 36 years   Krum Lekarski   Bulgaria
  Equestrian   1924-1960

**8** 36 years   Jacques Lafortune   Belgium
  Shooting   1924-1960

**9** 36 years   Nelson Pessoa Filho   Brazil
  Equestrian   1956-1992

**10** 36 years   Ian Millar   Canada
  Equestrian   1972-2008

*Unlike the other athletes with long careers, Hiroshi Hoketsu competed in the Olympics only twice, once at the age of 23 and not again until he was 67 years old. However, he also qualified to represent Japan in the 2012 London Games.*

# 6 Women with the Longest Olympic Careers

**1** 32 years    Cindy Ishoy (Neale)     Canada
                  Equestrian            1972-2004

**2** 32 years    Sue Nattrass           Canada
                  Shooting              1976-2008

**3** 28 years    Jessica Ransehousen (Newberry)     USA
                  Equestrian            1960-1988

**4** 28 years    Christilot Boylen (Hanson)     Canada
                  Equestrian            1964-1992

**5** 28 years    Christine Stückelberger     Switzerland
                  Equestrian            1972-2000

**6** 28 years    Kyra Kyrklund          Finland
                  Equestrian            1980-2008

# 14 Tallest Competitors

*All of the tallest competitors in the Olympics have been basketball players.*

M (Ft-In)

**1**   2.26 (7-5)     **Yao Ming**
                             **China**                     **2000-2008**

**2**   2.23 (7-3³/₄)   **Tommy Burleson**
                             **USA**                       **1972**

**3**   2.23 (7-3³/₄)   **Arvydas Sabonis**
                             **Lithuania/Soviet Union 1988-1996**

**4**   2.21 (7-3)     **Gunther Behnke**
                             **Germany**                **1992**

**5**   2.21 (7-3)     **Roberto Dueñas**
                             **Spain**                   **2000-2004**

**6**   2.20 (7-2½)   **Volodymyr Tkachenko**
                             **Soviet Union**          **1976-1980**

**7**   2.20 (7-2½)   **Viktor Pankrashkin**
                             **Soviet Union**          **1988**

**8**   2.20 (7-2½)   **Luc Longley**
                             **Australia**             **1988-2000**

**9**   2.18 (7-1³/₄)   **Janis Krumiņš**
                             ~~Soviet Union~~         ~~1956-1964~~

**10**   2.18 (7-1³/₄)   **Andy Campbell**
                             **Australia**             **1976-1984**

**11**   2.18 (7-1³/₄)   **Uwe Blab**
                             **West Germany/Germany 1984-1992**

**12**   2.18 (7-1³/₄)   **Eurelijus Žukauska**
                             **Lithuania**           **1996-2004**

**13**   2.18 (7-1³/₄)   **Frédéric Weis**
                             **France**                 **2000**

**14**   2.18 (7-1³/₄)   **Hamed Hadadi**
                             **Iran**                    **2008**

# 3 Tallest Non-Basketball Players

M (Ft-In)

**1** 2.17 (7-1½)  | Aleksei Kazakov | Russia
| Volleyball | 1996-2004

**2** 2.15 (7-0½)  | Marcin Nowak | Poland
| Volleyball | 1996

**3** 2.15 (7-0½)  | Stanislav Dineykin | Russia
| Volleyball | 1996, 2004

# 8 Tallest Female Competitors

M (Ft-In)

**1** 2.13 (6-11¾)  | Margo Dydek | Poland
| Basketball | 2000

**2** 2.10 (6-10¾)  | Uljana Semjonova | Soviet Union
| Basketball | 1976-1980

**3** 2.05 (6-8¾)  | Chen Yuefang | China
| Basketball | 1984

**4** 2.05 (6-8¾)  | Sue Geh | Australia
| Basketball | 1984

**5** 2.04 (6-0¼)  | Zheng Haixia | China
| Basketball | 1984-1996

**6** 2.04 (6-8¼)  | Olga Potashova | Russia
| Volleyball | 2000

**7** 2.03 (6-7¾)  | Anne Donovan | USA
| Basketball | 1984-1988

**8** 2.03 (6-7¾)  | Erzsébet Szentesi | Hungary
| Basketball | 1980

# 7 Olympians Under 5 Feet Tall

## 1 Lu Li, China, Women's Gymnastics, 1992

The winner of the uneven bars event at the Barcelona Olympics, 15-year-old Lu Li stood only 4 feet 5½ inches (1.36 m) and weighed only 66 pounds (30 kg).

## 2 Aileen Riggin, USA, Diving, 1920–1924

Aileen Riggin won the springboard diving competition at 14. She was also the smallest athlete at the Antwerp Games, 4 feet 7 inches (1.40 meters) tall and weighing 65 pounds (29.5 kilograms). She returned to the Olympics four years later, earning a silver medal in diving and a bronze in the 100-meter backstroke.

## 3 Joe De Pietro, USA, Weightlifting, 1948

Joe De Pietro's height was variously reported as 4 feet 8 inches or 4 feet 10 inches. Whichever figure is correct, his arms were so short that he was barely able to raise the bar above his head. Yet he was still able to win the 1948 bantamweight gold medal.

## 4 Aleksandr Voronin, Soviet Union, Weightlifting, 1976

At 4 feet 8¼ inches (1.43 meters), Voronin, an electrician from Kerekoo, was the shortest man in the competition. Taking an extra lift after winning the gold medal, he set a world jerk record of 311 lbs (141 kg).

## 5 Doug Herland, USA, Rowing, 1984

The coxswain for the bronze-medal-winning US coxed pairs team was 32-year-old Doug Herland, who stood 4 feet 9 inches (1.45 meters) tall and weighed 103 lbs (46.7 kg). He was born with broken hips, broken ribs and a broken collarbone as a result of osteogenesis imperfecta—brittle bone disease—and broke bones twice a year for the first eight years of his life. Herland discovered rowing at Pacific Lutheran University in Tacoma, Washington, where he earned a degree in social psychology. He went on to a career in social work, counseling handicapped and mentally disabled children, and establishing a rowing team for the disabled in Michigan.

## 6 Deng Yaping, China, Women's Table Tennis, 1992-1996

The biggest obstacle in Deng Yaping's career was not her opponents, but her height. When she was 9 years old she won a provincial junior championship but was denied a place on the provincial team because she was too short. In 1988, when she was 15 years old, she won the national championship, but was refused a spot on the national team because she was too short. The national coaching staff finally gave in and in 1989 Deng, still only 16 years old, teamed with Qiao Hong to win the doubles title at the world championships. In 1991, by which time she had topped out at 4 feet 10½ inches (1.49 meters), Deng won the singles world championship. At the Olympics she earned gold medals in the singles and doubles events at both the 1992 and 1996 Games.

## 7 Naim Süleymanoğlu, Turkey, Weightlifting, 1988-2000

Born in the small mountain village of Ptichar, in the region of Bulgaria with the highest concentration of ethnic Turks, Naim Süleymanoğlu was pound-for-pound one of the strongest men who ever lived. His father, a zinc miner, was 5 feet (1.52 meters) tall. His mother, who worked in a hothouse, was 4 feet 7½ inches (1.41 meters). Naim himself topped out just shy of 5 feet (1.52 meters). Short though he may have been, he was also strong. He set his first world record at the age of 15 and at the 1984 European Championships he became the second man in history to lift three times his bodyweight overhead. In 1986 he defected while in Australia. He was flown to London where he was met by a private jet belonging to Turkey's prime minister, Turgut Ozal. Upon arrival at the airport in Turkey, Naim kissed the tarmac and became an instant national hero. He went on to win three Olympic gold medals between 1988 and 1996.

# 12 Heaviest Olympic Competitors

**1** 210 kg (462 lbs.)    Ricardo Blas Jr.    Guam
Judo    2008

**2** 198 kg (435 lbs.)    Aytami Ruano    Spain
Judo    2004

**3** 190 kg (418 lbs.)    Marek Galinski    Poland
Greco-Roman Wrestling    1980

**4** 182 kg (400 lbs.)    Chris Taylor    USA
Freestyle & Greco-Roman Wrestling 1972

**5** 180 kg(396 lbs.)    Valentyn Rusliakov    Ukraine
Judo    2000

**6** 178 kg (391 lbs.)    Leonel Wilfredo Ruíz    Venezuela
Judo    2004

**7** 175 kg (385 lbs.)    Dmitri Nosov    Russia
Judo    2004

**8** 170 kg (374 lbs.)    Janusz Wojnarowicz    Poland
Judo    2008

**9** 165 kg (363 lbs.)    Carlos Zegarra    Peru
Judo    2008

**10** 163 kg (358 lbs.)    Leonid Zhabotynsky    Soviet Union
Weightlifting    1964-1968

**11** 163 kg (358 lbs.)    Pak Jong-gil    North Korea
Judo    1976

**12** 163 kg (358 lbs.)    Ernesto Agüero    Cuba
Weightlifting    1992

# 10 Heaviest Female Competitors

**1** 167 kg (367 lbs.)    Olha Korobka    Ukraine
Weightlifting    2004-2008

**2** 145 kg (319 lbs.)    Beata Maksymowa    Poland
Judo    1992-2000

**3** 145 kg (319 lbs.)    Urszula Sadkowska    Poland
Judo    2008

**4** 136 kg (299 lbs.)    Cheryl Haworth    USA
Weightlifting    2000-2008

**5** 136 kg (299 lbs.)    Reanna Maricha Solomon    Nauru
Weightlifting    2004

**6** 135 kg (297 lbs.)    Estela Rodríguez    Cuba
Judo    1992-1996

**7** 132 kg (290 lbs.)    Kim Na-Yeong    South Korea
Judo    2008

**8** 130 kg (286 lbs.)    Heba Hefny    Egypt
Judo    1992-2000

**9** 128 kg (282 lbs.)    Uljana Semjonova    Soviet Union
Basketball    1976-1980

**10** 128 kg (282 lbs.)    Tong Wen    China
Judo    2008

# 6 Athletes with Most Victories in the Ancient Olympics

**1** 12 **Leonidas of Rhodes**
192-meter Run, 385-meter Run, Race in Armour
164-152 BC

**2** 8 **Hermogenes of Xanthos**
192-meter Run, 385-meter Run, Race in Armour
AD 81-89

**3** 7 **Astylos of Croton and Syracuse**
192-meter Run, 385-meter Run, Race in Armour
488-480 BC

**4** 6 **Khionis of Sparta**
192-meter Run, 385-meter Run
664-656 BC

**5** 6 **Hipposthenes of Sparta**
Wrestling
632-608 BC

**6** 6 **Milo of Croton**
Wrestling, Boys' Wrestling
536-516 BC

# 14 Olympic Firsts

### 1 First Winner of Modern Olympics: Athens, 1896

James Brendan Connolly came from a poor Irish-American family in South Boston, Massachusetts. He was a 27-year-old, self-educated freshman at Harvard when he read about the revival of the Olympic Games. When denied permission for a leave of absence, Connolly dropped out and went anyway. His travel expenses were paid for by the Suffolk Athletic Club and by the proceeds of a bake sale organized by his local parish church. At 2 p.m. on April 6, the first modern Olympic Games were officially opened. Connolly was the last to jump in the triple jump competition and became the first Olympic champion in 1,527 years.

### 2 First Female Olympic Champion: Paris, 1900

Charlotte "Chattie" Cooper of Great Britain had already won three of her five Wimbledon titles when she traveled to Paris for the 1900 Olympics, the first to include women. She won the tennis tournament and was the first female champion of the modern Games. The first women to compete in the modern Olympics were Jeanne Filleaul-Brohy and Marie Ohier of France in croquet, also in 1900.

### 3 First Africans to Compete at the Olympics: St Louis, 1904

The 1904 Marathon included the first Africans to participate in the Olympics: Tswana tribesmen Len Taw and Jan Mashiani, and Bertie Harris, who was white. The three were members of a South African contingent who traveled to St Louis to act out two famous battles from the recently concluded Anglo-Boer War, as part of the Boer War exhibit at the Louisiana Purchase Exposition.

### 4 First National Teams: Athens Intercalated Games, 1906

The question of whether the 1906 Games should be considered official is a difficult one. Most of the participants thought they were competing in the Olympics, and in April 1906, the "Olympic Review," the official publication of the International Olympic Committee, published a special issue "on the occasion of the Olympic Games of Athens." However, in

1949, a three-man commission headed by Avery Brundage concluded that the 1906 Athens Games were not official and the International Olympic Committee has refused to reopen the issue since then. Despite the position of the IOC, the 1906 Olympics were the first to limit entries to athletes sent by national Olympics committees and the first at which there was a Parade of Nations.

## 5 First Athletes Village: Los Angeles, 1932

For the first time, the male athletes were housed in a single Olympic Village, while the women stayed in a luxury hotel. In the interests of international goodwill the US government suspended its prohibition against alcoholic beverages to allow French, Italian and other athletes to import and drink wine.

## 6 First photo-finish camera: Los Angeles, 1932

Official automatic timing was introduced for the track events, as was the photo-finish camera. In fact, for the first time, the results of a final were changed after the film of the race was reviewed. Originally Jack Keller of the United States was awarded the bronze medal in the 110-meter hurdles. When the revised results gave third place to Donald Finley of Great Britain, Keller found Finley in the Olympic Village and gave him the medal.

## 7 First Torch Relay: Berlin, 1936

The Berlin Games saw the introduction of the torch relay, in which a lighted torch is carried from Olympia to the site of the current Games. On July 20, 1936, fifteen Greek maidens lit a flame using the rays of the sun and a reflector. The flame was passed to Kyril Kondylis, the first runner in the 3,187 kilometer (1,980 mile) torch relay.

## 8 First TV coverage: Berlin, 1936

The 1936 Olympics were also the first to be broadcast on a form of television. Twenty-five large screens were set up throughout Berlin, allowing the local people to see the Games for free. The Berlin Games also produced the first noteworthy official film: *Olympia*, directed by Leni Riefenstahl. Although intended as a piece of Nazi propaganda, the film ended up as a celebration of the human spirit as well.

## 9 First Olympic Defector: London, 1948

After the 1948 London Olympics, Marie Provaznikova, the leader of the Czechoslovakian women's gymnastics team and the president of the Women's Technical Commission, refused to return to Czechoslovakia because "there is no freedom of speech, of the press or of assembly."

## 10 First Doping Test: Tokyo, 1964

The 1964 men's cycling 100-kilometer team time trial event holds a special place in Olympic history because it was the first in which experimental drug testing was carried out. A series of tests were imposed before and after the race. No athlete tested positive.

## 11 First (and Only) Defection *To* a Communist Country: Tokyo, 1964

The last-place finisher in the men's rapid-fire pistol event was Ma Chin-shan, a retired army officer from Taiwan. After the event, Ma took refuge in the Ginza office of the General Council of Chinese Merchants of Tokyo, requesting that he be allowed to return to mainland China to live with his parents, whom he had not seen since World War II. To this day, Ma remains the only Olympic athlete to defect to a Communist country.

## 12 First Drug Disqualification: Mexico City, 1968

The Swedish modern pentathlon team finished third, but was disqualified when one of its members, Hans-Gunnar Liljenvall, failed the drug test for alcohol. It was a common practice for pentathletes to steady their nerves with a bit of alcohol before the shooting contest, but Liljenvall, who finished eighth individually, was found to have a blood alcohol concentration well above the acceptable limit, despite the fact that he claimed he had only drunk two beers.

## 13 First Sex Testing: Mexico City, 1968

The Mexico City Olympics were the first Summer Games to include sex testing for women. A year earlier Ewa Kłobukowska of Poland, who had won two Olympic medals in 1964, had become the first athlete to fail a sex test—even though she passed a "visual verification" exam.

## 14 First Doped Olympic Athlete to Offer To Return a Medal: Moscow, 1980

Shortly after winning the women's butterfly bronze medal in Moscow, Christiane Knacke of East Germany underwent the first of three operations to repair damage done to her elbow by anabolic steroids. Her bones had turned to "crystal." In 1989 Knacke became one of the first East German athletes to speak publicly about the way her nation's sporting system really worked, describing her daily regimen of ten to fifteen steroid pills, shots of cortisone and procaine and, twice a week, intravenous drips of an unknown liquid. In 1998 Knacke was co-plaintiff in a lawsuit against former East German coaches and two doctors accused of damaging the health of their athletes. In the course of the trial Knacke became the first Olympic athlete to volunteer to return her medal because she had been doped.